GUJARAT AND THE GUJARATIS

GUJARAT
AND
THE GUJARATIS

Pictures of Men and Manners taken from Life

BY

BEHRAMJI M. MALABARI

GYAN

Published by

GYAN

Gyan Publishing House
5, Ansari Road
Daryaganj, New Delhi-110002
Phone: 011-47034999, 9811692060
E-mail: books@gyanbooks.com

Distribution Network
gyanbooks.com
India, USA, Canada, UK, Australia, France

ISBN : 978-81-212-3447-4 (PB)
First Published, 1882

2nd Impression 2020

Printed at: Gyan Press, Delhi.

GUJARÁT AND THE GUJARÁTIS:

Pictures of Men and Manners taken from Life.

BY

BEHRÁMJI M. MALABÁRI,

AUTHOR OF "THE INDIAN MUSE IN ENGLISH GARB," "PLEASURES OF MORALITY," "WILSON-VIRAH," ETC.,
EDITOR OF THE "INDIAN SPECTATOR," BOMBAY.

LONDON:
W. H. ALLEN & CO., 13 WATERLOO PLACE.
PUBLISHERS TO THE INDIA OFFICE.

1882.

TO THE

Honourable James Gibbs,

C.S., C.S.I.

MEMBER OF THE SUPREME COUNCIL OF INDIA.

My dear Mr. Gibbs,

It is now five years since I received your congratulations on the success of my "Indian Muse." Soon after was established an acquaintance upon a formal introduction by our lamented friend Sir Cowasji Jehangir. Looking back to-day on this, to me, long vista of years, I am rejoiced to find traces of your influence not only on my character as a citizen, but as a public writer.

As a friend and adviser of youth, I have often realised in you my ideal of a true English gentleman. There is no Englishman in India—official or non-official—for whom I cherish livelier feelings of esteem. But, above all this, you are known as one of the best friends of my countrymen. As Judge of the High Court, Vice-Chancellor of the University, Member of the Governor's Council at Bombay, and now a Member of the Viceregal Council, you have proved yourself as sincere a friend of India as of England.

For these reasons, and in the hope that these sketches may call up some pleasant memories of your long and honourable connection with Gujarát, I have presumed to borrow the prestige of your name as a sort of passport for my pictures of that most interesting province.

With best respects,

I am, yours sincerely,

BEHRAMJI M. MALABARI.

BOMBAY, 1880.

PREFACE.

The page of the social and domestic life of the people of India is almost unread by Europeans. There are many reasons for this. First, there is the difference of language. Very few Englishmen have sufficient knowledge of any Indian language to converse with Indians with ease and fluency. Then, there is the deficient education and seclusion of Indian women, which cuts them off from social intercourse with English men, and renders their meeting with English women productive of very meagre results. Gravest of all, as a bar to free intercourse, is religious prejudice. This operates even where friendship exists between Englishmen and Indians. Over every avenue to real cordiality, the Hindú and Muhammadan have written up: "Yes. To smell pork! To eat of the habitation which your prophet, the Nazarite, conjured the devil into. I will buy with you, sell with you, talk with you, and so following; but I will not eat with you, drink with you, nor pray with you." It has been said that the way to an Englishman's heart is through his stomach: well, the people of India cannot penetrate to English hearts that way. Caste sits before every Indian door and forbids the European to enter. The very shadow of a European pollutes the food of a Bráhman; and though an Indian may enter a European's house of prayer, the sacred places of the Hindú may not be profaned by the European footstep.

The story of Indian domestic and social life can be set forth only by the pens of Indians themselves, and these pens have many restraints upon them. Pages, therefore, such as these which are here presented to the English public, deserve to be welcomed. The author possesses a remarkable knowledge of the English language, and combines with it an amount of candour and freedom from bigotry which is rarely to be met with anywhere. In these sketches of Indian life will be seen the struggles which clever and ambitious Indians, who have but a meagre patrimony, must undergo, first to educate, and then to support themselves. Here, too, will be seen evidences of the friction which exists between the governing and the governed race. It is to be hoped that the *hauteur* of the one and the irritation of the other are decreasing; but the European who goes to sleep with his boots in an Indian gentleman's lap while travelling in the same compartment of a carriage on an Indian railway, is, it is to be feared, not wholly extinct; and wherever he exists he spreads around him an atmosphere of discontent in which good feeling finds it impossible to breathe.

Among the more general and lighter descriptions there are many sketches that will be new to English readers, as, for instance, the manner in which the people of India enjoy their holidays, the elephant-fights in the arena at Baroda. Many of these more interesting passages have drifted into the later chapters, and might be overlooked unless pointed out by reviewers. Of pure literary interest is the chapter on the Hindú epic, the Rámayana, which the author, struggling, perhaps, a little beyond his depth, compares with the Sháhnámah, and even with the Iliad.

What is said about English law may not, perhaps, be acceptable to English readers, and its soundness may be contested, but amongst Indians there would be a universal consensus as to its truth. The law's delay is in India an intolerable grievance; and it is certainly the fact that in the first mutiny the English judges were the most frequent victims.

The portraits of Indian notabilities seem to be drawn from the life, and will, no doubt, be thought by some to be recognisable; and it may be learnt from them that it is not always those Indians who are most countenanced and raised to the highest posts by the English authorities, who are most acceptable to their countrymen.

It will be seen that the author, although a very much younger man, is a friend of Lutfullah and his fellow-townsman, and these sketches have something in common with the autobiography of the older writer. May the *débutant* be equally fortunate with the English public!

E. B. EASTWICK.

CONTENTS.

GUJARAT

AND

THE GUJARÁTIS.

INTRODUCTION.

PERMIT me, gentle reader, to briefly explain the genesis of this little book. Starting on my pilgrimage in the too early twilight of life's day, I have often stumbled into dry nulláhs*—very dry and dismal, and with very steep sides. And in groping my way to reach the other side, I have badly barked my shins. But it is matter for thankfulness to be able to say that in none of my stumbles have I broken any bones. However bad the fall, I have always managed to pick myself up; and, with the rope thrown by friendly hands, have struggled up the stony hill-side. These "roughs and tumbles" of life have become

* Empty water-courses.

a part of my nature, and I have often felt a vague sort of conviction that life would be scarcely worth living without some prospect of having to "rough it."

A Poor Beginning.

I began life at twelve, giving private lessons. It was a poor beginning—the task of coaching big hulking lads was so dreary. At sixteen I became a regular teacher. I had seen enough of the world before this—the world of India, of course. I entered upon my new duties, therefore, with hearty interest. The work did not feel a drudgery for some time; but two or three years after, my migratory instincts again asserted themselves. I felt that I wanted a change. I had taught and studied children long enough, and I thought I must now study "children of a larger growth."

A Tempting Offer.

At this time I was offered the joint-editorship of a local (English) weekly. I jumped at the offer, and submitted it to a few friends whom I used to consult on matters beyond my management. These gentlemen, each and all, scouted the idea, and strongly advised me to keep where I was.

My Troubles.

Here began my troubles. I had already been favourably known as a versifier; and with the overweening confidence of youth, thought I had the right and the power to enlighten the public on political and other topics of the day. There was nothing for it, however, but to bow to friends' decision, once having sought their advice. During the next two years I had the most miserable time of it. They made me a morose, disconsolate verse-monster. I scribbled English verses by the yard; and after destroying the bulk of them, ventured to publish a few pieces. But no end of verse-writing could compensate for the glorious chance I had missed of becoming a journalist and public censor. However, I received fresh overtures soon after. This time I gave my elderly advisers to understand that I meant to act for myself, though I should be very glad if I could do so with their consent.

Struggles of a Cheap Newspaper.

It was a cheap weekly, hitherto owned by two partners, cousins, one who had given it money, the other brains. Two more partners were added, my friend N. bringing money, and I supposed as supplying brains. The work was fairly divided —the first proprietor, D., a small clerk, undertook business management. N. was to help D., and also to make himself useful to us—my friend P. and myself—in the literary business. For a week or two all went on smoothly; but we soon felt the necessity of discussing our position. N. was a man of temper, and among other things "compositors" did not take kindly to him. I received frequent complaints as to his harshness; but knowing he had brought us a thousand rupees I could do nothing more than appeal to his good sense. One Saturday night Mr. N. was given a "proof" to read. He corrected it; but instead of entering corrections on the margins, poked his pen into the body of the "composed matter." The compositor almost fainted at sight of the "proof" he had to revise—he could not follow the corrections, and the paper was delayed next morning. On Sunday, when we four proprietors met, I gently asked Mr. N. to be good enough to enter corrections, in future, on the margins of the proof-sheet. N. glared at me for what he took to be an insult, and replied that he had paid 1,000 rupees to be his own master—that he would do just what *he* liked, and would not be bullied by people who had not contributed a farthing. This sneer was passed over by me; but the co-editor winced under it, and replied hotly to N.'s insinuation. What threatened to be a bad quarrel was, however, soon made up; and we all adjourned to an adjoining hotel to discuss the future of the paper and a substantial breakfast provided for the occasion.

Editorial Vagaries.

But by-and-bye we two editors could not quite agree between ourselves. I was for treatment of social questions chiefly; my friend P. affected politics. We settled this difference by confining each to his own *forte*. Our ignorance, even in this, was as boundless as was our arrogance. But was it not glorious to criticise and ridicule the highest men in the country? What a privilege for too-early-emancipated school-boys! Nothing could be easier than my share of the literary work: I turned into prose, every week, two of my versified social essays, of which I had a plentiful supply at home. Did poet ever sacrifice his substance as I did, in those days, in the public interests? My sweet sonorous hexameters surrendered bodily to the manipulations of the deity P. D.! No martyr could do more. My friend P. wrote political essays. He was decidedly better-read than I. Certainly he took pains with his essays; but how could a young man of less than twenty overtake topics which baffle the grasp of practised veterans? One day, writing, I believe, of the battle of Plevna, P. asked me what was meant by "the Porte." I said "the Porte" was the Sultan of Turkey's principal wife. P. thought it was only the European title of the Khedive of Egypt. We often thought in that curious way, and often wrote ourselves down, in our own paper, a pair of conceited jackanapes. And when, next morning, we found out our mistake, we accused each other of ignorance, obstinacy, and so on.

Editorial Amenities.

This could not last; and one evening P. suggested, in Council, that our capitalist partners should get a few reference-books for the editor's table. Mr. N. refused to pay four our "extravagance." I submitted, as chairman, that we were neither of us "extravagant," and that Mr. N. was wrong. Hereupon he charged us with indulging in soda-water with office money. P.

replied. "If some fellows eat plantains (or bananas) with office money, I don't see why I may not drink a bottle of soda when thirsty." Here, by way of diversion, I suppose, N. said he wanted his thousand rupees back. P. asked him fiercely if he meant really to be so "perfidious." N. replied, with equal ferocity, that he wanted to get rid of "r——ls." "Very well," said P., taking up N.'s new turban and throwing it out of the window, desiring its owner to leave instantly, on pain of being sent after the turban by the same means of exit. But N. did nothing of the sort. He took P. by the throat, and demanded the satisfaction of throwing out *his* turban. "It is my right, give me my right, you r——l, and then I'll leave." Here they closed. They tugged and lugged, tore each other's hair and clothes, and mauled each other very prettily. It was with the utmost difficulty that the young Tartars could be separated. And the two—once intimate friends and college chums—have never since been on "speaking terms." That evening, in the presence of friends, servants, and neighbours, who had come up on hearing of the fracas, I wept tears of anguish, in my editorial and presidential chair, at all my hopes of fame and fortune having vanished so suddenly and so cruelly.

But crushing as the disappointment was, it enabled me to cast about for some equally powerful distraction. I had long cherished the hope of visiting Gujarát and Káttywár with some definite business views. And having at this juncture received an offer from a friend, I accepted it thankfully.

A Poor Programme.

This personal explanation has been given, reader, to warn you against expecting too much from my book. Now that you know me, I know you will not be too exacting. If you are curious to revel in the luxury of deep and learned research, I must frankly refer you to *Oriental Memoirs*, Forbes, Briggs, Ferishta, and such others, with whom my acquaintance is slightest of slight, barely sufficient to make me know my place. If you want to refresh, and at the same time to enlighten your mind, you had better turn to the picturesque details of the gifted *padre*,* Heber. Should you wish to have correct statistics and authenticated accounts, I could safely recommend

* Applied, in India, to all European preachers or priests.

you to pore over Mr. J. M. Campbell's famous *Gazeteers.* In these prodigious results of editorial labour you will find a forest of facts and figures which you can traverse leisurely, till you become another Dr. Hunter,* a prince of particulars, a very king of quotations. But if you care to have a fresh account of, perhaps, the least known but most interesting parts of Her Majesty's Indian Empire, of the inner life of an important people, their habits, customs, manners, the moral and social forces at work among them; then you are welcome to these pages, such as they are. You will have to be content with rough, hasty sketches, but generally taken on the spot—sketches from real life. I would not promise you much of system and order—because, you see, this is not an Official Report. Many of these sketches appeared, at the time, in the *Bombay Review*, and are all the better for having received a few touches here and there from the very able and accomplished editor. Not a few of them were, indeed, undertaken at the suggestion of that veteran Anglo-Indian journalist. These sketches, and a few more contributed to other papers, are here

* Dr. W. W. Hunter, Director-General of Statistics to the Government of India.

put into shape, intermixed with extracts from letters to friends and the contents of a rough diary—all strung together on a rather slender narrative thread.

I do not mind confessing, reader, that this is a poor sort of programme. But it is, perhaps, as well it is so. I may also prepare you for a little exaggerated expression, wherever the writer is "intense." But you will not find cause to question my *bona fides*—in spite of occasional levity, degenerating at times almost into what may appear to be flippancy. I do assure you that no writer meant to be more serious. If you follow my sketchings in the spirit and the letter, if you read between the lines, you will not find them all mere caricatures.

SURAT:

Its Fabled Origin.

. . . . " Something ails it now."

We left Bombay for Surat—I and my old servant Rasul—on the 13th of March 1878. Rasul was lent to me by a friend with whom he had spent many years in pleasant travelling. Surat is as good as my " native land," I having lived there from two to fifteen years of age. Its *genus loci* has been hallowed to me by association. The bones of a hundred ancestors are this day bleaching in the awful chasms of the Towers of Silence. Memory is besieged by the shadows of a thousand incidents when I find myself in the midst of old haunts, where, for an hour or a day's pleasure, I have passed months or years of bitter privations.

I know Surat intimately, from end to end, and notwithstanding the utmost ingenuity of patriotic bards and encomiasts, and the good-natured credulity of European *savants*, I do not think we can give Surat a fabled origin, linking her name with the glorious Souráshtra of old and making her one of the territorial galaxy which shed lustre on the arms of the valiant Rajput who swayed the destinies of, perhaps, twenty million human beings scattered over an area of more than fifty thousand square miles, and who traced his descent to the early Aryan fathers, the first discontented wanderers from the cradle land of our race. Vanity and self-love seek to identify this town of Surat with the far-famed Souráshtra which has been in existence time out of mind, and which embraced, perhaps, a hundred times the area of Surat. By some curious trickery of nomenclature, that which was known as Souráshtra is now come to be known as the peninsula of Káttywár, whilst others say that is Souráshtra on the site of which now stands Junághar, the capital of the Bábi Mahomedans. Surat may be a feeble and corrupt imitation of Souráshtra. Taking it any way, Surat was nowhere before the thirteenth century A.D.

Strange Vicissitudes.

It seems to have been built under Mahomedan auspices. It derived its former importance from its maritime situation, which afforded peculiar facilities not only for a vast sea-borne trade, but for hordes of well-to-do Mahomedan pilgrims sailing for Meccá. Surat has a curious and touching history; but this is not the time to call up visions of its past glory. Its career reads like that of the beautiful eastern slave, whom chance leads from one enamoured master to another, till the lovely captive has well-nigh lost her power to please. From the Ahmedábád Mahomedans, probably its first owners, it passed into the hands of Akbar, "first in war, first in peace, first in the hearts of his countrymen." But the deputies of the Grand Mogul could not retain the prize long; it passed successively into the hands of the mercenary Dutch, the fiery Lusitanian, the marauding Marátta, till the same chance placed it in the hands of masters who, hailing from the land of the free, claim freedom and justice as the objects of their mission to the East.

Surat of To-day.

Surat was a right jolly place a century ago, though even then it was in the afternoon of its glory. But "something ails it now." Its rapid ruin since can be traced to disastrous fires and floods, to the drying up of the Tápti, and to the rise and prosperity of the island town of Bombay. Surat of to-day is a shadow of its old self, its stout commercial spirit gone, the well-to-do of its citizens grovelling in indolence or pleasure, its social morality decayed and still decaying. The British are doing much to infuse new life into this prostrate capital of their original possessions in the Western Presidency. Enlightened and equitable administration of justice, well-worked medical and educational agencies, wise schemes of municipal impovement; these are all tangible reforms, and have a leavening tendency on the almost deadened national conscience. But the instincts of the people seek repose: it is incompatible with a true Surti* nature to keep pace with the march of progress. The labouring and agricultural classes have ample security of person and property; but I doubt if they enjoy that progressive prosperity which is the true criterion of a settled and enlightened rule. The fact seems to be that England is losing India

* Native of Surat.

with too much of law. The laws are too many, and too fine to be equitable in a community of mutually antagonistic classes and conflicting interest unused to such laws. And worse than the laws themselves is the working of them. Except in this, I do not think the people have any real cause for grumbling; and I am sure they seldom grumble, my poor, primitive peace-loving Surtis.

A few Honest Growls.

Coming to a class higher, I mean the middle class, what strikes the observer most is this: the rising generation are given every facility and inducement for acquirement of a fairly liberal education. Such education naturally widens their vision and gives play to their innate aspirations. But when they attempt to assert their position as politically and socially the equals of the ruling class, "these natives" are ridiculed for their presumption! Not only are our educated men so many political pariahs,* but even in ordinary social matters they are made to feel their inferiority. Those thousand little social charities, which might, perhaps, reconcile them

* Degraded homeless outcasts.

to standing political disabilities, are withheld from them as a matter of course. In public, as well as in private, the best of natives must "know his place," when in the presence of the white Sahib. It is the old, old story, of might being the better of right. It may be allowed that some distinction of the sort is inevitable. But really, it is neither necessary nor expedient to keep up this spirit of exclusiveness which is growing into another CASTE.

One more growl whilst I am in this stern preaching mood (I seldom preach) at the levelling policy of our officials. No doubt, there must be one law for rich and poor. This policy is unexceptionable in the abstract, and the higher sphere of affairs. But in practice, in the minor details of life, where the rich can feel and the poor *cannot*, it would be obvious injustice to make no distinction between the high-born and the low-born. This proposition may shock the philosopher; but as the world goes, I am afraid it holds good as much in Europe as in India. If it is the interest of a wise ruler to see the poor rise, it is equally his interest to see that the rich do not fall. Here in Gujarát we know of hundreds of young men of rank and talent who are treated by the officials with studied indifference. And what is the result? The flower of the generation, finding no scope for their talent, and no respect for their birth, degenerate, by degrees, into profligates and malcontents. In a country where rank and title are the prizes of life, those who claim a titled ancestry are literally worshipped by the masses. The people themselves are loyal to the core, though much puzzled by sudden and trying administrative changes; but the number of the educated high-born who feel they are neglected or despised, is on the increase. Let our Collectors and Judges see to this. I do not wish to meddle with politics here; but this particular complaint is so universal in Gujarát, and indeed throughout British India, that a mention of it could not well be avoided. A word to the wise.

Local Celebrities.

I made a very brief stay at Surat, and saw only a few of the local magnates. The most important amongst these may be considered the Nawáb of Belá and Meer Gulám Bábá Khán, or as they are popularly called, Bará (big) Sáheb and Chotá (little) Sáheb. I made the latter's acquaintance under somewhat painful circumstances. Travelling together one day, I learnt by accident that my companion was Meer Gulám Bábá. There were four of us in the compartment—Meer Gulám, his secretary, a European, and myself. Now, it so happened that the European, not knowing Meer Gulám, went to sleep with his booted feet in Meer Gulám's lap. The Meer, unwilling to provoke a quarrel, quietly moved further from under the insulting encumbrance. The European hereupon accused him of having disturbed his rest, and fired off a volley of *ear-splitting* abuses. The poor Meer held his tongue, though I could see from the working of his face that his blood was up. But the European, some vulgar bully, thus emboldened, took the Meer by the arm and attempted to push him out of the carriage. Here I interfered, and after a good deal of explanation, I got the European to desist from annoying the nobleman. The man went to bed again, muttering "I don't care a hang who he is." I hinted to the Meer that he could have done better; but he mildly replied in Hindustani, "We have had our day; these people have their day now, you see." After this philosophic remark, we dropped the unpleasant subject, but became very fast friends for the day. We exchanged some fine oriental compliments at parting, but have never met since.

The other Meer, a rival, I never got to know except as a curiosity. He is said to be a good-natured, pleasant-spoken gentleman, much given to what may be called pleasures of the palate.

Amongst Parsi celebrities of Surat is Khán Báhádur Burjorji Merwánji Fraser, a fine, pleasant old gentleman, who has run through a fortune in a very fashionable way, but not without behaving handsomely in making gifts to his native city, as is duly described in Murray's new *Handbook of India* (*Bombay*), and other records of the time. Shett Burjorji is a Khán Báhádur, let the reader remember. Surat boasts of other Parsi notabilities too; but as I do not know them personally, I cannot introduce the reader to them.

Notable amongst the Hindus is my friend Ráo Báhádur Jugjiwandás Khushåldás, the Full Power Magistrate, a sturdy old gentleman, honest and plain-spoken, a terror to evil-doers. I should not, also, forget the Surat editors, celebrated throughout India by their connection with the great (License-tax) Riots Case. They appear to be the very embodiment of the "mild Hindu" type, but conceal a world of energy and determination under a rather unpromising exterior.

But my best friends at Surat are the Irish Presbyterian missionaries, Dixon, Wallace, Montgomery, Taylor—alas, they no longer *are*! William Dixon, my own revered master, died quite a young man. You could see at first sight that he was a scholar and a martyr. He effected much good at Surat; and though death too soon cut short a career of brilliant promise, his influence is felt even now to be at work.

William Wallace was our Bible teacher—a man of great benevolence and learning. I have never seen a man so gentle in spirit and so unruffled under provocation. His life was a blessed example to us all.

Much differing from Mr. Wallace, but actuated by the same motive, was the Rev. Robert Montgomery. Mr. Montgomery was, I believe, the oldest Presbyterian missionary to Gujarát, and spent the very best days of his life there. He died at home, in the fulness of time, at the patriarchal age of three score and ten, leaving behind the memory of a virtuous and well-spent life to be cherished by three generations of men.

The deceased was a most successful preacher of the Gospel. He hated all underhand and dubious means; and rather than fire up the imagination of his audience by the glitter of false hopes and impossible promises, he preferred to reach their conscience by making Christianity a necessity of man's fallen nature. His Christianity was of a peculiar character, like himself, pleasant, practical, and conciliatory. Wherever he could, he cheerfully fell in with the views of his opponent; where he could not, he would not mind pulling Satan himself by the beard, keeping himself and the adversary all the while in the best of humours. An anecdote is current in Gujarát of how the good old man would sally forth of a Sabbath morning, enter an unknown village, preach against the stone-gods, be set upon by the mob, and incarcerated for his audacity: how he would hold forth from his prison—now in muscular Hindustáni, reminding the populace of their unlawful conduct and its consequences; now in suasive Gujaráti, laughing at their despicable mode of warfare; and then suddenly asking for a drink of water, and directly going off to take his forty winks; falling to the recital of some quaint but touching prayer on awaking; till at last he would win the hearts of the people, issue forth, all smiles and bows, snap his fingers at the heathen priest who had instigated the rabble, and set out for home, often after a supper of warm milk and bread, escorted by the very men who had, a few hours ago, put him into the cow-shed prison! Such was Mr. Montgomery, the missionary.

Yet one more. The Rev. Van Someren Taylor. This very day, 27th June 1881, as I am sitting down to record my sense of his worth, I hear of his sudden death at Edinburgh. I had not the honour of being one of his pupils. But Mr. Taylor did that for me which he scarcely could have had the opportunity of doing for many others. To him I am indebted for my success as a Gujaráti writer. He was my first literary guide and friend. He was the first to approve what had been neglected by many others; and but for his encouragement, I am not sure if I could at all have ventured to publish my works in the face of general discouragement from other friends.

Mr. Taylor was essentially a missionary, a devoted and indefatigable worker, a genuine scholar, and a genial friend. I believe that the success of the little colony of Christian converts at Borsad* is mainly due to Mr. Taylor's exertions and influence; at any rate, he is acknowledged its most faithful friend. To his many other acquirements, Mr. Taylor added a very intimate knowledge of the Gujaráti vernacular. His Gujaráti grammar is the best for students of all classes, and is, I believe, a standard book. He wrote excellent Gujaráti verses, and has published one or two volumes. Besides the fine Christian sentiment running through them, his lines are remarkable for purity, warmth, and simplicity. Many of them I have heard sung with very good effect. In his work as a missionary and a citizen, he won confidence and sympathy whereever he went; and though very quiet and retiring by nature, he was ever ready to advance, by word and by deed, the cause of education and enlightenment. In the case of many a struggling young man, Mr. Taylor's kindly encouragement hss been actually the making of a life of usefulness.

Another Gujarát missionary of much promise was the Rev. Mr. Wells, who also died at a

* A little town near Ahmedabad.

comparatively early age. He, too, was a great Gujaráti scholar and has written several works in that vernacular, which are not only popular, but are recognised as first-rate school-books. Mr. Wells was a very zealous, active man, and known for his rough practical benevolence.

Of the European officials, the best remembered men by this generation are Mr. T. C. Fere, the collector *par excellence*, and Mr. H. M. Woodlark—*the* judge. Surat is greatly indebted to Mr. Fere for numerous practical reforms. Stern and almost overbearing in his official relations, he despised false popularity, and though sometimes carried away by over-zeal, his honesty of purpose has never been questioned. Though smarting under some of his hasty measures, the Surtis readily acknowledge that "Fere Sáheb" has been the second founder of the city.

Mr. Woodlark is popularly known as "the Model Judge." He is no less a favourite with the official circle than with the public. He is "as good as a native, *one of us*," the people explain. I know of no greater compliment that could be paid to an official. And this praise is amply justified by Mr. Woodlark's love of the people, and his readiness to identify himself with every movement, private or public, for their advancement.

I must not forget two other popular officials —a Judge and a Collector again. The former, a native, Mr. Satyendranáth Tagore, is one of the ablest civilian judges, and his decisions are remarkable for their legal acumen and close reasoning. Coming of a race of reformers and benefactors, Mr. Tagore very well sustains the traditions of his family. Wherever he goes, he devotes his best endeavours to the enlightenment of his countrymen. He is the idol of the Gujaráti people. In private life he is simple and modest, quite a *Sádhú*,* as a friend describes him. Mr. Tagore is, I believe, the first native Civilian who passed the competition in England.

Another official is Mr. A. Lendhill. A good deal of energy and good sense has characterised his administration of Gujarát. Mr. Lendhill has read the native character pretty accurately, and he seems to know equally well how to apply his knowledge. The first thing almost that he had to attend to on his arrival at Surat was a formidable conspiracy of the grain-dealers to run up

* An ascetic.

prices. It was a sight to see the Collector walk up to the grain-market, button-hole the leading dalâls,* and lecture them out of their unholy league. Nothing stronger passed between them than friendly remonstrance, but it had its effect; though the more forward of the brokers freely quoted Bentham, Mill, and other advocates of Free-Trade. Mr. Lendhill is an out-and-out Anglo-Indian, as was his learned and highly-respected father, Harry, of that ilk, who compiled a valuable work on the castes of this province.

Let me not omit here Sayed Edroos of Surat, who is an Honourable and a C.S.I. This Moslem of many titles was in the Governor's Council for some time, but his legislative career was blank as a sheet of blotting-paper—or at best imprinted with the impressions of others. He cannot discuss any subject (1) because he is ignorant of English, and (2) because his ideas of his duty are the reverse of original. He thinks he serves his country best by nodding assent to whatever falls from the Sáheb's lips. Is it strange, then, that the Sáheb should love him dearly?

* Brokers.

Is it strange, then, that the collectors should try to give Sayed Edroos another lease of life as councillor to Sir James Fergusson? But this sort of happy-family arrangement will not do in these days—at least, I trust, not in the days of Sir James. The Sayed Sáheb is an exploded myth. He has ceased to believe in himself, and even his existence has become a matter of doubt. The Gujarát people, therefore, will have none of him. The Presidency protests against the contemplated jobbery of a second term for the Sayed. They say Let us have anybody else,—Mr. Cumu Sulliman,* or even Ismal Khán, butler to the Collector of Cobblington; but no Sayed Edroos—they have had enough of his name in official reports of "members present." Let him live retired—

"The world forgetting, by the world forgot."

As worthy a man as the Sayed is a certain Mohlá† of this province. The Mohlaji is at present in hot water. He is the head of a

* A wealthy and enterprising upholsterer, and good friend to impecunious subalterns.

† Mussulman leader.

Mahomedan sect very numerous in Gujarát and Bombay, and is, therefore, kept in good condition. For a long time he was considered the safest and most liberal banker in Gujarát; and people of all classes deemed it a privilege to leave money with the Mohláji. Many a poor widow disposed of a house or other property, and entrusted the assets to the Mohlá. About ten years ago something was found wrong with the Mohlá's affairs, and creditors flocked to his holiness to withdraw their money from under the Mohlá's trust. But this was no easy work. The Mohlá begged for a reprieve. After a good deal of bickering and yielding to threats of exposure, some of the Mohlá's friends undertook to wipe off the debt by eight annual instalments. But creditors allege they have not yet been paid back anything to speak of. The Mohláji again asks for time; but the creditors are indignant and threaten to "proceed." Poor old Mohlá! He is so much married! And that, too, on set purpose. He marries young ladies of fortune, so that he may be enabled to meet his heavy and long accumulating liabilities. But somehow or other the money seldom reaches the creditors. In the meantime, his reverence keeps up his personal establishment in grand style, though he has just issued orders for shutting up a religious academy hitherto working under his auspices. This is false economy, to be sure; but what can you expect of a poor beggar like the Mohlá when the Imperial British Government practises, sometimes, a similar method of retrenchment? The Mohláji is looking up and about; and, with the help of a few friends from Bombay, may again "tide over." But there is little fear of the creditors being paid in full. The Mohláji and his family are too "civilised" for any such folly. His holiness, now over eighty, has married another "wife"—a buxom widow with thirty-five thousand rupees. I forget if this is the Mohlá's eleventh or twenty-first "wife." But what matters it? So long as there is money, the Mohlá thinks, "Let the cry be, still they come."

Only one more good Surti, my dear and honoured friend, Moonshi Lutfulláh Khan. To my acquaintance with him and his, I owe much of my chivalrous respect for the Mahomedan character. Moonshi Lutfulláh is "a noticeable man, with large grey eyes." As scholar, linguist, and author, Mr. Lutfulláh is well-known in these parts, and even in England.* To the latter country he accompanied the late Meer Jáffer Ali Khan of Surat. Over twelve years ago I used to be almost an inmate, now and then, of the Lutfulláh family, thanks to an intimacy with his son, Fazal. I have enjoyed some of the happiest hours of my life under his hospitable roof. Moonshi Lutfulláh was an old man when I knew him; he must now have obtained the patriarchal age.

SIGHTS.

There is not much to be seen at Surat, except, of course, the new Hope Bridge, the Cowasji Jehangir Hospital, the Killáh (castle), the Park, perhaps the two cotton mills, the Band Stand, the High School, and the Andrew's Library.

The Tapti Bridge, or as it is popularly named, the Hope Bridge, in honour of that energetic Collector, is a recent construction. It connects Surat with Ránder on the opposite bank. The bridge is a fine strong structure, and is no doubt a great convenience to the people. It cost over seven lakhs. There are many larger bridges in

* See his Autobiography, a remarkable political memoir, edited by the eminent Persian scholar, Mr. E. B. Eastwick, C.B.

India; but to the stick-at-home Surtis, their bridge is a marvel of human ingenuity. I am not surprised to be told that some of them worship it and offer sacrifices to the presiding genius.

The Hospital is an admirable building, due to the liberality of the late Sir Cowasji Jehangir Readymoney, the well-known Parsee benefactor of Bombay.

The Killáh is a glum bit of stone-work, which stands firm as a rock against the violence of the elements. It is a Mahomedan structure.

To the building of the fine High School, Mr. Sorabji Jamsetji Jeejeebhoy contributed a large sum. Mr. Kharsetji Furdoonji Párakh, too, has one or two charitable institutions at Surat standing to his credit—the Párakh Dispensary and the Industrial School.

The Andrew's Library is a very useful institution; but it is badly off for want of funds, I am told. It is a pity that Bombay, knowing To to be so, will not save this institution much approaching difficulties.

The Band Stand is on a pretty pleasant site, to which *gorá loke* (white people) drive by one entrance and *kálá loke* (black people) by another.

PHILANTHROPIC MILL MANAGEMENT.

The local mills here were started on the most philanthropic and magnanimous principles, no end of interest on limited investments, and absolutely no future "calls." Even the wide-awake Bania (money-lending class) swallowed the bait; and it is a sight now to see him hauled up so tight and breathing so heavy. Matters have gone to the court, and that is no compliment to the management. Wise citizens, who detest every form of investment, except lending to impecunious artisans on the security of their families, are laughing slyly over this *contretemps*.

SCENES AT A MILL MEETING.

The Directors of the Jáffer Ali Spinning Company at Surat seem determined to ruin the concern. They agreed to disagree among themselves. The division was unequal, having a majority on one side and a minority (but that with the president) on the other. The bone of contention is poor Vakil (Advocate) Goolábdás. This veteran Vakil, more sinned against than sinning, suspected a "leetle" underhand work, and with the instinct of the lawyer he set about ferreting out the game. He could do this best as a director; so a director he would be, swore Mr. Gooládbás, and a director *was* he after some strenuous opposition. Now, this detective director has been putting awkward questions to some of the Aryan managers, who had it all their own way, headed as they were by a Mahomedan nawab.* Well, the Aryans have their own arithmetic, and Mr. Goolábdás cannot reckon in it. At a recent meeting Goolábdás said so, plain and plump. I can well see that firm Mongolian face of his, immovable and unmoved by the loudest vituperation. He wanted *facts*; they gave him "abuses." He bowed, they kicked their shins against the benches; he grinned, they roared; he said "gentlemen," they replied "r——l"; and so on and on, till the president lost patience. They want not Vakeel Goolábdás, but he *does* want them. Strong are his opponents, leading luminaries of the law. But he minds them not, this servant of *Gooláb.*† He asks, "Why spend rupees fifteen on this? I know an old barber could set it to right for rupees three." But the answer is merely a cackle of denuncia-

* Generally, an *innocent.*

† Goolábdás=slave of the rose.

tion. The end of it all is "in the womb of futurity," as Hindu graduates put it. Suffice to say, that it is a very pretty domestic quarrel in *embryo*, and that when the little dragon is born, it may, like the divine Sanishchar,* devour its own family. And that is what the Directors of the Jáffer Ali Mill want.†

A Season of Plenty.

Poor Surat shared the fate of all the neighbouring districts during the recent famines. Then again the *water famine* was proving too much for her when Jupiter Pluvius luckily became more favourable and more reasonable. His cloudy majesty is at present (latter part of 1881) exceedingly obliging. He comes and goes to order. The wise men of Surat wonder if the prospects of the *khedú*‡ could have been brighter even in the golden age. Everything is cheap, especially rice, *ghee*,§ and *tarkári*.|| The grain-dealers who, two months ago, entered into a secret compact to starve the poor, and who, only the other week, sat with all the insolence of

* Saturn. † This was written two years ago.
‡ Cultivator. § Clarified butter. || Vegetables.

"shop," are fearfully down in the mouth. They are now to be observed paring their nails, scratching their heads, and so on, and receive the ugliest customer with elaborate attention. In a word, they enjoy a season of plenty down here; and if my eyes have not deceived me, I have seen a well-defined smile lurking in the countenance of one of the municipal commissioners. When you see that, you may be sure the creature is in the best of moods; for in his normal frame of mind, you can trace not a sign of emotion in the commissioner's face, which is all cheek and chin. Indeed, the plenty is not so plentiful as in the days of the Nawáb, when my dear great-uncle used to maintain a family of fourteen, in peace and comfort, on rupees seven a month. And even from this pittance, my good aunt, his wife, was able to buy him a boxful of snuff, a pocket-handkerchief, and a pair of goatskin shoes every nine months. In those days *ghee* sold at fifteen pounds a rupee. Those are called "the fifteen-pound days." To-day, even though they look upon it as a very good year, *ghee* is less than four pounds the rupee. And *ghee* is everything to the Surti—his present happiness and his future bliss.

A Zealous Official.*

I was told the other day of our excellent young postmaster here. He is the very pink of a postmaster, and the way he stands on his dignity is stunning. His idea of asserting his authority is to fine the wretched peons right and left. These men are paid about seven rupees (fourteen shillings) a month, out of which the "paternal" Government makes it incumbent on each man to buy a red coat a year, a pair of shoes twice a year, turban, trousers, umbrellas, &c. Part of what remains goes towards the Good Conduct Fund. From the residue the peon has to maintain wife and family, father, mother, children, cousins, aunts, &c., in that irreproachable respectability which befits a servant of the Paternal British Government. "Hard lines," you will growl, reader. But I have not done. A peon tells me he is now fined about two rupees a month on an average. So what he earns is five rupees, out of which he has to attend to each one of the duties, private and public, that I have just enumerated. The postmaster is very likely a good man; but

* Written two years ago.

he overworks his men, and for the slightest error, such as he commits a thousand a day, he cuts the poor wretches in the tenderest, and, alas, the slenderest part! Sir Richard Temple could have made an excellent license-tax collector of my friend the postmaster. He is a typical instance of what we call here "a zealous official" —the man who, be he Native or European, brings the Government into utter disrepute by resorting to petty high-handedness like this, very often in order to curry favour with arbitrary and unscrupulous superiors. Such men are, unhappily, not few nor confined to a limited area. They are scattered over the whole Empire, and are doing damage to the *préstige* of the Government wherever they are.

BROACH.

We left Surat on the 16th March, my friend Rasul and I, and arrived at Broach after two hours' journey by the B. B. Railway. Close to the station we found the Rustomji Jamsetji Dharamsálá,* and here we put down ourselves and our baggage.

Rustomji Jamsetji Jeejeebhoy.

Poor Mr. Rustomji! His princely progress through Gujarát is still remembered by the people, who fervently bless his name for numerous quiet charities. In spontaneous and hearty good-will towards man, he was no way inferior to his sire.† Talk as one will of his "blindly

* A resting-place, literally "a house of charity."

† Sir Jamsetji Jeejeebhoy, first baronet, the world-renowned philanthropist.

lavish expenditure" and that sort of cold-blooded philosophy, one cannot divest oneself of the thought that the unhappy gentleman was shamefully jilted by fortune. What is a matter of more poignant regret to a generous heart is that his own people were far from grateful to him in his fallen fortunes. I fail to see the wisdom of the policy of the Parsi friends and others when they voted him a sectarian memorial. To my knowledge several Hindu and Mahomedan friends were ready and anxious, in fact they offered, to mark substantially their sense of admiration for this truly catholic lover of men. But his Parsi friends set themselves resolutely against all such proposals; no one can tell for what reason. It were foolish to conceal what is not a secret, that poor Rustomji Jamsetji had a greater claim to the gratitude of all sections of society than his late lamented and handsomely endowed baronet brother. But there is a proverb among us—"All bow to the rising sun—none to the setting." Rustomji Jamsetji most resembles the late Sir Cowasji Jehangir, with this difference, that the former had nothing of the cold, at times almost sordid, spirit of calculation which characterised the princely donations of the latter. All his charities were the offspring of generous impulse and an almost reckless disregard of consequences. Many "philanthropic" Parsis have died, and many may die hereafter (God have mercy on their souls!), but none probably have died so widely regretted and so long remembered as poor Rustomji.

The Rustomji Dharamsálá, though a really handsome, well-divided building, has not a piece of furniture it can call its own—not one single chair or piece of bedding. Could not some Bombay Parsi buy the Dharamsálá, say, three hundred rupees' worth of small conveniences?

The Great Man of Little Broach.

Seeing that the Dharamsálá was merely an enclosure of bare walls, with hard chunam flooring, I wrote to my friend Desái Kaliánrái Hukumatrái, to help me with a few chairs. Desái Kaliánrái is the greatest among the Broach gentry, a municipal commissioner, a leading shett, a public-spirited citizen, and a general favourite with friends. The Desái is a man of taste, and keeps his house and grounds in excellent order. The worthy Desái came to my help with chairs, tables, and beddings, and so kindly did we take to each other, that I refused to make the acquaintance of others at Broach. My first impressions of Broach are thus recorded:—

The Address.

Broach, thou venerable relic of departed commercial activity, father of far-famed Gujarát, once the proud emporium of the trade of Gujarát, Káttywár, and Rajputáná, cradled by the holy Narbadá and sanctified by the presence of the sacred Sukaltirth, I walk thy dusty, musty, spongy surface with a gentle gingerly tread! Hail land of pugilists and prudes, hail hoary dust-town, miniature Cottonopolis, all hail to thee!

An Afternoon Pastime.

One cannot help loving this dear old town with all its drawbacks. While a man is there, he feels as if he were treading his grandpapa's well-preserved stomach after tiffin. This is a favourite pastime among natives: their afternoon meal is the most copious of all, after which, feeling a little uneasy on having swallowed about two pounds of rice and the other concomitants, the elders of the family lie flat on the back, and invite the young hopefuls to pommel and promenade on their ample, capacious, middle regions. Their version is, that they give that exhilarating exercise to their progeny out of love (the venerable sinners!), but everybody knows it is all a sham. Well, then, one feels while walking the streets of Broach that he is hugging an old welcome friend, as if he were clasped in the arms of old Father Christmas, with a cloak of dust on his shoulders. Dear old hen-pecked Broach!

CHARACTERISTICS.

Yes, the science of *henpeckery* is carried here to perfection. It is studied universally. The town itself is henpecked by that termagant of a river, the Narbadá; the husbands are henpecked by their better-halves. Even the lower creation share the same fate; the dog, the horse, the bull, are tame as—a Turkish pasha; the other sex, bold, pushing, forward. Nay, even high Government officials do not escape this terrible discipline; their mistress, the Bombay Government, sits heavy on them.

A PRUDE.

I went a-marketing here, once upon a day, "in the merry month of May"; I approached a dairy-shop, and seeing a pot of boiling milk (rather partial to this liquor), asked the woman sitting there how much she would take for a *ser** of her milk. She glared at me in answer, got up from her crouching posture—I could see she was a short woman, with a shorter petticoat, and a shorter temper still—she got up, I say, and asked, in gasping tones, "Is it asking for the milk you are after? And asking *me*! Ar'n't you ashamed? Ask my *this*." Her "*this*," I saw, was her "old man," sitting in the inmost recesses of the shop, and eating curds on the sly, if I guessed aright. A Hindu woman will die rather than address or speak of her husband by his name; she will say "I say," or "my this." If they are an elderly pair, the wife will describe her husband as "father of my" (naming her eldest born). The husband does the same by her; and it is delicious to hear these old creatures chatting cosily of an evening, "I say, mother of ——" "Yes, father of ——, what is it?"

But to return to the milk-maid. I humbly said, "I only ask if this milk is to sell." "Don't ask *me*," she shrieked; "milk and no

* About one pound, more or less.

milk. Marry come up, asking a stranger woman! Ask my *this*, did you hear?" Her "this" was inside, I said, and there he remained. I listened to her with Socratic patience, and then left her, merely remarking, "Pray thee, good woman, do remove the milk from under thy glance; it is turning sour." I need not add that I walked very fast after this towards my lodgings. The encounter took place last year. I hope there are not many such women at Broach as my sweet-tempered milk-maid.

SIGHTS, NATURAL AND UNNATURAL.

The visitor will be struck here by the number, more so by the noise, of the ginning (cotton-cleaning) factories. There is not much of other business to be noticed. Amongst sights, the best are the river Narbadá, the Kabir Bur, some old Dutch tombs, the band-stand, and recreation grounds. Perhaps the most noticeable sight in the streets is the snobbery of men and the prudery of women, also the happy family relations between the cart-driver and his bullock. The animal is kissed, embraced, lashed, and imprecated by turn. "Go on, bullock of my heart, go on, thy mother-in-law's darling"; "Will you go or not? you lazy widower, you son of a widow." These are the sounds the ear continually catches, interspersed with whacking sounds, twisting of tails, cutting of flesh, &c. Broach badly wants a Society for the Prevention of Cruelty to Animals.

But for its ginning factories, mostly under Parsi management—besides the large one of Messrs. Greaves and Co.—Broach would be an unspeakably dull place. Dulness is the prevailing characteristic of most Gujarát towns; at least, to one who has lived in Bombay, it feels so.

Broach was recovering from the effects of the Gujarát famine at this time. It was piteous to see hundreds of villagers—men, women, and children—begging from door to door, and swallowing anything that came in their way. Some of these famished wanderers were, I was told, substantial farmers only a few years ago, but successive failures of crops and the inexorable demand of the *Sirkár** had driven them into voluntary exile. In the document I give below, a copy of which I picked up at Broach, and

* Government.

which document must be read between the lines, may be found the views of the Collector, the Revenue Commissioner, and the Government, as regards remission of taxes in bad seasons.

A Remarkable Official Document.

From the Collector to the Revenue Commissioner, N.D.

"Sir,

"Looking at the wide-spread misery of the ryots, their distressing past and hopeless future, I respectfully submit that their arrears be remitted them, or at least the payment deferred till better times.

"I have the honour to be,

"Etc. Etc."

From the Commissioner, N.D., to the Collector.

"Memo. 2,085,677 of February 1877.

"The undersigned read the Collector's *insane* letter with pity and disgust; and has done his duty by forwarding the same to head-quarters. Undersigned is afraid the Collector will have to pass a bad half hour with His Excellency, but it will serve him right."

—— ——.

From Chief Secretary to Government to —— —— Esq., Collector, ——.

"Sir,

"Your strange communication, forwarded by the Commissioner of your Division, has excited much amusement. His Excellency in Council vows and declares such unpatriotic proceeding on your part is highly reprehensible. But in consideration of your past meritorious services, your folly is forgiven; should you, however, repeat it, His Excellency will be forced to make an example of you. If you have so much sentiment about you, why don't you resign? You will have a crust of bread for your old age.

"I am sir, yours,

"Etc."

"Memo.—Whereas a certain District Revenue Official (name withheld out of consideration for long service) has dared to suggest the remission of our just and lawful dues, it is hereby notified for the general information of the whole Civil Service that His Excellency will visit with his utmost displeasure any such weakness, which may lead at any time, but for the vigilance of the Police, to gross crimes, such as riot, burglary, dacoity, and murder, and ultimately tarnish the fair fame of Britain. Times change, and with them must we. The people may die, that is the only means to the salvation of this conquered land. They may starve, languish, sell their children, or eat them. That is no concern of such high-minded Christian rulers as we are. We *must look to the remote future.* There we descry hoards of Afghans and Cossacks overrunning the fair fields of Cashmere. (Is not he our neighbour? and what is our duty by our neighbour?) And would it be Christian of us to rest before we have made a trans-Himalayan tramway, and till we take our formidable future foes home to Afghanistan and Siberia, wash the one and put the other to bed? Think over these complications before you talk of remission and this and that remedy."

This official memorandum, or, as they call it, "resolution," and the other brief but expressive epistles which accompany it, may not be found on Government records; but they will give to the uninitiated some idea of what we know as demi-semi-official arrangements, in which our newly developed "Imperial" policy finds occasional play. The *imperial* politician always looks to the "remotest future."

BARODA.

LEAVING Broach, nothing loth to leave, we came to Baroda on the 10th March. The capital of the Guicowárs was to me the Mecca of my pilgrimage.

THE APOSTROPHE.

Land of my birth! After twenty-four years of forced exile, I fly to thee. For a fourth of a century has my spirit yearned to see thee. For a full fortnight have I tried, on the spot, to conjure up thy past glories. But where are they, Baroda? Where are thy traditions, thy institutions? Where are the goody-goody stories which soothed me to slumber and thrilled me into infantile action? Above all, where are thy great institutions, such as the Sáthmári in which human beings were trampled under the elephant's foot (just for the *fun* of it, you know), where alleged offenders were buried alive, thrown down steep hills, pinned to the wall, rolled in barrels nailed inside? Where are thy *Holi* festivals, during which a hundred hired houris* frolicked in naked charms in the palace compound, and invited, by a thousand arts, the whizzing liquid of the royal *pichkári*? † Where are the marriages between doves‡ and the attendant festivals? Where are the crusades against cats, because one of the feline tribe breakfasted on the feathered bridegroom? Where is thy bracing fever, thy benignant cholera, O land of my birth? Gone, gone are all thy glories, gone for evermore! And instead I see the jail and the court-house, parks and palaces, roads and tanks, schools and colleges; and that monster of a Municipal Commissioner! But enough of interrogatory apostrophisation; it leads to bad blood and bad grammar.

* Very brown nymphs.

† Syringe. Mulhár Ráo Guicowár used to play at this very delectable game.

‡ Khanderáo Guicowár celebrated the marriage of his two favourite doves with royal pomp.

Description of a Durbar.*

A Durbár was held last year in honour of the youthful Guicowár having attained a certain age. The Dewán Sáheb was absent in the district, his duties therefore devolved on his Parsi coadjutor. Half an hour before the Guicowár arrived, the nawábs, the sirdárs, and páttidárs, and a host of other feudatories flocked to the Nazar Bágh. The court officials received them. On entering the state-room, each looked about to see if he had the right seat reserved for him. Your Spanish snobocracy could not be more punctilious in their "reserved-seat" etiquette. It was a sight to see old Kawáb Squaretoes Sakkar-Missari exchanging fiery glances with young Sirdár Hukká-Chilam Pán Supári. I looked on steadily till my thick upper lip curled up in contempt and my nose expressed my unspeakable disgust at their silent squabble. They simultaneously read my thoughts, and turned upon me with a fierce look which clearly said, "You intruding upstart! What have you to do with *our* concern?" That glance killed my æsthetic being; but still there I was, a living monument

* A court and political reception; a sort of levee.

of hardened humanity. But that day I made up my mind, that if I ever went to a Durbár again, I would look as grave as a chancery judge, whatever more exalted people did. Soon after came the Guicowár, as intelligent and fine-looking a young fellow as was ever called upon to grace a *gádi**; as cool and collected as if to this "greatest favourite of fortune of our times"—as Sir Mádav Ráo aptly describes him—his present life and his life of five years ago made a very little difference. His Highness was shortly after followed by the British Agent and his staff. When the appointment of Mr. Philip Sandys Melvill to Baroda was first announced, it was considered by the Bombay officials especially as rather out-of-the-way, rather a *jobbish* appointment. But the Government have been amply justified in their choice. There are few officers in the whole range of the Indian Civil Service who could discharge the duty of the post with greater tact and delicacy. Mr. Melvill's principle seems to be, never to interfere hastily with the Durbár concerns, and a most healthy principle it is. In private he is as humble as he is

* Throne.

amiable, one of the very few official Englishmen in India who are not ashamed to own the dusky children of the soil their brethren.

But to return to the Durbár. Well, the Resident sat, and with him the whole assembly. And then rose three noticeable personages from the floor on which they had been squatting. Two muddy-complexioned nymphs,* and the bear-leader, that is to say, the music-master. The former ethereal beings I dare not describe; the latter was a short, healthy Mahomedan, not much under four hundred pounds avoirdupois. I need not say he is a man of great *weight*. The dusky *houris* sang a few snatches in a clear vigorous monotone, accompanied by instrumental music on half-a-dozen *porcelain cups and saucers* by the healthy Mahomedan. The music was not intended for man; so I cannot be a judge of it with justice. It soon ended, to our relief, and was followed by the rubbing of attar† (which has a sweet sickly odour, and a most tenacious regard for your handkerchief) and distribution of pán supári.‡ Before the Durbár broke up, a tall, lank courtier stepped forward, and offered his

* Dancing girls. † Otto of roses.
‡ Betel leaf and the nut.

stereotyped good-wishes to His Highness, the beginning and, in fact, the gist of which I translate *verbatim et literatim* for the reader :—"May you bathe in milk, and may you (the future Ráni, that is) bring forth sons." Thus ended the Durbár of 1878.

THE PEOPLE AND THE DOGS.

From prince to people is a natural transition. The capital of the Guicowárs has a population of two lakhs of folk, consisting of men, women, and children, with a thick sprinkling of Páhriá dogs. The men may be divided into two classes—the snobbish and the sheepish. The former perpetually chew pán supári, wear huge turbans, and drive about in the tiniest carriages dragged along by wee little bullocks, an inch or so smaller in size than our Bombay goats. The more bloated the face, and the smaller the carriage and bullock, the readier is room made for the owner by the awe-struck pedestrian. Women may be divided into three classes—wives, widows, and prudes; the first rule their husbands, the second rule their shops, the third may have been intended to scare away the small boys and dogs, and generally go about veiled and without shoes.

They are very helpful to the Police, in that way, and honest citizens avoid them somehow. The little boys of Baroda may be described as "sad dogs," and the dogs as "gentlemen at large." These gentlemen seem to enjoy more privileges than their biped brethren. You will see one of them of an evening basking and luxuriating in the sunshine and street dust, his red tongue lolling out, absolutely refusing to make room for the state carriage, or any other carriage, until he is taken hold of by his *southern extremity** and flung bodily into the neighbouring basket of sugar cakes. Even under such trying circumstances his serenity is undisturbed.

H. H. THE LATE MÁHÁRÁJÁ KHANDERÁO.

It is said the late lamented Máhárájá Khanderáo Guicowár was very partial to this race of philosophers. His late Highness was a genuine "ruler of men," brave as Rustom, and munificent as Jamshed, though perhaps not so wise as Solomon. He had strong likes and dislikes. But his failings were always amiable. One of these was, that he thought himself a born Esculapius. He had a remedy for all diseases, known

* The tail.

and unknown, and used to physic everyone about him. He used to experiment on a large scale. The shortest way to his favour was to go and say you had the belly-ache—by far the most usual complaint among the Barodites. Well, His Highness would straightway repair to the dispensary, and return with a large bowl containing some vile mixture, which you must quaff at a draught and without giving the slightest indication of a wry face. On the contrary, unhappy patient, you must smile while drinking the royal nostrum. If you do not grin in the most approved court fashion, you are a ruined man. Well, after you have swallowed the poisonous stuff, make a low bow to the royal physician, and retire to the adjoining room. Going to eject the dose on the sly ? Do not attempt it, poor deluded wretch, there are two royal eyes gloating over thy misery. Go to sleep over the potion, though thy inner man may be on the fire of h——l the while. Return in half an hour to report progress; smile and simper and bow and scrape and loudly bepraise the medicating genius of thy master. Then go thy way, thy fortune is made. In this direction His Highness was not less busy than my Aunt Charity. His Highness also knew some occult science, such as alchemy which means, I suppose, the science that treats of extracting sunbeams from cucumbers.

Disposal of Dogs.

But to come to the gentlemen dogs again. I fear they make it too hot for "His Highness's" other loyal subjects, and must either be banished, or the municipal commissioner ought to give them a uniform and set them to some "Imperial" work. The Afghan war has not yet quite ended, and the Zulu war may begin anew. The illustrious Ráma had Hanuman's monkey-army to fight his battles with Ráwana; why may not Baroda send to one of the frontiers a contingent of its canine cavalry?

Summing-up.

To sum up, Baroda is a good place enough, but it is dull, dull beyond description. There is no living here; it is a mere humdrum existence. Between the people and the "upper ten thousand" there is no sympathy. You have no such institution as Society.

Exhortation.

How is it there is no missionary here? I demand. Import one, ye powers that be; he is indispensable to progress and enlightenment. Get up popular lectures and street-preaching. " Steady internal progress," and all that, is very well, but let the people learn to *enjoy life* under your administration. In their present state they are almost justified in looking back. Let them forget the past. The " glorious " reign of rapine and plunder and the degrading superstition, they must be taught to hold in horror. Give them something on the strength of which they may fondly look forward. Let the agricultural interests of your people claim your deepest consideration. Get up cattle shows, and agricultural shows, and vegetable shows. Get up, if not fine, industrial arts exhibitions.

The Viscount, the Sáthmári, and the Popinjay.

Attend all ye who, &c., to a soul-stirring account of the Baroda Sáthmári, which implies an elephant fight, but really means much more than that. In the year of grace 1879, 12th day of April, it pleased my Lord of Hinchinbrook, a Government guest, to ask to be shown the elephant fight. To hear a live lord is to obey ; and instantly were issued thundering despatches from the acting Dewan's department to "all concerned," namely, one parrot, two elephants, eight buffaloes, two rhinoceroses (I am not quite sure if these officials are not called hippopotamuses, but both are bad, long words, and might be fairly interchanged), twelve rams, and sixteen wrestlers, a superior race of animals, who looked almost men, short and sleek and close-shaven. These doughty champions met at about five on the eventful evening, at a sort of house in the heart of the town, variously described to me as a palace, a bakery, and a charnel-house. I believe it was a palace in ancient times, when "horses were kings." At present, it is a skeleton house, exceedingly seedy and sensitive, but with an air that eloquently reminds one of better days. Adjoining this house of mystery is a spacious compound, the battle scene, that is to say, and surrounding it are the menagerie and stables. The *tamáshá** opened with an acrobatic exhibition. A man stood on a rickety frame-work of wood, resting on a table, another man taking somersaults on the arms and shoulders of number one. I do not very well remember this part of the

* Public show.

performance, but have a vivid recollection of the concluding part, when the wooden framework came to grief, and with it the two jack-pudding snobs. It was a relief to know that both escaped serious accidents, one having broken his pate, the other only his shins.

Then came the accomplished parrot, who flourished his miniature sword, with his beak of course, bent his bow and shot his arrows, and, what is more amazing still, loaded his tiny cannon with gunpowder, lit the touch and—fired! The feathery hero wrought wonders. The skill of a British general is nothing to the versatile genius of this gymnast, archer and artillery soldier. Indeed, that parrot is a genius! May this record immortalise thee, O Prince of Popinjays!

The rhinoceroses gave each other very warm reception. About this time last year, when His Excellency Harun-Al Raseid* graced the *sáthmári*, these sulky warriors would not *close*, though every gentle persuasion—such as poking into their eyes, nose, and other tender parts, the long-pointed *bhálo*†—was exhausted. Lord Hinchinbrook was more fortunate. Old Rhinos fought

* Sir Richard Temple. † Lance.

for him, as I said, and fought valiantly and well. The elephants, too, "went in for it" right cheerfully, and it was a sight to see these black moving hills of flesh tugging and lugging and heaving away as earnestly as if, on the issue of *their* contest, depended the scientific rectification of our frontier. Poor beasts! And yet why *poor* beasts? Are they not considered the paragons of womanly beauty by the Hindus? "Oh, elephant of my heart," was the tender exclamation with which our ancient fathers used to greet our great-grand-dames during courtship and honeymoon. Ask Sir Mádov Row, who is an authority on Hindu literature, from politics to poetry. And yet your modern Mary Ann would not relish the compliment if her Brown met her behind the kitchen door with, "Ho helephant of my 'art!" But I am sure the ancient *Munis** and *Rishis*,† the venerable sires to whose genius we owe the Vedas and other Shástras, did address their "old flames" as above, when in a frolic mood.

The buffaloes and rams butted away beautifully. Brisk and energetic was the meeting of

* Sages. † Seers.

the bovine heroes, and their parting, oh! so very slow and unwilling.

But before finishing this catalogue of intelligent fighting brutes, the faithful historian should not omit the wrestlers—bless my eyes, how very like *men* they look at times! They first make each other a make-believe bow, then shake each other by the paws, and then close. They rub and scrub and curry-comb each other till both drop on earth, where they go through a process of mutual kneading, and finally they mix, these fat, living butter-barrels, and there you lose their identity; you cannot, for the life of you, say which is which. And here ends my description of the *sáthmári*.

But let me just run you off one screed. I was asked last year by a great man, a man of advanced views, what I thought of the fight. I praised the affair as faintly as a *devoted* husband praises his mother-in-law, and then gently insinuated, "But don't you think, Sir ——, it is a barbaric if not a barbarous pastime?" That insinuation cost me a fine lecture, in the course of which I was told of the great power such exhibitions have to excite our martial instincts. I blushed (in imagination) at my stupid want of enthusiasm, and later on, when I read a work in which the Parsis are eloquently exhorted to go to and conquer Persia, I said to myself, says I, "The Baroda *sáthmári* is the only thing that can rouse my slumbering patriotism." Hence my second trip to the capital of the Guicowárs.

Official Dignitaries.

In the course of the two visits to Baroda, I was able to make the acquaintance, more or less, of all the official dignitaries. Sir Mádav Row I saw during the first visit, with two or three members of his council. It is impossible, of course, not to be favourably struck with such a man. My visit lasted less than half an hour. At Baroda also I had the honour of the acquaintance of the Resident, Mr. Melvill, and of Major and Mrs. Nutt. As I have caught hold of the Baroda Administration Report for 1877–78, I think it may be best to give, in a few lines, my impressions about these gentlemen individually, in connection with their official work. To begin at the beginning.

H. H. Mahárání Jamnábái, C.I.E.

This august widow of the illustrious Mahárájá Khanderáo, seems to be extremely popular with her people. Bráhmins worship her more fervently than they worship Bráhmá. According to official reports, she is a highly intelligent woman, and extremely *dharmi.** She is, of course, at the head of the palace, and the palace expenditure having been left to Her Highness's control has happily increased by about a lakh.† Last year's item stands at sixteen lakhs and odd (£160,000). There are several departments of the palace—the household, kárkhánás, and dharmádagá being the principal. Each of these costs considerably over six, four, and four lakhs, respectively. With the utmost respect for Her Highness's prudential instincts, I submit the dharmádagá items are disastrously heavy. The kárkhánás include the jewel establishment, the elephants, horses, bullocks, fireworks, sporting establishments, dancing girls, and the athletes, that is, the animals employed in the arena. The dharmádagá is maintained for giving *khichri*‡ to the poor and gifts to the Bráhmins. Looking to the item under this head, I do not wonder at the report that some of the *mendicant* Bráhmins of the royal

* Charitable.

† A hundred thousand rupees.

‡ Rice and *dál* cooked together.

household are *millionaires*. But next year we are promised wholesale economy. We all remember how Her Highness was invested with the Imperial Order of the Crown of India. That evening Mr. Melvill proposed Her Highness's health at a royal banquet. In returning thanks the gallant Dewán broke out into lusty eloquence, likening Her Highness to Venus. But, it may be remembered, it was to the Venus of Astronomy, not of poetry, that the sage poet-politician likened his royal mistress. The Mahárání is doubtless a remarkable woman—she is firm of hand and strong of will. She is said to be a capital horsewoman, and fond of riding out into the open districts, and all that sort of sport. She is equally fond of music and dancing; and she is the mother of little Tarábái, married recently to the Sáwuntwári chief.

H. H. Siájiráo.

His Highness the young Máhárájá is the object of Ráni Jamnábái's instant and constant solicitude. The Agent, the Dewán, and the tutor are agreed in thinking him an exemplary youth of his class. His arithmetic is necessarily weak; but it must be remembered that none of his ancestors had a genius that way. And if he had an arithmetical turn of mind, why should he have been reserved for a *gádi?* His progress in languages is, however, satisfactory. He is now reading the *Children's Friend*, a book without an equal. Why should he not read a little of Chesterfield now and then? His Highness is also studying Chemistry, Political Economy, and Geography. All this while his physical development is being taken care of. In the midst of all this good-natured progress-puffery, I am much gratified to find Mr. Melvill's sober testimony as to the young Guicowár being hitherto "untainted in his moral character." That was three years ago; H. H. is now married and a father into the bargain. It looked almost impossible that a youth, with Siájiráo's private surroundings and his unfortunate physical precocity, should long remain untainted; but the official testimony must be accepted.

THE EX-GUICOWÁR MULHÁR RAO.

This gentleman is said to be doing as well as could be—we half think better than while he was in *hukumát.** His expenses, ordinary and ex-

* Authority.

traordinary, are being regularly supplied to him. Dr. Seward* treats him and his family, we are told, with a "combination of firmness and tenderness."

The Governor-General's Agent.

Of Mr. Melvill's worth and abilities I have spoken elsewhere at length. Let us now see what the Dewán has got to say of him. And who better able to speak of the Agent than the Dewán? Sir Mádav Row, after gratefully acknowledging "the generous confidence and uniform support" accorded to his administration by the Government of India, records the following brief acknowledgment to Mr. Melvill:—"The administration is deeply indebted to Mr. Melvill, who, as Agent to Governor-General, does all that is possible to give effect to the high aims and to follow the great principles of the Government of India." From all that I know of Baroda affairs, I can honestly bear out Sir Mádav Row's opinion of the Agent of the paramount power. Mr. Melvill has nothing of the petty intermeddling spirit which, unfortunately, characterises the generality of Political Agents; and

* The Ex-Guicowár's keeper at Madras.

being above local prejudices, he discharges his duties of arbiter between the State and its vassals with a calm impartiality which seldom leaves room for appeal. Though ready and anxious to help forward the good work inaugurated by Sir Mádav Row, he never yields an inch where principles require firmness and consistency.

The Rájá Dewán.

This veteran administrator is an *élève* of the Madras University, a Maráthá Bráhmin by race, and a Tanjorian by birth. He owes much of his early education, I believe, to Christian missionaries. These facts may prove instructive to the cockneys whose feeble wit is never tired of railing at "the benighted presidency," and at the efforts of foreign *padris*. I know little of young Mádav Row's academic career; but it must have been far above the common run, to judge from the fact that soon after leaving college he was taken in hand by the Director of Public Instruction, Mr. Evan Powell. He seems to have started in life as a schoolmaster, and sometime after is said to be in Government employ. At this stage he attracted the notice of one of the Arbuthnots, at whose recommendation, probably,

Mr. Mádav Row came to be tutor to the first Prince of Travancore, and ultimately the Dewán. This prince, now Máhárájá, is considered, an educated and accomplished sovereign, and an enlightened ruler. This is, no doubt, partly due to the influence of His Highness's tutor. It was for his successful administration of Travancore, I believe, that Sir Mádav Row was knighted by the paramount power. He was then invited by the Máhárájá Holkar to take charge of his State as Dewán. Here he remained for some years, and managed to secure the esteem and goodwill of, if not the Máhárájá, the British Government and the people.

Sir Mádav at Baroda.

Early in 1875, on the deportation of Muhlár Rao Guicowár, our Government cast about for a pilot capable of steering Baroda, a most unseaworthy vessel, clear of the dangers and difficulties surrounding it. Their choice fell on Sir Mádav Row, and it has at least partially been justified. Indeed, it would not be transgressing truth if I said, on his own authority, that in the past three years this able Máráthá minister has worked wonders. He has almost cut through formidable rocks of Girásia* and Sirdár† claims, crossed the shoals of internal and external opposition, refilled the sands of the almost run-out revenue glass, bridged over boundary chasms,‡ spread the light of education where once "reigned and revelled" the gloom of ignorance; the judicial, financial, and sanitary "chaos," he has reduced to "order," which, Edmund Burke tells you, is "the foundation of all good things." Instead of the army of athletes who expended their brute force in wrangling with brute creatures, Sir Mádov Row introduced an army of intellectual wrestlers who fight their foes in their several provinces with faithful courage. Mulhár Ráo's Baroda was the most uncleanable of Augean stables; but with their brooms and mops and spades (no offence, gentlemen, this may be a fine Sanskrit figure) the enlightened warriors have swept away all abuses, and made it all "sweet and clean" for young Siáji Ráo and his little family of eighteen lacs. §

* A vassal, generally a small landed proprietor.

† A military vassal.

‡ Boundary disputes between neighbouring states.

§ 18,00,000, population of Baroda.

ADMINISTRATION DETAILS.

But to come to the particulars of the year under review—1878. On the outset, I am favourably impressed by the Dewán's endeavours to "conserve the rights and privileges" of his State. These endeavours have culminated in the reduction, to its minimum point, of the active interference of too many British officers (neighbouring, I believe) in the internal administration of the State. This is a great triumph for Baroda, and equally creditable to the persistent representations of the Durbár and the liberal good sense of the paramount power. Oh that other native States of Western India were half so handsomely treated! And oh that these States deserved to be so treated! But interjections are wasted upon Government officials and native Kárbháris.* In the year under review, the Dewán obtained the loan, from the Bombay Government, of the able Civilian, Mr. Joshua King, for the settlement of "girás" disputes. The Minister also confesses to having invested to some extent in municipal dead stock, an arrangement sure to benefit the live stock of Baroda in

* Managers of native States.

the end. In the same year were sanctioned or expended Rs. 2,30,000 for medical buildings, of which the New Jamnábái Dispensary costs Rs. 86,000, and is pronounced by Dr. Cody as "unsurpassed at least in this country," in its management for the "comfort, convenience, and privacy of the patients." Dr. Cody may be right in his estimate of this gem of a dispensary. But I, too, have seen dispensaries in Káttywár, which are, and will remain for a century to come, quite "unsurpassed."

An Unsurpassable Dispensary.

For instance, there was one at Máliá. It was in a nice little hovel, and was conducted on catholic principles; for, not only was it free to light and rain, but even beasts of the field and birds of the air found free access to it. For some time, I was told, the dispensary had not been working; but I found that this assertion could not be borne out; for I myself saw a number of respectable-looking mice experimenting with the surgical instruments, and a number of big stalking spiders surrounding the blue bottles with a fantastic network. I have no right to recommend a study of this "unsurpassed" dispensary to Dr. Cody, now that he has been so politely feasted and toasted, and bowed out of Baroda.

FINANCE.

In spite of liberal disbursements under all heads, it is gratifying to see that the Dewán so well keeps up his financial position. Soon after the assumption of office, he roughly estimated the normal revenue of Baroda at about 110 lacs, and the normal expenditure at 105 lacs. The receipts for this year, I note, amount to 120 lacs, which is more by 10 lacs than what the Dewán first estimated. The disbursements for this year are 122 lacs, which is more by 17 lacs than the original rough estimate. Both the receipts and the disbursements were, however, mainly influenced by the bad year on one hand, and the consequent extraordinary expenditure on the other. Last year's financial statement is a better criterion, in which I find the receipts to be 133 lacs, and the expenditure about 105 lacs. The amount invested in Government notes stands at one crore and two lacs* at the end of the year under review. Altogether the financial position

* £1,200,000, reckoning Rs. 10=£1.

is most satisfactory. The report gives promise of curtailment in several departments, especially the palace and the military. This is a healthy move. But the double marriage at Baroda has absorbed a fat fraction of Sir Mádav Row's cherished hoards once basking in the sunshine of 4½ per cent. interest.

THE RÁJÁ DEWÁN AS A WHOLE—THE BRIGHT SIDE.

The Rájá Sir T. Mádav Row is an avowed admirer of Anglo-Indian statesmanship, and his administration thus far of one of the largest native States in India has been thoroughly British in character. Whether this administration—a most interesting experiment in itself—has been or is likely to be a complete success, time alone can tell. Sir Mádav Row went to Baroda with a reputation for rare political ability, and he has given ample proof, at least, of his industry and perseverance. Sir Dinkar Row and Sir Mádav Row were the likeliest men for the coveted prize. Baroda was then bordering on anarchy, thanks to Mulhár Rao's gross misconduct. The finances were at a low ebb; the administration of law and justice was arbitrary and uncertain; and, to be brief, both State and society, were completely demoralised. It required a strong hand to restore the *prestige* of justice and law, and to check the sirdárs, zemindárs, and other hereditary hangers-on in their career of oppression on one hand, and extravagance on the other. The public, the Maráthá people especially, had made up their minds as to the appointment of Sir Dinkar Row. The Government of India, however, nominated Sir Mádav Rao, who was generally understood to be the more liberal-minded statesman of the two. But somehow this appointment did not please the public of Western India. Sir Mádav Row came on the scene as a friend, but the Guicowár subjects instinctively, perhaps unjustly, called out "save us from our friend." The attitude of both Maráthás and Gujarátis was rather ominous, and it no doubt damped the spirit of the ardent administrator, whose career had hitherto been a series of triumphs. To add to the discomforts of his position, the Government of Bombay "looked with a severe eye" upon the intruder from the south, whom Holkar had only recently found to be too "advanced" for his slow-going subjects. But the fiat had gone forth, and Sir Mádav alone could rescue Baroda from anarchy. He had only a short time previously afforded Lord Northbrook* great pleasure by his astronomical lucubrations. He was generally allowed to be a man of talent, one of the most educated men in India, with a will and capacity for work. Thus came His Excellency to Baroda, conquering and to conquer. Luckily for him, the Government sent a local Agent and Resident who was well qualified by temperament and training to second His Excellency in every detail of administration. The Dewán of Baroda had, indeed, good cause to be thankful for the appointment of Mr. P. S. Melvill; and the recent rumour of Sir Mádav Row's resignation simultaneously with the approaching retirement of his friend, the Political Agent, although unconfirmed, takes some colour from the fact of their cordial and intimate relations.

Sir Madav Row on setting to work, formed a ministry of some of the ablest native servants of the Government of Bombay. He skilfully distributed the work of administration, reserving to himself the supreme control of affairs in every

* Then Viceroy.

department. He requested his subordinates to find him as much money as they could by honest means. The result was, that within a year the Dewán was able to show a surplus. Arrears of State dues were recovered, fresh contracts were made on advantageous terms; sirdárs and other idle pensioners were told to shift for themselves; the Ráni-mother (Queen-Dowager) and the Guicowár elect were informed that they must not exceed their already liberal allowances, and that the State would not be responsible for any extravagance in which they might indulge. Having procured finances, the Dewán entered upon a series of reforms, revenue, judicial, municipal, and educational. A glance at his elaborate annual reports will show that Sir Mádav Row has done more than was anticipated. He has changed the face of Baroda. He has introduced various reforms, developed industries, and encouraged individual enterprise. Two years ago in "letting off" a couple of marriages, he exhibited the resources of the country and gave to European visitors a taste of Oriental hospitality such as is seldom offered even at the durbárs of Rájás.

THE SHADOW SIDE.

But in spite of all this prosperity, Sir Mádav Row's administration of Baroda is far from popular either with the Maráthás or the Gujarátis. Sir Mádav Row is not only an avowed admirer of Anglo-Indian statesmanship; he is a servile imitator of the same. He worships routine and centralization. The result has been disastrous, as it could hardly be otherwise in a state where the masses are yet struggling with poverty and ignorance. What can be more exasperating to the poor illiterate *khedu*,* used to direct appeal and rapid decision, than to have to carry his grievance from his village to the town, and thence to the district, and finally to the capital. Another fault in the Dewán is that he insists on exercising direct control over the minutest departmental detail, even to the employment or dismissal of a sepoy. His municipal and other reforms are confined to the principal towns. The Mofussil† is a howling wilderness. Roads, irrigation, and all other essentials of material progress are conspicuous by their absence. The people, all Gujarátis of the "mild Hindu" type, are committed to the mercy of the Maráthá officials—men not only

* Cultivator. † Country districts.

unacquainted with the concerns of rural life in Gujarát, but destitute of all sympathy with the people. The sure and short road to popularity at head-quarters is increase of revenue. To the unscrupulous official nothing is impossible in this direction. The Bombay papers have reported many instances of oppressive taxation introduced on frivolous pretexts, and various taxes of the kind are still levied, although the nominal reasons for them no longer exist. Sir Mádav Row has sense enough to see that, with the people arrayed against his administration, he has no chance of ultimate and permanent success. Intelligent and beneficent as that administration has been, as compared with the state of things which preceded it, there is yet lacking in it, as in its "Imperial" model, many of the qualities essential to efficiency.

Popular disaffection is already finding vent in newspaper articles and in anonymous pamphlets, in which the writers accuse Sir Mádav Row and his co-adjutors of crimes the most repulsive and hateful. These may be all—no doubt some of them are—a tissue of malicious fabrications, but they augur no good to the now very much-embarrassed ministry.

KHÁN BAHÁDUR KÁZI SHÁHBUDDIN.

This able revenue officer is a Mahomedan, and was once upon a time in British employ as Mámlatdár. I can trace him only so far back; his official identity beyond that is to me shrouded in mystery. That he was once a school-boy and so on, I allow; but his personal history I shall reserve till he retires, or at least becomes a member of the Legislative Council. From a mámlatdár, Kázi Sháhbuddin came to be a Deputy-Collector. He then entered the service of His Highness the late Rao of Kutch. Since then, I believe he has been at Baroda. He can, therefore, be fairly supposed to have a greater knowledge of the "ins and outs" of Baroda than any other brother officer of his. Kázi Sháhbuddin has a remarkably clear head, and his revenue administration of Baroda would do credit to any English Civilian in India. In the dismal history of Mahomedan management of public affairs in this part of India, Kázi Sháhbuddin's official career is the only "shining part." The flourishing state of Baroda revenues, and the comparative ease with which they are collected, speak much for him. "With a rare mastery of details, he knows and appreciates large principles, and applies them with judicious modifications, to the existing state of things." So says Sir Mádav Row, and he ought to know what he says. Kazi Sháhbuddin is well known for his pleasant manners and accommodativeness, and during the recent scarcity in Gujarát he discovered a vein of philanthropy as charming as it was original. He kept under his protection several famine refugees, and is said to have been wonderfully hospitable to them.

Khán Bahádur Pestonji Jehángir.

This Parsi official commenced his career, years ago, under the auspices of the British Government; and since his entrance into public service up to this day he has been recognised as, perhaps, the ablest native officer in the department under which he has served. He is best known in this Presidency as Settlement Officer; and as such he has always commanded the approval and confidence of his Government. He went to Baroda, six years ago, with a reputation for ability, independence, and rectitude. His duties at Baroda are of a most delicate and complex nature, involving the awards of very considerable sums of money; and he discharges them with a judicious care that often entitles his decisions to the respectful acceptance of both parties. The department over which Mr. Pestonji presides is, in many respects, the most difficult, and it certainly could not be in better hands. In the course of the year under review the Settlement Department is reported to have disposed of 1,067 cases, some of them involving immense labour and judicial acumen.

KHÁN BAHÁDUR CURSETJI RUSTOMJI.

This gentleman, a Parsi also, is a *protégé* of the British, under whom he has occupied several judicial posts. He has a very respectable knowledge of English law, and is a fine Maráthá scholar. He is a slow, shrewd, and competent officer, and at present occupies the important office of "Chief Justice"* of Baroda. He presides over the Varishtá Court, and transacts business in relation to original and appeal suits with much discrimination. Mr. Cursetji Rustomji is assisted as Puisne Judge by

* High, or Chief Commissioner.

RAO BAHÁDUR JANÁRDAN SAKHÁRÁM GADGIL, very well known for his power of manipulating figures, in which business he has rendered himself useful to the Dewán. Mr. Gadgil was some years ago connected with Bombay journalism, be it whispered gently. Under the Varishtá Court there are, in all, 123 inferior tribunals, with 126 judges, which, to be mathematical, gives the satisfactory ratio of 1·024390 judges to 1 court. Among these finely decimalised administrators of Guicowári law may be mentioned the well-known Mr. Ambálál Sákerlál, Mr. Raoji Vittal, and Mr. Gunesh Shitárám Shástri. The cost of the whole judicial organisation for the year is put down at Rs. 3,73,000, against which there is a set-off of Rs. 2,81,000, in the shape of stamps, fees, fines, &c.

RÁO BAHÁDUR VINÁYEKROW J. KIRTANE.

This zealous officer I have been industriously and impatiently looking about for, till I find him sadly mixed up with the Police. Mr. Kirtane is a quadrupal officer, managing the *Khángi*,* the General, the Educational, and the Police

* Guicowár's private purse.

Departments. He seems to be a most efficient and able officer, and has rendered very good service to the Dewán in the matter of police organisation and reform during this year. Sir Mádav speaks with cordial approval of "the rare amount of knowledge, thoughtfulness, and sustained though unostentatious energy" which this officer has expended on the discharge of his onerous and multifarious duties. The strength of the city police force is represented by 1 superintendent, 8 inspectors, 72 subordinate officers, 245 peons,* 20 sowars,† 4 detectives, and 42 men on office establishment. Besides the usual police expenditure of Rs. 95,508, an extraordinary grant of Rs. 13,923 was made this year. Mr. Superintendent Tubák, generally known in Bombay, has been thanked by the Dewán for having guarded grain-shops during the recent scarcity.

MR. G. F. H. HILL, C.E.

This gentleman is State Engineer at Baroda, and the Department under him has done "very creditable work," to judge from former reports. The total outlay by Mr. Hill's department during

* Constables. † Mounted Policemen.

the year is Rs. 6,37,000. His office establishment has been materially strengthened, and special addition has been made for purposes of account and audit, which will cost annually Rs. 18,000. An additional sum of Rs. 25,000 was also sanctioned for fair weather roads in the Amreily Division. This latter amount, the Dewán Saheb says, was partly spent "usefully," and partly, I should say, "wastefully." Sir Mádav Row forgets that nothing under the sun is perfect. However, His Excellency is not behind-hand in Oriental compliment. He says, "Mr. Hill may be congratulated on the excellent manner in which *several* of his subordinates have served the department"! So he may. Besides Mr. Hill, the State Engineer, Baroda has a "Special" Engineer,

Mr. Crosthwait.

This gentleman seems to have rendered signal service to the State in connection with the water-supply and drainage works, and also in devising means to restrain the floods of the Viswámitra—an annually recurring danger. It is satisfactory to learn that the bunds (embankments) erected by Mr. Crosthwait have proved very useful. Mr.

Crosthwait is also reported to have investigated the means of lowering the floods; and it is to be hoped that his suggestions may prevail. Sir Mádav Row's allusion to the durability of the old "unscientific" bridges is very apt in this connection. It is a foregone conclusion with all, I presume, that the old works executed by practical native engineers, are far better, at least in their usefulness, than the æsthetic "lumps of sugar" we now see springing up in all parts of India. These latter afford an illustration of engineering science *run mǎd*.

MR. DINSHÁ ARDESHIR TALEYÁRKHÁN.

A name very well known as that of an ardent and honest political reformer. As a journalist Mr. Dinshá has done much good service, at the same time making himself very unpopular with the *ultra-patriotic* class, whose dictum is "Let a hundred people die under native misrule, rather than ten of them be saved by British interference." Mr. Dinsha's persistent and manly exposure of the management of the native states of Sucheen, Dharampore, Káttywár, and even Baroda, has resulted in great public good; and his waging war single-handed upon such fearful odds is, in itself, indicative of the moral stamina he possesses. Besides editing the *Gujarát Mitra*, he has written innumerable pamphlets, and I do suspect he has dabbled in blank verse! But in spite of the latter weakness, which comes natural to all (even Bacon and Franklin have perpetrated some glum atrocities of the kind), I hardly know of any native journalist of Western India who is his better in perseverance and devotion, though there have been some capital native journalists, too, in the past generation.

Since the assumption of ministerial office by Sir Mádav Row, Mr. Dinshá has been working under him as Municipal Commissioner of Baroda, in which capacity he is reported to have rendered a good account of himself.

"That officer is full of genuine zeal, and diligently looks after details with care and thoughtfulness. He has made steady approaches to order and system in the operations of his department. He has overcome, with temper and tact, the natural apathy or positive resistance of the people concerned. Indeed, he may be said to have achieved a certain measure of popularity for his department. I have heard expressions of appreciation and thankfulness from even such citizens as are distinguished for intense conservative ideas. And strangers visiting the city at distant intervals have borne testimony to progressive improvement in terms satisfactory and encouraging."

So says Sir Mádav Row, and the Agent bears him out. This is another refutation, if needed, of the vulgar prejudice that journalists never make good men of business. Mr. Janárdan S. Gádjil is another member of the fourth estate whose services to Baroda have proved valuable.

Mr. F. A. Elliot, C.S.,

is the tutor to His Highness the young Guicowár. This excellent officer has succeeded very well in his delicate, if not arduous work. His report of the progress made during the year by his princely pupil is in itself a certificate of his own high abilities and character. The young Guicowár was fortunate in having secured the services of such a man for his guide, philosopher, and friend.

The High School is flourishing as well as it could under Mr. Tait. That officer is highly spoken of for his abilities and zeal. The Baroda High School matriculated four of its students last year (1877), two of whom entered on a collegiate course, with a scholarship of Rs. 20 each. The Guicowár *Sirkár* have also founded several scholarships and prizes for lower standards, and Kázi Sháhbuddin bestows two scholarships on deserving Mahomedan students. Not the least noticeable feature of State Education in Baroda is the establishment of the "Anglo-Indian Institution," for European and Eurasian children. This is a most desirable institution, and I am glad the Agent takes especial interest in its welfare.

The vernacular schools are flourishing under Mr. Bhogilál Pránvullub Dass, a well-known man with whose *name* strange liberties seem to have been taken—perhaps with reason.

One of the most useful agencies of the Administration is the Medical Department, virtually, I presume, under the control of Dr. Bhálchandra, the hero of the Cæsarian section.* It is curious to see how kindly Hindus have of late been taking to the medical profession. They seem to be most successful in the line, too; decidedly more so than the Parsis. That is

* He has performed sixteen operations known by that name.

owing to the fact that they do not become quite *biláti* * in their treatment. There are in all six medical officers in the Baroda territory, among whom Dr. Bhál stands pre-eminent for his rare abilities and tact. "He is specially conspicuous for popularity, and has earned confidence at the Palace," says the Dewán, and this is saying a good deal. The profession ought to be proud of Mr. Bhálchandra. The other officers, too, are doing much useful work in various sections, especially my friend Mr. Rustomji Hormusji.

I do not think I have omitted any officer except the argus-eyed Appáji Rámchandra, whose close grasp on the Guicowár's money-bags is making "itself felt more or less in all departments." Ráo Sáheb Appáji was the right man in the right place, and the heads of all departments stood in awe of him. In him was centred the glory of good works at Baroda. Mr. Motirám Goculdáss, too, is a likely man—quite a gem of a treasurer.

Non-Official Magnates.

Of the non-official notabilities at Baroda, Gopál Row Myrál, the renowned banker, or his

* Europeanised.

heir, stands first. He is the Rothschild of Baroda, and knows—at least his book could tell you—much more about the Guicowárs than anyone else could. Among the *Sirdár* class the Nawáb of Baroda is eminent. The Nawáb Sáheb is hospitality itself. Some time ago he gave a "supper party" to the *élite* of Baroda. Knives, forks, and spoons were introduced for the first time; and though the guests may be supposed to have handled them freely, these instruments of torture did grievous mischief to the worthy host and his heirs. Medical aid was immediately required. Let us draw a veil over bleeding tongues and chopped fingers! The poor Nawáb Sáheb left "this world of woes" almost a year ago. He was a very popular man.

EN ROUTE TO AHMEDABAD.

On the 1st of April 1878 we left for Ahmedabad. The poor famine-stricken people came to us in crowds wherever the train stopped, looking more like apparitions than beings in flesh and blood. About Dákore, Umreth, and other adjoining places, the distress seems to have been very severe and general. Still the prospect that lay before the eye was pleasanter than we had hitherto seen.

In the carriage we occupied were a Vakil and a philosophic Shráwak. The Vakil had an opera-glass, which he seemed to mistake for a telescope. He said he espied Ahmedabad through it at the distance of about 60 miles. This the Shráwak said he could not see. Whilst these two were wrangling, the train stopped at an intermediate station, and in came a Hindu gentleman, a Bania, big, great, and eminently ugly. He had his little son with him,—his "only son," thank goodness. He was the very image of his father,—big, bloated, pock-marked face, without any visible eyes, and excessively nosey. The train stopped at a certain station again, and the Bania prepared to alight. He first handed over his kit to the porter, then that ugly boy of his, so very leisurely, that before he found time to drag his own carcass out, the engine gave the whistle. The Bania's wife, who had just issued from one of the third-class carriages, gave a shriek on seeing her lord's danger. The man turned pale and yellow by turns. Meantime half a dozen Parsi officials rushed to his assistance. "Come to my arms," said one ugly fat fellow to the Bania. But the Bania would not accept the loving invitation. "Stop the train," he cried hoarsely. At last they got the motion considerably slackened, and that Parsi again said, "Come to my arms." The Bania replied, "Stop it altogether." And stopped it was. The Bania stepped out, and we started. That Bania is a *Sowkár* *; I afterwards

* Money-lender.

ascertained that he was a Desái,* and was on a visit to Ahmedabad. He came from Billimorá.

LOCUST-DESÁIS.

This Desái, or the family of the Desáis rather, are petty officials under the Guicowár, and possess holdings in Nowsári, Gandevi, and Billimorá. The revenue and other exactions of former Guicowárs were hard enough to bear for the poorer people of these parts; but the Desáis, taking advantage of the misrule of later days, seem to have added their own taxes and imposts to those already existing. And these iniquitous exactions have, it is said, been levied until now when the unhappy peasantry and traders are absolutely unable to bear them.

It is curious to see how these Desáis' imposts were first brought into existence. The Desái, for instance, had, in a prosperous year, a superfluity of grain. He left a few maunds † at the house of each of the villagers, and after a short interval billed them for the grain—at fancy rates. This was sharp practice enough. But that was only the beginning. Next year the Desái forgot

* Small hereditary dignitaries.

† A Bombay maund is about 28 lbs. avoirdupois.

to leave the grain for the family, but a sum similar to that paid the year before, when the grain had been left, had to be paid over again! And thus came the grain-imposts into existence. This practice seems as infamous as the robbing of the people by the Turkish village tyrants. As is the case with grain, so with everything else of which the Desái had once a superfluity. The superfluity could not often recur; but the imposition of Rs. 500 to Rs. 600 was made first annual, then, I suppose, eternal.

After a good deal of clamouring on the part of the more intelligent of the townsmen, the Dewán of Baroda seems to have deputed a Náyeb Subhá to investigate the nature of the discontent which had become general throughout the three towns above referred to. This Náyeb Subhá, the *Gujarát Mitra* informs us, made himself and family the guests of the Desái, and it was at the Desái's place and in his presence, where he could smile or frown at will, that the Subhá held his court of inquiry. If this be so, nothing could be more reprehensible even in the Guicowár territory. But getting over all these cruel hindrances, the writer in the *Gujarát Mitra* has been able to record the following disclosures made in the course of inquiry. The facts may convey some idea of the desperation into which the poor people have been driven :—Parsi shopkeepers of Gandevi deposed that the Desái has been, for years, exacting from each Rs. 51 a year. Parsi boat-builders of the same place have been paying the Desái Rs. 5 on every craft prepared, besides fuel, timber, &c. Those who pleaded inability were deprived of their tools, and thus left without the means of earning a livelihood. Some Hindus, whose business it is to weigh loads of fuel or other things, were taxed Rs. 40 a year, and are now taxed Rs. 260 a year! On one bale of tobacco the Desái exacts Rs. 21. From the Mussalman weavers he takes fifty yards of the cloth they weave. Some years ago the Desái had a *nautch* * party, and he wanted cloth for a pavilion. That grant of cloth has been made perpetual! Besides, the poor fellows have to pay something in cash too. Hindu weavers have to supply sixty yards of cloth. The butcher, too, has to contribute Rs. 25 a year towards the Desái's maintenance, as also the dyer in a similar sum. The Vanjárás † have to pay a certain sum

* Performance by hired dancing-girls.

† Or Brinjaris, itinerant grain-carriers.

per bag of grain. All these taxes are alleged to be the Desái's *own*, over and above the Guicowár's. The Guicowár *Sirkár* has its house tax; the Desái has a corollary to it, named the *choolá* tax, or tax on cooking-fire, of Rs. 2–8 a house. Then comes the Márwári, who has to pay the *jájam* or carpet tax; also the *ghee* tax. That is, these Shylocks of the village had to present to the Desái so much carpet and so much *ghee* a year. But when the Desái had too much of carpet and *ghee*, he asks for their equivalent in money. "We paid some years," depose the epigrammatic Márwári. "We don't do so now: *our will.*" That is sturdy common sense, and once in a way we sympathise with the obscene miser.* The Dheds had to pay hide tax, that is a substitute in coin for the hides of animals they skin from time to time. They now plead inability. The fishermen, too, are not left out of the list, poor miserable creatures, barely able to eke out a "bellyful" of seeds, fish, or anything that comes handy! They, too, are utterly unable to oblige the Desái.

* The Márwári—sordid money-lenders.

BILLIMORÁ.

I have seen Billimorá and the adjoining parts, and am assured by respectable informants that the account I give above of the Desáis' exactions is substantially correct. My trip to Billimorá was not quite uneventful.

RAILWAY SPEED, ETC.

I left for bunder Billimorá by mail train. The train went at *high speed*, I am told, which, on ascertaining it, I find to be about twenty miles an hour. Compared with bullock hackeries, Mr. Duxbury's * dragweight is much faster, to be sure. But it is *nothing*, speaking absolutely; because I am told that the strain of any greater speed would be too much for the yielding soil. It is, however, to be noted that what is wanted in speed is made up for by the noise. The carriages hobble along with ominous squeaks that indicate chronic rheumatism. The engine seems to be suffering from constipation, and the faint and sickly sobs it now and then gives are heartrending indeed. Then the dust, the clouds

* The energetic Traffic Manager of the B. B. and C. I. Railway.

of dust that assail one on the line. Let the authorities take hold of the fattest and the rosiest of the station-masters and rip him open. Thus dissected, the creature will emit such overwhelming volumes of dust as would cover a hundred Duxburys with shame and remorse. Insomnia and dysentery are said to be inseparable from railway service. And what wonder?

Public Roads and Personal Experience.

Immediately on alighting I entered the town of Billimorá. It was a moonlit night, and I preferred walking. In the mofussil I generally walk, as, in driving, there is a chance of dislodging the liver. Billimorá dust is no way inferior to that of Broach—it is subtle, light, and knee-deep. The road leading into the town is said to be a *made* road; it may have been so before it was recently unmade. There is a romance about the road. A few years ago His Excellency the Rájá, Minister of the State, was driving on it at night, when, by some mishap, the *ghari* * upturned and deposited His Excellency's whole weight in the dust. That was a

* Carriage.

great fall. The noise awakened the housewives. The Rájá-Dewán, at his time of life, was not able to pick himself up. So when the women came up to the scene of the fall, they saw a well-dressed old beau grovelling in the dust, with sowárs and sepoys chattering and bowing at a distance, as is their wont. Then said a spinster old, approaching the figure in the dust. "Brother, what are ye about?" And he replied, "Sister, go thy way; the night is dark, and I am the Dewán Rájá. Think not I have fallen; I am merely trying, by personal experience, to see if the road requires repair." Then asked a maid of twenty-three, looking archly at the fallen figure, "Old man, art thou satisfied?" "Yes, my child," replied the pious Rájá, picking himself up by main effort. Before entering the *palki*,* the Dewán turned round and said, "Good people, do not bother me with a petition; I know you need a good road, and will give you one."

Such is *personal* experience. How much I wish that a Legislative Councillor had now and then a fall, a Town Councillor now and then a

* Palanquin.

shower of "dirty Jupiter" in the streets, a Police Commissioner set upon by rabid dogs!

How Roads are Made.

This road was first made by H. H. Khunderow. Mad Mulhár Rao, on coming to the *gâdi*, paid a visit of state to Billimorá. Now, Mulhár Rao, as we all know, is a man of honour. So he refused to enter the town by the road made by his brother. He ordered a special road to be made for him in a *few hours*. The officers mowed down fields, telling the owners that His Highness the Guicowár was to *sanctify the soil* by driving through it. Mulhár Rao drove through the road thus improvised, and paid Rs. 25,000, which went into the officials' pockets, the owners of the fields making the best of the half-destroyed harvest. On this wise are Public Works conducted in native states.

Billimorá Proper.

Billimorá belongs mostly to Parsis, who have a Tower of Silence there, and other religious and social institutions. The Dustoor* cannot

* Parsi Levite.

live there, and so far Billimorá is blessed. The Parsis here are respectable people, very fat and very prayerful. There are Hindus and Mahomedans too. But the bulk of the population consists of the fisher people, low-class Hindus, dark, thick-skinned, and very poor. I stood on the main road for about two hours one evening to feast mine eyes on the beauties of nature: then I retired to bed, and dreamt vividly of Dante's *Inferno*. Billimorá does not boast of rural beauties—pariah dogs cannot pass under that title. But fish is cheap, and plentiful, and good. Now and then you can get a pull at the toddy* flagon. But the liquid is too sweet to be the genuine article.

Billimorá is under a magistrate, a very good man, a relative of the Subá (Chief Commissioner). This magistrate is said to be a very strict man, and as he fines people right and left, he might look to be a Subá very shortly. He is a reformed Hindu, I am glad to say. Under the magistrate there is a Parsi Foujdár,† an energetic and obliging sort of man, with about fifty policemen and 500 street dogs. This latter force may pass

* The palm juice.

† Police inspector.

under the name of Sir Mádav Row's *Canine Cavalry*. I am told Sir Mádav Row offered this cavalry, as well as the gold guns of the Guicowár, to Lord Lytton when the Afghan war was at its height; and though the Dewán is said to have been in earnest, Lord Lytton took it for a joke. Sir T. M. has ever since been in disgrace. Thus goes the story which Sir Mádav alone can verify or contradict.

IN TO AHMEDABAD.

But to return to the train taking us to Ahmedabad. We reached the station late in the evening, and finding a shigram waiting for hire, thrust ourselves and luggage into it. We were driven over excellent roads to the "Káranj," a delightfully-situated house belonging to Mr. Cowasji Muncherji Káranjwálá. I was very kindly received by my host, and passed a very agreeable fortnight under his roof. Mr. Cowasji is noted—as was his good old father before him—for loyalty and liberality, qualities rare enough in the mofussil. He has always been a friend of the people, and ready to promote every scheme of public usefulness. He is honorary secretary to various public institutions; and in the consideration of all public measures his advice and suggestions are always sought by the authorities. Every visitor to Ahmedabad returns charmed with Mr. Cowasji's hospitality and the range of his local knowledge of all conditions of life. Among his many acts of public service, those by which he will be longest remembered, and which ought to have received some substantial recognition from an appreciating Government, are his exertions during the flood at Ahmedabad a few years ago. Those who have read the accounts of his continuous efforts to save life and to support the rescued at considerable personal risk and expense, are of opinion that Ahmedabad could not be sufficiently grateful to its benevolent and public-spirited Parsi citizen.

Sights.

Next morning my excellent host took me out for sight-seeing. Ahmedabad is rich in sights. The remains of Mahomedan architectural art are "magnificent" even "in their ruin." The mosques and mausoleums, tombs and tanks and pleasure-grounds, vie with each other in grandeur and beauty. Nor is the Hindu style of architecture less attractive. For eight days consecutively did I *do* the town, often with mine host for guide, sometimes with a Mahomedan guide picked up in the streets. Mr. Káranjwálá knows Ahmedabad probably as no other living man knows it. So much has been written about the architectural importance of this Mahomedan capital, that I have nothing new to add, and I hate borrowing. Of recent accounts, the best is Mr. T. C. Hope's spirited historical and descriptive sketch.

Making Friends.

This day I had the pleasure of making the personal acquaintance of my friend Rao Sáheb Mahipatrám Ruprám, Principal of the Gujarát Training College. Mr. Mahipatrám remained for over an hour, and a long and very interesting talk did we have together. Mahipatrám Ruprám is a notable man—an educationalist, reformer, and patriot, a man of much literary taste and ability. He has done and suffered more in the cause of social reform than any Hindu I know of in Gujarát. He is quite earnest in whatever he undertakes, and, for a Hindu, wonderfully persevering. After the death of the heroic Karsandás Mulji, Mahipatrám has been perhaps our only Hindu reformer deserving that title. Of "lip-reformers" there is no lack at Ahmedabad, or in

India; but the genuine man is only too rarely met with. With a truer education than hitherto, I hope we shall have really earnest workers in the field. May the example of Karsandás's noble life be always before my countrymen! Mr. Mahipatrám introduced me to Mr. S. N. Tagore, the well-known Hindu civil servant. Of him I have spoken elsewhere. He was Sessions Judge at Ahmedabad for a pretty long time. The Ahmedabadis speak of him in the highest terms, not only as an official, but as a gentleman and friend. Indeed, I have all along thought that Satyendra Náth Tagore would have still better adorned the Pulpit than the Bench. But as he does credit to both functions, it would be churlish to repine.

Next day came Mr. Bholánáth Sárábhái, a Rao Báhádur, a Sirdár, and an esteemed Government pensioner. Mr. Bholánáth is an elderly gentleman, and ranks among the reformers. But age has taught him to be cautious, and I do not wonder that he is not such a favourite with the ardent youngsters as with men of his own time. But all the same he is an estimable old gentleman, and if he can do good by "word of mouth," he will not be silent.

That evening I had the honour of a call from my friend Khán Báhádur Cooverji Cowasji Sabáwálá, the Deputy-Collector, a sensible practical worker, with a character for independence which few native officials can boast of. Mr. Cooverji is a man of the old school. He hates idle talk. Not given to insincere profession, and too rough-hewn by nature for mere sentimentalism, he is a terror to our "civilised" dandies. He will gladly shake an honest labourer by the hand, but holds the scented "exquisite" in horror. Mr. Cooverji bears a high reputation in the official circles.

Next in order came Rao Báhádur Mukunrái Manirái, the Sub-Judge, a very quiet unobtrusive man. He is seldom heard of in public, but is none the less earnest in the work of popular enlightenment. I believe Mr. Mukunrái is a very studious man. His official career has been blameless, and he is popular enough in the profession.

Having very little time left on hand now, I gave a hasty call to Rao Báhádur Nuggershet Premábhai Hemábhai. Sett Premábhai is the leading Hindu here, and was a millionaire before the days of the share mania of 1864–5. He was once a Member of the Bombay Legislative Council. He showed me several ancient Persian documents, proving that his ancestors were holders of great jagirs* from the Moghul Emperors. Mr. Premábhai is by no means a poor man, even in these days. Personally, he is a worthy, amiable, asthmatic gentleman. Professionally, he is a *Sowcár*, an astute man of business for all his airs of innocent simplicity. Sett Premábhai is a Jain Shráwak by caste; and a few years ago he more than amused his friends by marrying himself and his eldest son to twin sisters. It would be interesting to determine the degree of consanguinity between his progeny by the new wife and *his son's* progeny by her *sister* AND *daughter-in-law*!

I also called upon Mr. Cursetji Mánockji, the Small Cause Court Judge, son of the famous Mr. Mánockji Cursetji, the friend of kings and princes. Mr. Cursetji appeared to be a very interesting and intelligent man. But if he were to appear in his usual dress before one of our Dustoors, he would send off his reverence into fits of hysteric vituperation. Mr. Cursetji dresses

* Landed estates.

like a European, and does not cover his head—which is a scandal unto a Parsi.

I must not omit Kavi Dalpatrám Dáyábhái, the blind bard of Gujarát. Kavi Kalpatrám is a popular Hindu Gujaráti poet, and has written much of the sort of "poetry" that we can have in the country. He has a great rival in Kavi Narmadáshankar Lálshankar of Surat. This latter seems to have more *power*, the former more simplicity and grace. The aged Dalpatrám gave me a very warm greeting, and would not let me leave him without a formal benediction.

Before leaving Ahmedabad I had the pleasure of making the acquaintance of the Rev. Mr. Gillespie, of the local mission, to whom I was introduced by my late lamented friend Mr. Joseph Taylor. And now enough of acquaintances and friends, and enough, for the nonce, of Ahmedabad too.

THE PEOPLE.

HINDUS.

The Hindus of Gujarát are divided into several castes, the most considerable, on the whole, being the Vaishnavas, the followers of Vishnu. They are merchants, traders, vakils (lawyers), and gentlemen at large. As merchants and traders they are even now most successful; but the vakils, with few exceptions, are mere petty-foggers; the gentlemen at large are easy-going, well-preserved individuals, who live and die to themselves. The enterprise and honesty which once characterised mercantile dealings are unknown to men of the present day. Transactions involving enormous sums were once carried on in Gujarát verbally; and some of my readers may have heard of the Gujarát *Sowcár* who received a large advance of money *on a hair of his moustache* as a pledge! But those days are gone from

Gujarát. To-day the best-cultivated beard will not get the best known *Sowcár* a loan of Rs. 10. We see mutual distrust and petty jealousies amongst traders. Commercial morality is at a low ebb, as in Bombay. Let me give the instance of a Hindu merchant of extensive credit who took the benefit of the Insolvency Act some time ago, and thus ruined hundreds of widows and orphans who had entrusted their little all to his care. When these unlucky wights besought him for some relief as *charity*, the *Sowcar* mildly said to them, "My dear creatures, why do you want money? You are poor and can beg. Can I beg? And knowing this the *Sirkár* (Government) has relieved me of liability to you. But do not, I pray, think that I am happy. No, no; with your money I have to settle their dowries on my daughters," &c. &c.

A very pleasant way of settling dowries, to be sure! But instances of fraudulent insolvency are common both among the Hindus and Parsis. We have insolvents who have "taken the benefit" of what we call "the white-washing Act," half a dozen times each; and after each "white-washing" the insolvent has suddenly come into a fortune, with which he endows his wife or mother or a religious institution! He often builds houses, opens a new business, or goes in for "philanthropic" pursuits with the money he has so miraculously obtained soon after having been "whitewashed." He has no thought, even then, of the hundreds whose homes he has made desolate by his refined rascality.

This merchant is one of the Vaishnava sect, to which belong Baniás, Bhattiás, Márwáris, and others. Besides indulging in gross idolatry, these people deify the heads of their Church, who are about thirty-seven in number, scattered over Gujarát, Káttywár, and many other parts of India. The deified priest is the Máháráj,* the visible incarnation of Vishnu-Krishna, to whom every pious Vaishnava dedicates his or her *tana, mana, dhana* (body, mind, and property), and not only his or her body, mind, and property, but of all those over whom he or she may have contrel. This is the essence of Máhárájism, and yet, as all the world knows,

The Vaishnava Máháráj of the Day

is a spurious character; for, though he may claim to be the lineal descendant and visible

* Literally, Great King.

incarnation of the protecting deity, he is susceptible, perhaps more than ordinary mortals, to pain, pleasure, love, hatred, and other emotions. Pinch him, and he will roar; tickle him, and he will grin; gratify his desire, and he will worship you; baulk him of it, and he will put you out of caste! He is born a "lord" of ancestors the Lord knows who, and at a very tender age he lords it over a seraglio of intellectual ladies whose husbands are men of highly liberal marital sentiment. It is a wonder to many how the Máhárāj lives in such a princely style. It is thus:—The Máhárāj has a first-rate taxing imagination. Sir John Strachey * is a mere novice to this accomplished tax-master. The following are supposed to be among the few known imposts the Máhárāj derives from his devout followers:—For homage by sight, Rs. 5; for homage by touch, Rs. 20; for the honour of washing the Máhárájá's toes, Rs. 35; for the credit of swinging him, Rs. 40; for the glory of rubbing sweet unguents on his body, Rs. 42; for the joy of sitting with him, Rs. 60; for the bliss of occupying the same room with the Madana

* Late Finance Minister of India.

Murti,* Rs. 50 to 500. For the pleasure of being kicked by Máháráj or his attendants, Rs. 11; for the privilege of being lashed, Rs. 13; for the performance of *Rási Kridá*,† Rs. 100 to 200; for *Rása Kridá* performed by proxy, Rs. 50 to 100. For the delight of eating the cud of *pán supári* thrown out by the Máháráj, Rs. 17; for drinking the water in which the Máháráj has bathed, or in which his foul linen has been washed, squeezed, and wrung, Rs. 19. He also levies many other minor taxes on the events and necessaries of life, such as birth, marriage, death, cloth, silk, sugar, &c. The late Mr. Anstey‡ said he would not touch a Máháráj "with a pair of red-hot tongs." Quite right; it would be desecration of the tongs. The Máháráj is a very pious man a week before he dies, and when he dies he goes to where the rest of us do not—that is, to Kailás. He generally dies without issue, and without a groan.

Having described the average head-priest of the Vaishnavas as he actually is, I may also

* Madana Murti, the Image of Cupid, as the Máháráj is named by fair worshippers.

† Literally, the Essence of Pleasure.

‡ The renowned barrister.

give a brief sketch of the career of the late Jivanlálji Máháráj, of Gujarát, who is now supposed to be a saint in the Vaishnava heaven.

The Late Jivanlálji Máháráj.

The Vaishnavas of Western India went into mourning the other day, out of respect for the memory of Jivanlálji Máháráj, one of their "great lords." Jivánlálji Máháráj died of "some disease," and, so far, it is not satisfactory, I fear, for his numerous devotees to learn that their "great lord," the ever-youthful and immortal, should have succumbed like an ordinary mortal to mere physical ailment. What the "some disease" was I have no curiosity to know; but many will guess that it was an accumulation of the after effects of what Englishmen in other spheres of society designate "gay life."

Jivanlálji Máhárái was born 51 years ago. There is a profound mystery always overhanging the personal affairs of the Máhárái. That mystery shrouds his birth, it shrouds his life, and I 'll be bound that same mystery shrouds his death. We know that he was born in 1829, visibly of human parents; but some hundreds of thousands of his worshippers assert, on their solemn oaths, that Jivanlálji Máháráj existed ages before he was born, and that ages before that event did he carry on that amorous traffic with his fair devotees which is essential, in the Vaishnava creed, to the salvation and beatification of the degraded female soul. Thus Jivanlálji was a philanthropist before he was born; but those "deeds of merit" could not be visible to mortal eye. His life "here below" and its many exciting incidents are better known. At ten years of age he could tell a maiden from a matron; at that tender age could this incarnation of the divine Krishna Chand warm the iciest of fair worshippers; he could toy with their toes in amorous wantonness; he could ogle the most virtuous prude into a smile of ineffable happiness. The wondrous boy! What could he not do?

At twenty, Jivanlálji was an old man, and took to studying Sanskrit and patronising female education among his people. This was a great triumph for the "reform party," who shed tears of joy and wrote odes belauding the Máhárájá's liberality of sentiment, and voted him a handsome memorial. This, by the way, irresistibly reminds one of the old rhyme, recounting how, when another illustrious pleasure-seeker fell sick, a "monk he would be"; but how, when he grew well, "the d——l of a monk was he"! The Máháráj and his worshippers afterwards found out that they were not quite agreed as to the meaning of "female education," but that mattered little. Jivanlálji Máháráj is spoken of as having been "the best among the brethren." I hope this assertion is meant as a compliment, though I very much fear the being "best" among Vaishnava Máhárájás is at the best a sorry way of spending one's life in these days. But we cannot judge of these exalted personages from our own standard. It is enough for us that they *die* sooner or later; and we are thankful for their thus doing the community the only favour in their power. What becomes of them after death it would be idle speculation to enlarge upon; but if I am to trust Vaishnava traditions, death means to them the departure of the wearied soul to *Swarga*, where its sole occupation is—flirting with the spirits of those who were the choicest among his female friends on earth! The lover and the beloved there "drink delight" in each other's possession—they drink delight, and when their ethereal cravings are not quite satisfied therewith, they drink curds and eat cocoa-nuts. If this be a pleasant life—a life of love, flirting with spirits and browsing on curds and cocoa-nuts—I wish Jivanlálji Máháráj joy of his new life. Let those envy it who can. All that I would desire is, that the spirit of this great lord of ladies innumerable, this "friend of female education," this sainted patron of native arts and of Sanskrit, may not, in the other world, where the wronged are righted, encounter the meek and persecuted spirit of Karsandás Mulji.*

Europeans and others may think Máhárájism a foul superstition, a system of vile sensualism; but so long as it is sustained by the "odour of sanctity," it will hold in thrall tens of thousands of families in India within its embruted cult. The ritualistic orgies of the Vaishnavas are a "proverb of reproach" even amongst the superstitious and idolatrous Indians. Every sensible native knows that these priests "pollute their sanctuary," and in the name of religion desolate hearths and homes, and poison the fountain of domestic happiness. Karsandás Mulji, the truly

* The great Hindu reformer of Bombay, who died about 1869.

enlightened Bania reformer, waged war on the tribe of Máhárájá's twenty years ago. He was fiercely opposed by rich and influential bigots of his own class; but so well-aimed were his hits, that at last he drew forth the giants of iniquity from their impregnable stronghold. They dragged Karsandás to the Court of Law; but in the course of the trial such fearful disclosures were extorted from the Vaishnavas by the redoubtable Anstey, that the cause of the Máhárájás was damaged for ever. The highest tribunal in the land and the entire Indian press pronounced Máhárájism a sink of iniquities. But Karsandás Mulji died, and with him died that spirit of patient heroism which alone could cope with and triumph over bigotry, hypocrisy, and sin. Our friend the Vaishnava Máháráj is again relapsing into his old ways. His is a very tenacious creed, and until some providential visitation overtakes it, it will go on "conceiving mischief and bringing forth iniquity." It is unspeakably sad to find men and women, whose lives in other respects are regulated by the best domestic and social virtues, men of keen wits and women of pure habits, becoming so utterly infatuated by a vile tradition—a tissue of fantastic fables and transparent myths. It is a most incomprehensible psychological phenomenon. No husband is more jealous than the Hindu; no wife values her honour so high as the Hindu wife. And still, both make a merit of sacrificing the most cherished social privilege! What power of faith is theirs! But how perverted!

MAHOMEDANS.

THE Mahomedans were lords of Surat, and more or less of Gujarát. But at present, generally speaking, they are probably the poorest as a class. Their aristocracy live without aim or ambition, men crushed by their own "pride of birth," men who would borrow rather than earn, and starve rather than beg. They are ever ready to "grasp the skirts of happy chance." But that chance never comes to them. Their life is a round of inane pleasures and idle ceremonials, and the little substance now left to them is being exhausted in "playing the king." They are pining for the "good old times," and being desperate hopers they hope away life with astounding patience; they hope and hope and still they hope for "the good times coming."

Many, finding time hanging heavy on their hands, abandon themselves to low gratifications of the sense—feasting and dancing and carousing—in such "fool's paradise" they wile away time. They have a horror of honest work. Poor fellows! As friends I have always found them faithful and true. Most of them are in abject poverty, and to keep up some show of gentility—dearer to them than life itself—the head of a family at times acquiesces in the sacrifice which a too-loving wife or daughter feels bound to undergo. One might well excuse this mistaking of duty—the practice is very limited—as an act of true martyrdom on the part of the female; but it is impossible to contemplate the husband or father's share in it without loathing. To him, a confirmed polygamist, the matter may not look quite so serious.

Latterly I believe this class has been "looking up." Hoping and dreaming has already given way, in some notable cases, to more sober, practical ideas of life. Altogether, I do believe "a change is coming over the spirit of their dreams."

The lower orders of Mahomedans are—"unspeakable." They are made up of brag and blnster; and "truth often sticks in their throats." Like their betters they despise work, but, unlike them, will beg, borrow, or steal, with the utmost pleasure in life. They live in a world of—wine and woman. Many of them sleep by day, and make the night hideous by their drunken revels. But against all these vices, common to the Mussalman "about town," they set off some very fine redeeming traits. As friends and servants they are invaluable; and if you treat them kindly they will lay down life in your service. As a rule they are above that meanness, that petty intriguing spirit and want of gratitude so common among their neighbours. Mussalmans in the villages around Gujarát present quite another picture. Their manners and habits correspond to those of Hindus of their position, naturally enough, as they were originally all Hindus, and have mostly to deal with Hindus even now.

Meer Bakhtáwar Khan.

A Romance in Real Life.

As an instance of how the Mahomedan gentry of Gujarát have sacrificed what remained to them after the loss of their supremacy to their pride of birth, and as explaining how the mean, insinuating

Bania has risen on the ruin of his Moslem master, let me give here a leaf out of the unwritten autobiography of my Shráwak friend Nyálchand Nakhodchand of Ahmedabad. Says Nyálchand :—

"I entered the service of Meer Bakhtáwar Khan in 1840. The Meer was then about nineteen years, and only recently married to the beautiful daughter of the Buxi. Meer Bakhtáwar was by nature very reserved, and as he did not agree with his step-mother, his father gave him, soon after his marriage, a separate establishment. He bestowed upon his only son all the ancestral property he could — including houses, lands, ornaments, books, and a little of cash. The doting father also gave to his son a few "disputed claims" against the British Government for compensation. This last doubtful gift was to be reserved to the last and utilised when there was no source of maintenance left. Thus prepared, and fortified by a very respectable fortune from the Buxi, his father-in-law, Meer Bakhtáwar removed to his new residence with his wife and servants. The day after his removal he formally installed me his head *kárbhári*,* presenting me

* Manager.

with a valuable dress and the right to full management of all his affairs. He could not, and if he could would not, attend to any business —it was beneath him.

"The Meer passed his time in the zenana. He so devotedly loved his wife that he never gave her a rival. All the livelong day they were together, this infatuated pair, so absorbed in their new-born happiness. To me, an unmarried Hindu, the Meer's self-abandonment was shocking. He never left the side of his Bibi—she would not part with him. I had not the *entrée* of the zenana, but learnt from the servants that the master and mistress were inseparable. The Meer stole out of his inner chamber once in a fortnight or so, when he had to ask me for a large sum of money, or to go to the mosque. About seven months passed this way, when one day my master's father and friends paid the family a visit. It was this day I learnt that Meer Bakhtáwar expected a son and heir. Great were the rejoicings on this occasion. One day the anxiously-expected heir came to gladden the hearts of the parents and, as it seems to me now, to darken their hitherto brilliant course of life. The demands for money became more frequent. I met every demand with a smile. Sometimes I had myself to go out with money for the purchase of some nick-nack for the mother or the child. At such times I was not slow to use discretion, you may be sure. I had not seen the Meer's beautiful wife up to now, though it was over two years; but the baby was now and then brought out for a peep at the outside world. It was the most lovely child I have ever seen. They said the mother was growing lovelier every day. They talked of her as *The Angel.* This was her favourite name. I tried many means of obtaining a glimpse of her divine beauty, but it was not to be for years to come.

"My position in the household improved with the progress of time. The master had implicit faith in me, and I rewarded him by improving my opportunities. Not a rupee passed from my hands out of which I did not withhold a fraction for my own pockets. Not a piece of cloth, not an ornament, not a single article of luxury crossed the threshold, of which part was not diverted to my house. Poor men must live, and, if possible, I had determined not only to live, but to live to the best purpose, as I could see as early as now, that my master was running out of his fortune very fast. But it was not my business to advise or warn him till the worst came. This way we lived for seven years. I had already to tell my master that we had no cash left. We had to part with some ornaments, and were living upon the rents of two or three shops which we had to mortgage. One of these shops was mortgaged to myself unknown to the Meer—it stood in my uncle's name. About this time I myself married. I need not say that my master and mistress paid the expenses—about Rs. 3,000—of my marriage. They parted with their ornaments—these people seem to me to part with things as cheerfully as when they buy them—to help me. They thought very highly of my honesty and diligence; they also knew that I was very useful in 'raising the wind' and disposing of superfluities. For the Rs. 1,000 my master had to borrow I would bring him 700, part of the rest being considered interest already deducted, the remaining part going to me. At home, too, not a single day passed when I did not earn something more than the stipulated pay. I had my black-mail upon everything bought or sold, borrowed or mortgaged.

"One day the master's son would come behind and ride on my back. In so doing he would do damage to my coat. Well, this coat I would show to the parents who, to encourage the boy to learn a little of fun and freedom, as they explained, would on no account scold him. But when I cried and said I was a poor man and had a family—I had become quite free with my master—they would laugh at my plight, and present me with a piece of longcloth, saying, by way of apology, that they would give away a thousand pieces of cloth rather than that their darling be checked in the free exercise of his faculties! One day the little urchin would empty the contents of an ink-bottle on my turban, and straightway would I go to the drawing-room, dripping with the liquid. The delighted father would clap his hands and describe my misery to the wife inside, who would laughingly order me to buy another turban! Well, I was nothing loth. Many a time since have I invited the boy to play me some such trick, and right handsomely have I got the parents to pay for it!

"But now Meer Bakhtáwar was about Rs. 15,000 in debt. There was scarcely anything left to pledge or to sell. I prevailed upon him, therefore, to curtail his expenses. This he did. It was a trial to him not to be able to afford to his wife and child those thousand and one little luxuries they had enjoyed so long. But the wife was perfectly contented with his love and devotion. The boy was too young to notice the difference in their circumstances. But even now our monthly expenses were Rs. 200, my own pay Rs. 40, and we had no visible source of income. I was therefore told to dispose of such things as I could. This I did, carrying most of them to my house, and paying what price I liked. There were some splendidly mounted swords and daggers, some exquisite paintings, some rare and magnificently illuminated Persian manuscripts, which I thus transferred to my house. My mistress took her misfortune much to heart; but her husband was of good cheer. He knew that his father would not last long, and that he would be sure to leave him something. But the old man did not die. To add to the misery of suspense, the son and heir fell sick. The parents' anxiety was terrible. Night and day the Mahomedan doctor remained by the side of the little sufferer, and night and day prayed the priest for his recovery. The parents hovered over the child in agonised suspense. The mother gave me her last ring, her husband's wedding gift, to sell. But no earthly power could save the child—he sickened and died. The father's life seemed to go out with the son's. The mother suffered, too, but she had something still left to cherish in this life. A servant now came to ask for money; I had none to give. My master was too much prostrated to think of such things. In this her cruel extremity the mistress came to the door of the room (outside which we servants were assembled). She asked to see me. This was the first time I saw her. She was in her 'sleeping dress'; her beauty of person was truly divine, and recent sufferings had hallowed it with that dignified composure before which the most supercilious could not help bending his head. I bowed to her, trembling from a hundred little agitations in my heart. She swept a haughty glance over me, and asked if I could not bring money. I pleaded inability, but promised I would try. Then she whispered, 'See, Nyálchand, you must save your master's honour, so don't go to his father's house. But give my boy a decent burial; have you nothing, *nothing* left to sell?' She shut the door before receiving my reply, and I went out for money. I could spare none, nor borrow any; the only chance was with the old Meer. I went to him with the news of his grandson's death. He was himself sick unto death, but without asking any question he ordered Rs. 100 to be given me.

"In two weeks more the old Meer died, leaving property to the extent of about Rs. 20,000 to his unhappy son. My master never recovered from his melancholy. I was given power to dispose of the property just inherited. I realised the value, paid off all standing debts, most of them in my favour, and put about Rs. 4,000 in my master's hands. I further undertook to appeal to the Government, but nothing seemed to rouse him. Friends advised my mistress to dispense with her establishment, and to live within her income, but she would not listen to it so long as her 'lord' lived. She accepted my resignation, agreeing that I should improve my prospects after so much suffering in their service! I assured her of my life-long devotion, and my daily prayers for the well-being of herself and her husband. Being a woman of singular abilities and resource, she wrote to the Governor's wife, in Persian, telling that lady of her misfortunes, and of the claims of her family. Her touching story moved the officials who heard of it. The case was not worth looking into, but Government sanctioned an annual grant of Rs. 500 to the Meer for his lifetime. He seems to have entirely forgotten the past. He scarcely recognised me. I am now a rich and highly-respected merchant—so high up in the world that I cannot visit my master any longer. My lady is said to have grown gray-haired; but neither premature age nor her past sufferings, the gloomy present nor the blank future, can lessen her devotion to her husband. She seems to live for and in him. She is his sole attendant —the servants attend to minor duties. She is charitable even now, and on every *Jumá* (Friday) she gives what she can to the needy and suffering. I do not feel quite satisfied with myself when reviewing the past, but then, you see, *a poor man must live!*"

PARSIS.

GUJARÁT was long the head-quarters of the Parsis, especially so Surat and the adjoining towns; and it can now boast of some "very good" families. But the Parsis of Surat have fallen upon evil days. The Shettia class, that is, the aristocracy, became, by training, lazy, listless, gregarious creatures, grovelling for generations in one and the same groove. They cannot understand patriotism, and though charity is the very basis of their grand old faith, they are utter strangers to that greatest of divine graces. Their notion of charity is the giving away of alms, the distribution of money—their own and anybody else's—to the deserving or undeserving, with some object, often that of earning popularity or official favour. That comprehensive virtue, which inculcates a spirit of justice and generosity and total forgiveness, they lack the faculty to appreciate. They know not, the bulk of them, the true nature of charity. No doubt our Shetts are loyal to the British Crown; but to what ruling power have they ever been disloyal? Loyalty is their policy, their interest. Excepting in this matter, the Parsi Shett of Surat is an honest, peace-loving citizen. He seldom beats his wife, and is otherwise a very pious, moral old gentleman, with a few "old-gentlemanly vices," and many old-gentlemanly virtues.

There are Parsi Shetts in Bombay, too, a shade better than those in Surat. They are more civilised, so to say, but all their civilisation does not save them from priestly influence. Five to twelve Parsi Shetts compose what is called a *Puncháyet*.

The Puncháyet and the Shett.

The Puncháyet is a highly respectable body, but it seems to be a body without a soul; for none of its many members, it seems, can call his soul his own. The Puncháyet Shett is often a prim old individual, well shaven, well washed, and well scented. This faultlessly white being walks as if he were a basket of newly-laid eggs. He seems to be in dread of progress, of the very motion of life. Sloth is his idea of the fashionable. His limbs move very cautiously and very slowly, as if at every stage there were concealed Sir Richard Temple to chaff him about his "blue blood." He hates action of any kind. He hugs indolence, rejoices in its company, and revels in its seductive bosom. When, once in six months, he is required to attend to a little public business, he helplessly turns to his steward and asks, broken-hearted, "Oh! what's to do again?" as if only an hour ago he had done some tremendous deed of heroism for his country! The Shett sits down with a grimace, stands up with a yawn, salutes with an ogle or with a rather original parting of lips, which process he flatters himself is a smile. He is sensitively nervous about his health. He will not get out of his carriage till a few minutes after it has stopped; this is to avoid any internal agitation which might follow a hasty descent. He cannot go to sleep without a stout cotton pillow tied round his "food-bag."* Except in

* Stomach.

these respects the Shett is a very worthy citizen, and a thoroughly loyal subject of Her Majesty. But he has no strength, no stamina. He can look no man in the face.

The Parsi a "Hebrew Jew"!

There would seem to be pretty good ground for Dr. Wilson's startling theory that the Parsis are one of the lost "Ten Tribes." There are many striking points of similarity, many common weaknesses and common virtues between Hebrews and Parsis. The difference between them to-day seems to be that the Parsi life is infinitely less intense and less patriotic. A Parsi may be a Hebrew with the vices and weaknesses of the lower class of Hindus. For this deterioration he has to thank climate and marriage with Hindu women. Scarcely any Parsi living can claim to be of the pure Persian "blue blood."

Our "Forlorn Hopes."

It is in the middle ranks of life that we can perceive materials for "a mighty, puissant nation." If this glorious middle class goes on educating itself, it may one day realise the future which has been predicted for it by the ancient seers. Besides keeping abreast of the rapid advance of arts and sciences, the people have to learn patriotism and to abjure priestcraft. Above all, they have to create or organise a new national church, founded on the simple tradition of *good thought, good word, and good deed*, bequeathed by Zoroaster. Let them weed their scriptures of its verbiage, and let them defy the threats of the Levites. Let them see that neither greatness nor happiness is to be achieved by a compromise with the conscience.

The Orthodox Parsi at Prayer.

But for true national greatness, sincerity in all we do, and some rational scheme of life for "here and there" are essential. Unfortunately for him, the Parsi is either insincere or irrational. In the most solemn business of life, at his prayers and devotions, the Parsi makes a droll figure. I mean the orthodox Parsi. To him prayer is as necessary as food, and the time for it recurs oftener than the time for his meals. The minute he is out of bed the orthodox Parsi shakes himself free of all idle reveries, the remnants of the night's dreaming; and unfolding the triple cord * round his waist, turns his face

* The *kusti*.

to where the sun has just risen, and giving the sacred badge three vigorous flaps, he cries out in choice Zend, "Defeat, defeat to Shaitán," * so that the author of evil may not venture, later on, to molest the pious man on his path of duty. Shortly after he takes his bath, and then commences the regular prayer business. He has his prayer-book in Zend text and Gujaráti character, out of which he recites an appropriate prayer or two either before the kitchen fire, before the blazing censer in the drawing-room, before the sacred fire of the neighbouring temple, and even in one of the central fire-temples—this according to his circumstances or the degree of the devotion he possesses. At other times he prays before the sun, the moon, the stars, the well, the river, the sea, the plant, the tree, the mountain. He sees nothing wrong in some of these improvised keblás,† and I do not see what right *I* have to make him see otherwise. My business is with the quantity of his devotions. These are five in form, according to five natural divisions of his day. In quality these devotions are good and

* Satan.

† Mediums or things facing which the Orientals offer prayers.

healthy, but they are hopelessly "mixed." Very often there is a long piece for quiet reading and meditation, which the pious Zoroastrian drawls out line by line with well-executed ejaculations and the approved nasal twang, but without the vaguest notion of what he is doing. This is a sorry exhibition, and to the younger generation it is becoming a farce. An educated person, with power to discriminate between right and wrong, cannot help repudiating idle formularies which consist in mere mumbling over an extent of jaw-breaking jargon. And yet there are sensible men in the community who cannot understand why a spirit of infidelity, a feeling certainly more dangerous than mere passive indifference, which in itself is ominous enough, should prevail in the Zoroastrian world. The reasons are obvious enough. There is very little element of genuine devotion in the formularies as at present gone through. There is no intelligent appreciation of the recitals. The priest says his prayers for hire. He mumbles a certain quantity of jargon without indicating the least appreciation. There is no solemnity, no dignity, often no decency in the performance of the hireling priest. He knows it all to be humbug, and he gets through it as fast as he can, to see if he can give the benefit of his services to another credulous client soon after. And the devout layman! How does he offer prayers? He recites chapter after chapter of matter which he ought to read once in a way, which contains some excellent moral or philosophical dissertation, but which has as little of devotional merit as *Gulliver's Travels*! He does not understand a word of what he recites, and therefore he does so necessarily without any intelligent appreciation. He wastes from six to eight hours of his day under a mistaken sense of duty. What he wants is to thank his Creator for His mercies, and to beg of Him to continue these. Not knowing how to do it in language he can understand, he wades through his volume of bewildering phraseology containing learned discourses on matters astronomical, geological, metaphysical, moral, and social! Morning and evening he is haunted by visions of duty, and however oppressed at the prospect of the distasteful task before him, he gets through it with the patience of a martyr. But the attention, which is never wholly absorbed by such work, is apt to be disturbed and distracted. Hence it is not unfrequent to see the orthodox Parsi at prayer breaking out into abuse of his neighbour, into snatches of conversation or observation, and many other acts besides, which have nothing at all to do with the solemn affair in hand. The Zend prayer is always wound up with a personal supplication in Gujaráti. The devout gentleman is considerably relieved when he comes to this part of the edifying business. Here he at last understands what he says. And what does he say? Why, he thanks, in a sort of way, and as fast as he can, his Creator for his past favours; and then he asks for future blessings. True to his Asiatic instincts, he has "an eye to business," even in this solemn obligation of life. He prays not because it is his duty to do so, but because a prayer opens the way for a request! So he thinks, and so he acts. Who has not seen the orthodox Parsi of a morning or evening at the sea-shore? With what arts, what blandishments, he tries to seduce the Will Divine! How he bows, how he bends, how he kneels, how he promises and coaxes, threatens and bullies Heaven! How he scratches his nose in repentance, and holds up his skirt-corner in hope of receiving instantly the good things of life he prays for! And what decent man will not be shocked at this miserable travesty? If devotional services are a necessary institution for the people, let them be so; but why this public exhibition which exposes the community to the ridicule of all others? What presumption that a man should ask Deity to think of *him*, and HIM exclusively! The presumption becomes simply unpardonable when the supplicant descends to details such as asking God to get him good interest for his money, to provide his son with a suitable berth, and his daughter with an eligible husband! God is asked to be a match-maker and a broker; he is requested to be engrossed with the supplicant's affairs altogether, as if the Creator and Upholder of the vast and magnificent universe had nothing better to do than to devote His time to the affairs of an infinitesimal and insignificant worm-like man! The fact is the average orthodox Parsi has mistaken the scope and spirit of genuine devotion till he has drifted into a callous, selfish, presumptuous creature, unworthy of the name of Zoroastrian. And this is entirely owing to the mystery in which a crafty priesthood has hitherto shrouded his scriptures.

THE REFORMED PARSI OF THE PERIOD.

As for the young or, as he is called, the reformed Parsi, I doubt if he is a true Zoroastrian at all; he scorns everything that requires self-denial. It is often good to be independent, and I would not so much mind if the Parsi youth tried to live independently of any human religion, and at the same time to be an honest, useful man, desirous of leaving the world the better for his having lived in it. But it is not so with the average young Parsi. How could it be so, poor fellow, whilst he is in the transition period of his national existence, wavering and undecided at every stage of thought and of action? The Parsi youth's infidelity is directly and indirectly due to the Dustoors—the priestly class. The Dustoor is an hereditary functionary, and he thinks it his interest to keep the people grovelling in ignorance and superstition. In so doing the Dustoor, unconsciously perhaps to himself, remains ignorant and superstitious. I confess I bear the Dustoor no love. In revenge for the harm he has done to a great people, let me describe the worst of his class, now happily becoming extinct.

The Dustoor.

[His origin; rise; decline; his fall unfathomable; his ways of life; his sympathies, antipathies, and miseries; what to do with him.]

The Dustoor is the *ignis fatuus* of the dark ages of religion. Historians of free-thought consider him a myth, whilst the faithful claim for him a direct descent from the Magi * of old. If magi is Greek for maggots, then there is much sense in the latter interpretation, as the Dustoor's creed is, above all, very maggoty. But these interpretations do not at all settle the questions of origin. There is much doubt about the primary meaning of the compound or hybrid Dustoor. Some say it is a good Persian word meaning "pious leader" (*vide* Persian dictionary), others assert that Dusthoor, which is the correct rendering, means literally "the hand of Hoor." Max Müller lets off the Dustoor with the gentle hint that he originally came from Chinese Tartary. But M. M. is a wag. The intense *Rast Goftar* † can prove that Dustoor means the

* The wise men of Iran and Parthia.

† The leading Gujaráti weekly in Bombay.

10

most heinous offender against the law of God and man. But probably the most correct interpretation is that furnished by the broad and eclectic *Bombay Review*. That worthy reviewer has ascertained, by light of the most recent researches in Persia, that Dustoor is the father of that disastrous system of *dusturi** which is eating up the Municipality, the Commissariat, and every other Department of State. This is a hit. It shows how many others, besides the priest-ridden Parsis, are writhing in the cruel grip of the Dustoor. The Municipal Commissioner, the Commissary General, the Railway Agent, the Viceroy, the Secretary of State, all, all are under the baneful influence of this father of *Dustoori*. Worse still, the Ráo Sáhib Vishwanáth Náráyan Mandlik,† in his great work on Hindu Law, openly says that Dustoor means Custom. Cruel custom has been the ruin of India's social life, and Ráo Sáhib Vishwanáth Náráyan Mandlik, C.S.I., F.R.A.S., conclusively proves that the Dustoor is Custom itself! Truth is stranger than fiction.

Such, then, is the origin of Dustoor. There

* Petty but systematic bribery.

† A scholar, jurist, and prominent citizen of Bombay.

is absolutely no truth in Darwin's alleged insinuation that the genus Dustoor includes the hedgehog and the porcupine. Indeed, I cannot go so far as to deny that the Dustoor bears a strong resemblance to the "Ferocious Dooly." Members of Parliament are supposed to know all about it. But Darwin's supposed theory staggers me; and, as an admirer of the Dustoor, I cannot help saying that Darwin is the greatest and maddest of wags.

When the wave-worn exiles of Irán * first stood in the kindly presence of Ráná Jádava of Gujarát, there was no such thing as a particular Dustoor among them. Up to recently the Dustoor had a shadowy existence. But it waxed into such fierce light by degrees, that the Dustoor made it too hot for any sensible person to stand in his shadow. Then, by the law of action and reaction, as philosophers write, there grew up a new power in Parsidom—a Puncháyet. Then came a sudden change, a sort of depression, over the spirit of the Dustoor's dream. In its turn the Puncháyet, too, has become a thing of the past, making room for another social regeneration, the Ráhmumái. But this Mái,* too, is

* Ancient Persia. † Mother.

getting too old-motherly, and may have to defer to the pressing demands of the younger generation to have truth, *the whole truth, nothing but the truth.*

But even in his declining glory the Dustoor is not a personage to be despised. Far from it. He lives in better style than ever did old Friar Tuck. In eating and drinking he is thoroughly Garagantuan. He has all the animal spirits of a Rabelais without anything of his finely-concealed spirituality. They say the Dustoor never speaks while eating. Why should he, when what he eats is enough to make a feast for the gods?

The Dustoor can put on looks of portentous learning, but inside his head all is a Dead Sea, a Desert of Sahara. The most noticeable features of his dress are the muslin petticoat * and the cauliflower pugri.†

The Dustoor will never eat or drink with the Hindu or Mussalman, though he may take a cup of tea or a glass of ice-cream with a European official. He hates the Hindu or Mussalman, whose shadow is so polluting that the Dustoor has to soak his hirsute carcase in cow urine and

* His robe is very much like a huge female garment.

† Turban.

water for having crossed such shadow under certain circumstances.

The Dustoor Sáhib is very pious, and prays day and night for anyone that will pay him. He is chief mourner at a funeral, and gets handsomely paid. He is chief actor at wedding and other social parties, and is more handsomely paid. He is a good hand at match-making and match-breaking, and is most handsomely paid. These are his doors of income, or his "windows of income," as he modestly and sorrowfully puts it.

To the widow in affliction—that is, with a large property and no heirs—the Dustoor's soul goes forth with resistless ardour. Well endowed young widows are very wild creatures; but between the Dustoor, the doctor, and the lawyer, they are soon tamed into lambs.

The Dustoor has a tendency to poking his nose in everybody's concerns; and every honest man hates your prying, paltering, button-holeing busy-body. In this respect the Government is the most suffering victim of his persecution. He follows the Governor with odes, elegies, charms, and benedictions, and overhangs the august "presence" till the thing is "accepted with thanks." This note of acknowledgment the

Dustoor frames in a looking-glass or a mirror. It is said that Sir Philip Wodehouse,* who had a mortal horror of the Dustoor, actually contemplated an anti-Dustoori Act; but Mr. Gibbs,† who has a tear for every sinner, interposed, and said a J.P.-ship ‡ would do as well. I am not quite sure if the Dustoor is yet branded with those terrible letters of fire; but sooner or later he is sure to be a J.P. That is his *kishmet*.§ Poor man! It will be the last straw on the camel's back. May he be spared that last bitter humiliation. They have made him a Fellow ‖ already, lower than the Puttáwálá.¶

The Dustoor is afflicted by a fell disease, a most enervating and gangrenous tumour on each of his shoulders. The tumour has a very pleasant exterior, but there is no concealing the fact that it is noxious at the core. The disease is called *Shettia* by social doctors, and threatens to be the death of the poor Dustoor.

What to do with the Shett-ridden Dustoor in

* Governor of Bombay in 1875.

† Now Member of the Supreme Council of India.

‡ Justice of the Peace—an honorary office in Bombay.

§ Fate.

‖ Fellow of the University.

¶ A belted messenger.

order to save the Dustoor-ridden laity, is a serious question. We know of two remedies only. Assuming the *Bombay Review's* theory as to the origin of Dustoor to be correct, the best thing we could do with him would be to hand him over to Mr. Hyndman.* The Dustoor is at the bottom of the "bleeding" process, and we can guess how Mr. Hyndman would deal with the vampire.

The second best thing would be to send the Dustoor on a long tour in Europe and America in charge of a capable bear-leader. Such tour is sure to do the unfortunate patient much good, the best of it being that he would know his exact place in the world.

As to the *Rast Goftar's* (Truth Teller) clamours to have the Dustoor delivered up to him, I think that such a course would be wanton cruelty. The streets of Bombay are not made for bull-fights.

There are many other ways in which to utilise the Dustoor, such as damming up the breach in the Narbadá bridge, sending up to Kandahár for transport duty, to Simla for exhibition, to the Jamsetji Hospital for vivisection, &c. &c.

* An enthusiastic English writer on Indian politico-financial questions, who says India is being *bled to death*.

THE BORAS OF GUJARAT.

NEXT to the Parsis are the Borás (voharas—meaning literally, pedlars). They are Mahomedans and followers of Ali, but were originally Hindus. They are scattered over various parts of India, but generally gravitate towards Gujarát. The Borás have their Mohla, as the Parsis have their Dustoor, and the Vaishnava-Hindus their Máháráj. All three peoples are about equally priest-ridden. As a typical Borá, I have much pleasure in introducing my friend Adamji *bin** Didamji to the reader.

ADAMJI BIN DIDAMJI.

[HIS DESCENT, ATTRIBUTES, HABITS, MANNERS; HIS LOVE OF MAN AND FEAR OF GOD, WITH MANY OTHER THINGS BESIDES.]

Adamji *bin* Didamji is a compound product, as

* Born of, son of.

his name implies. He is often found loafing about the outskirts of Gujarát; but he is by no means a loafer. His forefathers were substantial Hindu farmers, somewhere between Kapadwanj and Viramgaum, what time the followers of the Prophet went from Ahmedabad lower down, with the sword in one hand and the Koran * in the other. As this is not a scientific paper, I shall proceed with a strictly personal history of Adamji, leaving further details of his origin to the faithful chronicler. Suffice it to say, for the present purpose, that Adamji comes of remote Hindu ancestry. He resembles the Hindu of Gujarát more in features than any other people. In habits he is milder than the mildest Hindu. He dresses like the Hindu, except in the matter of the *páyamá* † and the *pugri*. He speaks the language of the province with a peculiar accent. Frugality and simplicity are the leading features of Adamji's character.

My Adamji.

But to give a true picture of his character, it will be best to write of *my* Adamji *bin* Didamji. I made his acquaintance about fifteen years ago.

* The Mahomedan Bible. † Drawers.

He was then a flourishing young man of seventeen, and I was his junior by some years. Though I belonged to quite another race, Adamji took kindly to me from the very beginning. We met under peculiar circumstances. We were both suffering from a bereavement, and our sympathy was therefore very warm for each other. Adamji often invited me to dinners. When these dinners were private affairs they were extremely frugal. A handful of parched rice was thrown into the sands in which we were sitting, and one by one the individual grains were picked up by us during intervals of discourse. Adamji was, as a rule, my moral preceptor, and his morality was of almost a divine nature when we had to make shift with the parched grain aforesaid. He then talked of Heaven, and said the surest way to go thither was by conciliating the friendship of the Mohla,* but it would be pleasanter to begin with marriage than death. One day Adamji brought home his bride from Kapadwanj—his "brand-new wife," as Adamji told me in the pride of his heart. He gave us (me and other friends) a grand dinner on the occasion. A young buffalo

* The Borá's high-priest.

formed the backbone of the banquet. Good Surat *ghee* and sweet Bengal sugar lurked in every nook and corner of the big buffalo dish. *Kabobs* and *samosás*, *bhujias* and *hulwás*, roast and stew, sweet bread, and *pulow* and *berian* formed the other concomitants of this wondrous feast. All of us, about twenty mothers' sons, sat down to the repast, each one of the lot eating out of the same enormous dish. The blooming bride came at the end of the dinner to distribute flowers and *pán supári* * to the guests assembled. It is the custom among Adamji's people that the bride, under the circumstances, *must* be ogled. This we did with extreme unction. We peeped into Mrs. A.'s pretty face, and ogled with outrageous freedom. She gave back defiant smile for smile, whilst the "happy" bridegroom hung down his head and looked extremely foolish under this severe ordeal. But he soon after made up for his temporary humiliation by cold-shouldering us all and walking into his room with the bride and his and her aunts. It was about a week after this that I met Adamji again. I had also many occasions to see his Boo,† and

* Betel-leaf and nut.

† Borá or Mahomedan wife.

though she always kept herself *purdar nashin*,* Mrs. Adamji was not a bit of a prude. She chattered freely, and after the birth of little Adamji she did not hesitate to sit by the side of her husband's friends when he, the husband aforesaid, was near.

I had the melancholy satisfaction of seeing old Didamji, Adamji's father, die. He was about sixty years old at the time. He had made his peace with Heaven. Didamji explained to his admiring friends that, though he had not lived an exemplary life, having been only a shopkeeper, still he hoped he had a happy hereafter. He had invited the Mohla for over a dozen times during his lifetime, and had gone to His Holiness about a hundred times; and just before his death Didamji had paid a large sum of his ill-gotten gains to the holy intercessor, the Mohla, for a note of introduction on behalf of Didamji *to the address of the angel Gabriel.* The note ran somewhat on this wise :—"Dear Brother Gabriel,—My old friend Didamji *bin* Dosá it has been the pleasure of the all-wise Allah † to call away. I have honoured Didamji with my friendship for many a long year, and knowing his worth, I

* Under veil. † God.

beg of you to receive him hospitably, and to introduce him to the Most High with my respectful compliments." This note of introduction was buried with poor Didamji, and was no doubt taken by the deceased worthy on the day of resurrection, to Gabriel. And there can be no sort of doubt that "Brother Gabriel" *did* bring Didamji to the favourable notice of Allah, as Mrs. Adamji protested she had seen it all in a dream.

Adamji's life is a dead level of honesty, frugality, and simplicity—and so much the better for him. He is the thriftiest trader and shopkeeper in Gujarát. He begins life with selling matches, and generally ends with a substantial little establishment. In the beginning he can hardly earn one anna (1½d.) a day; and yet you will find Adamji lives happily, and saves something besides. I know of Adamji's countrymen maintaining themselves and their families on two annas a day. But however heavy the expenses, the income is never altogether squandered.

Adamji is prudent by instinct, but never miserly. In ninety cases out of a hundred he makes a true friend. Though gifted with a keen sense of the powers of money, he can make excellent use of it when he lists. Poverty has no sting for Adamji, nor riches an irresistible attraction. He is probably the shrewdest business man of the town; but in other relations of citizenship his simplicity is truly charming. It is guilelessness pure and simple.

But in one thing Adamji *bin* Didamji differs very materially from every other Gujaráti—he has absolutely no taste for politics. He is utterly callous as to the political management of the country. He has infinite faith in the Government, next only in intensity to his faith in the Mohla. The strongest political agitation in the country fails to strike a responsive chord in the heart. He is a lover of peace. He will put himself to any amount of inconvenience, he will sacrifice anything to secure peace. Peace to Adamji is a priceless blessing; and knowing that a discussion of political questions has a very disturbing tendency he will always refrain from politics. He neither hates nor loves politics; it is a question of stolid imperturbable indifference.

Such is Adamji *bin* Didamji; and whoever comes to know him well will agree that Adamji is, taking all in all, an exemplary man in every respect. As a son and pupil, as a brother or father, as a friend, his life is a lesson to his neighbours. As a citizen he is invaluable—simple, sober, prudent, and eminently loyal. Long live my friend Adamji *bin* Didamji, a worthy exemplar to the "educated" jackanapes of the generation.

LÁLIÁ "BOYS."

BESIDES Hindus, Parsis, Mahomedans, and Borás, there are numerous mixed and aboriginal classes in Gujarát, such as Dhers, Mahárs, Bheels, and so on; of which I shall here introduce only one, the Láliás as we call them. The Láliás or Surtis profess to be Hindus, but are Hindu only in name. They are as pushing and mercurial as the Parsis, and are mostly in the domestic service of Europeans and Parsis. Surat and Nowsári are their head-quarters, but the more venturesome emigrate to Bombay every year, where they take kindly to no other calling except to be "boys" (menial servants) with European families. They pick up a smattering of English with the blustering habits of their masters. They are particularly in request among bachelor employers, under whom they work, play, drink, cozen, return home, grow fat, and die. Their women are generally fine, sturdy lasses, highly developed in muscle and bone, and "sound in wind and limb," as they say in disposing of a girl in marriage. The Láliáns are brisk, handy creatures for indoor or outdoor work. They make masterful wives; and it is, therefore, easy to account for many a droll Rip Van Winkle in Gujarát villages. Instances are on the records of the police court where an outraged wife has tried "to whip the offending Adam" out of her husband for indulging in "heroic love." The Láliáns themselves, however, are no votaries of Diana.

CHARACTERS.—THE MÁRWÁRI.

In going through Gujarát the traveller is sure to come across a character who offers much scope for observation and study. Who has not seen the Márwári?—the professional usurer, so useful and so execrable!

His Infancy.

He hails from Márwár, and is a Vaishnava Hindu. At home, and up to eight years of age, the Márwári is the sprightliest little animal that ever kicked the mother who suckled him. He skips about like a wild kangaroo in the wantonness of unlimited freedom, returning at brief intervals to the warmth of the maternal breast. The little Márwári is kept at the breast till he is eight—till then parental affection is literally lavished on him. Eight is his weaning time;

and with true insight, as soon as he is weaned, he is sent off to these parts in company of an honest acquaintance.

His 'Prenticeship.

The little suckling is destined to be a merchant, and to a shopkeeper he is apprenticed at the first start in life. He is bound to serve the Shett for a number of years, to serve his person and his shop, to help at cooking the meals; he is bound to serve diligently and well, he is bound to *keep secrets*. If he give satisfaction for one year, he may expect a salary of eight annas * a month from the beginning of next year. Meantime he looks upon himself as a lucky dog if he can have for his two meals what remains after the master has dined—barely enough to keep body and soul together. But the boy who, only a month ago, led the life of an infant epicure, indulging every pleasure and every liberty dear to childhood, repines not at the change that has come over his bright young life. He slaves at his work heroically, bent upon learning the craft by which his master has raised a fortune. This alchemy the

* About a shilling.

young apprentice is determined to master, and to that end he strives with incredible diligence to ingratiate himself with his employer, and he succeeds. His half rupee pay is increased to Rs. 3 a month. He becomes the confidential *moonim*, the factotum, the *alter ego* of his master, and is entrusted with the sole business when the latter goes home for a holiday. The return of the chief marks a new era in the existence of our Márwári. He who was only the other day a thoroughly mercurial being, has now changed into a staid, sober shopkeeper. He opens a shop on his own account. His earnings of so many years will suffice for the purpose ; if not, he can borrow of his master, whose interest in him is not nominal. He can borrow from Rs. 50 to Rs. 100. Under more favourable circumstances he can borrow Rs. 500, though he seldom needs so much to start with.

THE MÁRWÁRI HIS OWN MASTER.

And now our Márwári has his own shop. He generally begins with salt, oil, grain, fuel, or other cheap nick-nacks. The Márwári never deals in anything which will not bring at least cent. per cent. profit. One might ask how he can have the courage, though his conscience is up to it, to ask double for such articles as oil, rice, fuel, &c. Well, it is thus:—The Márwári buys his articles of the poorest quality at the cheapest market. He buys when things go merely for the asking. He buys in the lump, and charges a heavy discount. He keeps shop in a locality from which the nearest market measures by the mile. He sells his goods on credit, and, of course, in retail. He weighs and measures as he likes, and the customer has only to smile and accept the article held out. His weights and measures are not of the latest make, and he often substitutes pieces of stone for standard weights. It is easy now to see how the Márwári earns at least cent. per cent. at his shop.

His Modus Operandi.

He allows credit to the customers till it has reached, say, a rupee; then begins the interest at two annas a month; then it becomes a book debt; then is required a security—an old ring, a few cooking utensils, some wearing apparel, &c. These are lodged with the Márwári till the lodger has drawn upon the shop for about half their value. Fresh security is now required if fresh supplies of rotten grain, adulterated oil, wet fuel, &c. are applied for. On all "reasonable" security he is ready to give, says the Márwári, but the customers must know that he has to meet his own liabilities. He charges heavy interest for the credit money, on the plea that he has to replace the goods disposed of on credit by new supplies for which he has to tell down cash, which he is forced to borrow. Besides, he turns to account the security lodged with him. He lends the ring, the clothes, the utensils, or the furniture to others, and charges for the use. He is not responsible for the wear and tear; if those who have lodged the articles with him object to their being used, why, they must close the account with him! *He* must live somehow! and so on, and so on. It is no use arguing with the Márwári, he will circumvent you everywhere. He lends and you borrow; it follows he should command and you obey.

His Mode of Recovery.

The Márwári will lend and sell on credit to the last pie compatible with safety. Infinite is his power of lending, so is his power of recovering. He manages to meet the debtor on pay day, on the very threshold of his office. He offers every facility to the debtor to earn money enough to repay. If the debtor seems to bear the Márwári's exactions with ease, he may be sure he will not be out of his debt. But the moment the Márwári finds difficulty in repayment, he sets about squeezing the last drop out of the unhappy wretch. He removes from the house everything worth removing. He appeals to the debtor's employers to give him the month's wages; he puts himself in communication with the debtor's rich relatives. He appeals to their *abru*.* He takes the debtor's wife and sisters and daughters in hand. He opens out new avenues of income for them. He sends some of them to factory work, others into domestic service. The Márwári does not scruple to put his victims to the vilest uses, so he can recover what he thinks to be his due. It is suspected that full half of the inmates of the brothels of Bombay are the victims of the Márwári's cruel persecutions, the female friends of the wretch who began his acquaintance with the

* Credit, honour.

Márwári with buying a pound of sugar on credit, and has ended that ill-fated acquaintance in the ruin of his manhood. When all this fails to satisfy the relentless fiend, he resorts to the Small Causes Court. He is a great friend of some of the underlings there, and those who know what a summary suit is, need not be told that the Márwári has the power to sell by auction everything the debtor may possess. He often buys up everything himself.

The Márwári's Victims.

The Márwári feeds upon the poorer classes of Hindus—our factory hands, house servants, and small handicraftsmen. His policy is the policy of the "long rope." He lends and lends till the man is completely in his power. There are Musulmans, too, in the Márwári's debt; and when he finds it is impossible to get anything out of a poor beggar, he sets him to steal. There may be many a notorious Musulman thief who is driven to the trade by the Márwári, who is his instigator and accomplice. The Márwári is invariably the repository of stolen goods. Parsis and Portuguese, too, the Márwári lays under contribution, especially clerks and mechanics. But these victims are apparently getting used up, so thinks the Márwári, and he scorns to deal with them. Europeans and Eurasians are not without the pale of Márwári's influence. He will lend when the banks fail a poor fellow. When the manager dismisses Augustus Hardup, of the G. I. P. Railway, the Márwári is his refuge. It is with the Márwári's money that Augustus applies for another place; it is with Márwári's money that Augustus woos and wins the widow Pereira with Rs. 10,000 under trust, left by the ugly old apothecary, her first husband. It is also with the Marwari's money that Augustus goes to Poona, Jubbulpore, and other likely places in search of employment—never to return. But the Márwári has security at least in the person of a friend of Augustus decamped. This worthy, an inmate of the workhouse, generally pays the Márwári with kicks and cuffs. He shakes off the "reptile" once for all, and after that is never troubled by the dun.

The Márwári as a Member of Society.

Thus lives the Márwári, buying and selling, lending and recovering, scheming, bullying, and going to court. His life is a continued struggle with his better part. But so successfully does he wrestle with himself, that before thirty he has ceased to be a human being. Before thirty he is a money-grubbing machine. He will do anything for money, get money from everything. He works greater havoc in the mofussil than in the Presidency towns. More minutes and reports have been written on the Márwári than on all the wild beasts and venemous reptiles put together. But the Márwári still flourishes. He threatens to be an evergreen.

The Márwári at Home.

Next to money the Márwári loves his home in Márwár, then his mother, then his wife and children, then his national music. The Márwári seldom smiles under Rs. 100, but the loss of a pie will bring tears into his eyes. He has not much religion in him; and though as a Vaishnava he is bound to visit the Máhárájás, he seldom does so, unless under inducement of a dinner or a loan. He has not much respect for his gods, and will prefer a Queen's coin to the best of them. In all his habits of life simplicity, that is, a love of cheapness, is the leading trait. He loves his holidays, and during the *Holi* the

Márwári abandons himself to full indulgence of the senses, but he takes care that the carousals do not cost him much in money. "Anything but money, unless it is *for* me"—that is the Márwári's motto. The Márwári makes a good friend so far as his advice goes. He marries late in life, and makes a loving husband and father, so far as love is love without money. He is too fond of hoarding to part with anything unless forced to.

A Solemn Warning.

There is hope for the wildest scapegrace buried in debt, if he has not gone to the Márwári; but once in the Márwári's clutches, not the wealthiest and the goutiest uncle can save him. The man who has escaped the Márwári's grip with a whole coat on may fairly claim to be the Finance Minister of Turkey.

THE VILLAGE HAJAAM.

ANOTHER curiosity, by the way, is the village Hajaam, the barber. No native can do without the Hajaam, and as he attends to many other little offices of life besides shaving, it may not be amiss to give an account of his "life and labours," in these days of cheap biography. The Hajaam in Gujarát is Hindu by caste; sometimes he is Musalman. There is no Parsi Hajaam. There are several little handicrafts at which the Parsi flatly refuses to work. He may be a professional gambler or thief, but a Hajaam or blacksmith—never. There are religious scruples in the way of his becoming a Hajaam. According to his Shástras * there is sin in paring the nails or picking up, clipping, or shaving the

* Scriptures.

hair. Very well. This is how the strictly religious Parsi shaves; he sits down to a Hajaam with a prayer to Ahurmazd,* probably to restore him his neck safe from the Hajaam's keeping, and an anathema against Ahriman.† He would not, for fear of having to endure the pangs of perdition, allow a single hair to go astray. As soon as the Hajaam has done his work, the religious Parsi collects all the shavings and buries them in a solitary place after certain vigorous ejaculations. Though this practice is said to be eminently philosophic, it has somehow fallen into disrepute; and Parsis of the day do not only disregard the practice itself, but have so far diverged from the original firmán‡ as to shave their chins and whiskers themselves. There is your wicked English education at the bottom of this revolution.

How the Hajaam operates on a Hindu.

But to return to our Hajaam, and how he operates upon an Aryan brother. The operation generally takes place on a Sunday noon, immediately after tiffin. Patient and operator squat

* The Parsi's God. † The father of evil.
‡ Commandment.

before each other, each chewing *pán supári*—a process which the ignorant might mistake, from a distance, for either making faces at the other. After discussion of the latest news, the Hajaam takes out his tonsors and falls to picking the hair of the patient's forehead. There is torture unutterable in this part of the operation; but be it said to the credit of both that the more vigorously plies the hand of the Hajaam, the more gratefully grunts the Aryan brother. The object is *high polish*, and both have set their hearts on that object. As soon as the tonsorial part of the operation is finished, the Hajaam presses the patient's head downwards; and meek as a lamb, the latter bows till his head is fairly ensconced in the Hajaam's brotherly lap. The water is now applied for a few seconds, and then is applied the trusty razor. As it moves backwards and forwards, the razor makes a distinct noise—a sort of wail complaining of the rough surface to which its edge is applied. When much put out, the razor sometimes makes a gash here or there; but the patient being persuaded that a little blood thus drawn averts apoplexy, submits to the razor's vagaries with cheerfulness, encouraging the Hajaam every time there is a gash, with a vigorous smack of the lips, as if to say the owner of the lips entered into the fun with all his heart. It takes about an hour to shave a well-developed Aryan. The razor has to glance north to south, east to west, to see that all is smooth as an ivory ball. This much ascertained, the Hajaam takes a handful of lime-juice and rubs it on the newly-shaven cranium with a smart air of superiority. The patient smarts under this operation just for a moment, but, knowing it to be for his own good, he is the last man to complain. But the operation is not yet complete. The head is as smooth and shiny as ivory, if not more so. But there is something yet to do. There are the cheek-bones to be similarly treated, the hair on the upper lip to be touched up, the hair in the nose and the ear to be picked out, for, with Oriental charity, every respectable Aryan cultivates hair in both these organs to a considerable extent. After the picking, clipping, and shaving are over, there is the nail-paring. Then follows the shampooing. Here the Hajaam puts the patient in various positions, and rubs and scrubs and currycombs with a smart vigour that would do good to the heart of a veterinary surgeon to witness. After half an hour thus employed, the patient is released, and the Hajaam is paid about a pennyworth of copper on the assurance that the operation will "answer" fifteen days.

His Miscellaneous Duties.

Thus plies the Hajaam at his principal work. He is good at many other jobs besides. He is the hereditary torch-bearer of the village, and has the honour of lighting in or out the Collector or his young man. The Hajaam is also a good pleader; not a High Court or District Court pleader, please, but a *pleader*—that is, he pleads the cause of the enamoured youth before his (that is, the e. y.'s) divinity. The village Hajaam is the priest of Hymen, and his wife is the accoucheur-general of the village. This is a fair division of labour between husband and wife.

The village Hajaam is also a good herbalist, and in this respect a more trustworthy person than the modern L. M. and S.*—he never poisons his patients.

The village Hajaam labours under one sad

* Bombay Licentiate of Medicine and Surgery—a passed medical man.

infirmity. He has a very loose tongue. He is an incorrigible gossip. The best use you can make of your enemy's secret is to entrust it to the Hajaam. If you want the secret to be most widely known, just say you give it him in the *strictest confidence*. He will rush off to the bazaar* directly he leaves you, and will not rest till the whole village knows the secret, of course with due exaggerations, but in the *strictest confidence*.

But though the village Hajaam is a great "spendthrift of his tongue," he never dabbles in politics. He has an idea that the Police Superintendent is the natural enemy of those who discuss politics, and that he has the power of hanging any such person in the back part of the jail at the Collector's command.

* Market quarters.

THE VA'QUIL.

ANOTHER "character," as busy as the Hajaam and about as popular as the Márwári, is the mofussil Vakeel (Pleader), or, as Persian scholars would call him, the Va'quil.

The Va'quil may be described as a column of vapour issuing from the Ocean of Emptiness. When condensed, after repeated manipulations, by the Professor of Law, and mixed with a strong solution of *brass*, the thing is rolled up before Sir Michael Westropp,* who licks it into shape, generally after tiffin. The exercise is said to be very exhilarating for both parties. As soon as Sir Michael has licked into shape and breathed life into it, the Va'quil starts up as if from a

* The Chief Justice of Bombay.

state of *Nirvana*,* rubs its eyes, stretches its arms, and, shuffling out of the "august presence," passes the rest of the day in chuprásis' † company. Under cover of night the Va'quil steals homewards, and hiding its guilty head in the bosom of its greasy quilt, it cries for relief.

His First Start.

Next morning the Va'quil is placed in a cage on a fashionable road, where it can be handled, from a safe distance, for about Rs. 3. The fee rises from Rs. 3 to Rs. 30, according to circumstances. But it is very seldom that the fee comes. This process of the Va'quil's profitless exhibition is technically termed "vegetation." In this state it remains from six to twelve months, when it begins to bud forth into something like human appearance.

The Va'quil with the Márwári.

At this stage the Va'quil is taken in hand by a Márwári, or such another worthy recognised by the Court as Dalál ‡ or Mukhtyár. But its

* Absorption, the Buddhist theory.

† Court peons. ‡ Law broker.

existence is not yet generally recognised. It has more leisure than it cares to have, which it devotes to the columns of the *Amrita Bazár Patrika*,* the pages of *Malthus*, of the *Sarvajanik Sabha*, or the *Theosophist*.

He Dabbles in Politics.

The Va'quil is now about thirty, and has already joined several free institutions where it can sit cross-legged and read the newspaper and discuss the leading article with friends. This it does in the evening. Occasionally it borrows a Famine Report, on which it pores for nights together. The result of this lucubration is a lengthy critique on Sir Richard Temple's administration, especially his famine and forest policy. At times the Va'quil draws a caricature of the late Governor, and, when it can afford to do so, it buys cheap photographs of him, Sir John Strachey, and others, which it hangs in its room head downwards. The practice may or may not have a significance.

The Va'quil Retires.

At forty the Va'quil becomes staid and sober. Its youthful exuberance, which found vent in

* The most popular Indo-English journal in India.

elocutional antics in obscure reading-rooms is now exchanged for argumentative criticism of the measures of Government, at public meetings. It also takes to strictly religious and patriotic modes of life—disposes of its offspring in marriage, retires to "the original town,"* encourages indigenous art by using everything that is made in India, and generally dies at the age of sixty. The Va'quil dies, as a rule, in "fairly good circumstances," though it does not live so. Formerly it used to migrate into the mofussil immediately on coming out of the larva state, but the Collector and his brood of assistants having made the districts quite unendurable for it, the Va'quil seldom goes further than Poona on one side or Ahmedabad on the other.

His Composition, Nature, etc.

As a chemical compound, the Va'quil may be analysed into butter, brass, and asafœtida.

Physiologically it takes after the kangaroo, and has much of that intellectual force which is believed to be derived from constant indulgence in vegetable marrow.

* His birthplace.

Phrenologists are agreed that the most prominent characteristics of the Va'quil are the bumps of combativeness, of secretiveness, and obstructiveness.

SCENES IN A SMALL CAUSE COURT.

Swearing and All.

Having described the Pleader or Va'quil, I might as well record here some trying personal experiences in the Court of Small Causes—experiences which more than confirm the popular belief as to the "glorious uncertainty of law," and which may be of use to some unwary simpleton like myself.

I once perpetrated a book. It was a wonderful book that, no two critics agreeing as to its merits; but it brought in a good deal of money, a good deal of praise, and vast deal of abuse. Amongst the many other things this wondrous book of mine brought me was a Small Cause Court summons. The poets sing of "death and doom." I had a very vivid idea of these unwelcome twins when the summons was put into my hands. I went about my business with the poor knees knocking together; and, though friends assured me that I had nothing to be down in the mouth for, I felt a vague foreboding of the goods and chattels at home being sold by auction, and myself being sent to jail for at least six months. In those moments of trouble I did not think well of my poor book. Why *would* it be written by me, the unlucky thing? It was all the book's doing. The suit was for recovery of Rs. 200, or something like 60 per cent. of the value of copies sold, for their *delivery in town* and such other services. I have paid more handsomely for still lighter services, but could not do so this time. It was not a question of will, but of power. I and my friends proposed all manner of compromises, but the man was obdurate. He had made up his mind to milk his cow dry. He had retained the services of a Vakeel, and nothing less than Rs. 200 and counsel's fee would satisfy him. In a word, there was nothing for it but to go to Court and contest the claim. So one fine day off I go to Court with a number of friends and followers. At first it felt as if one were going to his own funeral. We paused at the door of the Court, and, looking round to see if the eye of the public was on us, we rushed in breathless with suppressed excitement. Inside we were besieged by a number of daláls offering their services. I had no occasion for such services, as my friends said there was an excellent Vakeel to plead the cause. But the case was to come on late in the day; and as the feeling of horror subsided by degrees, I allowed myself to be taken to various parts of the court-house just to divert my thoughts. At every step almost we encountered a knot of Márwáris engaged in hasty but animated conversation with the harpy of a dalál. These, we were told, were concocting a story to ruin some poor debtor. False documents, false witness, and perjury were here gone through in open daylight, and almost in the presence of the judge. The Márwári seldom gets a Vakeel to conduct his case. Between himself and the Mooktiár they can hoodwink justice quite successfully.

Summary Suits.

From here we moved on to the court of the last judge, a native gentleman. His Honour had just then a case before him. A house-owner was asking for the removal of his tenant, a poor Portuguese. The Bible was given and the oath mumbled. Then asked His Honour of the defendant:

"How many months?"

"Seven months, Sir," replied poor Caitan.*

"How many rupees a month?" asked His Honour again.

"Five rupees, Sir," replied Caitan.

"Decree for Rs. 35, with costs, time up to the first," drawled His Honour turning to the clerk.

"Call next case," continued the Judge, asking for another case to be decided.

"But, Sor, me paid two months rent reg'larly," whined Caitan.

"Appeal to Full Court," drawled His Honour, turning condescendingly to the man.

This was a "summary suit," we were told by our guide. It was. We waited for two other cases. We saw a good deal of swearing by the Book, and a good deal of audacious and easily-detected lying gone through in rapid succession.

* A favourite name with the Portuguese, or rather Goanese.

But except for the Judge's frown, we noticed no other punishment for false witness. All this was far from reassuring to me, and I once more requested friends to compromise with my persecutor, as the case would be soon coming on. Negotiations were opened, but now the pleader on the other side told my friends he "could not conscientiously advise his clients to withdraw." We saw we had to take our chance; but there was some hope in the judge before whom we were presently to stand, being reputed a patient and impartial man.

We entered the room, and on our pleader asking the interpreter where His Honour was, that pompous functionary declared, "The *Court* have gone to drink." There was no time to laugh over this interpreter's joke, for the "Court," alleged to have been in such undignified occupation, had already returned. The Judge fell to business as naturally as the child falls to its dinner of sugared milk. The complainant, my persecutor, was administered the oath. He promised by the life of every one of his 330,000,000 gods to tell the truth, "and nothing but truth." The Judge asked the interpreter if the complainant had been sworn. "Swored, your

Honour," vociferated that obliging official. Then the complainant was asked to say what he had done for the defendant to earn Rs. 200. Hereupon, the man who had just a minute ago solemnly pledged himself to truth, gave utterance to a number of lies appalling in their magnitude. I and my friends were astounded. Complainant deposed to having witnesses to corroborate the statement that he had done enough to earn Rs. 200 on sale of the books worth Rs. 600.

His Vakeel looked triumphant, mine was quite crestfallen. I was shivering as if with the ague, and a young friend actually burst into violent gesticulations at the man perjuring himself with such malignity of purpose. The Judge then asked for a few particulars. Among these the complainant, unfortunately for himself, stated that he had procured for the ungrateful defendant a loan of Rs. 100, at 36 *per cent. per annum.*

"Is this to be one of the *services* entitled to a honorarium of Rs. 200, Mr. ——— ?" asked the Judge, turning with benevolent surprise upon the plaintiff's pleader.

The game was lost. Client and counsel looked extremely foolish. Every remark they hazarded after this miscarried. Witnesses for the plaintiff were at last called. Like true men of the world, these Aryan gentlemen had already vanished! Taking their cue from the turn affairs had taken, all of them had bolted except one, and this man in his evidence damaged the complainant's case, whispering to him after every pause, "I told you I would tell the truth; I have to face my Maker." The Judge having done taking his notes, the complainant's counsel opened his speech. This Aryan orator began somewhat in this strain:—

"Although my client is *confounded* here and there, I have reason to believe that he is an honest man; also elderly. The defendant is a mere lad who owes much to my client. He more than once offered to compromise. Why, if his conscience did not prick him? Having made these general observations, I now leave the matter with your Honour, only remarking in the end that my client has a large family," &c. &c.

The defending counsel, knowing full well that in certain cases silence is golden, merely said, "I can do no better than leave the case entirely to your Honour."

The Judge awarded the plaintiff something like Rs. 30, which, seeing that he had promised a much larger sum to the pleader who had picked up his case, was a sore disappointment. The Judge passed severe strictures on the complainant's conduct, and his judgment was received with delight by all save two in the room.

But I have not looked upon the issue of the case as a success. What I suffered that day in mind I have not yet forgotten. Even in the hour of triumph I wished I had never gone to Court. What a ruin I had so narrowly escaped! But for the Judge having been patient and considerate, for his having that day assumed the double *rôle* of judge and counsel, it is impossible to tell where I would have been. And though the dark visions of bankruptcy and jail were the offspring of my morbid imagination, there is no doubt that, with a hasty and inexperienced judge, I would not have been able to clear myself of the many charges foisted upon me by the baffled fiend. Since then, in the plenitude of my experience, I have warned all from going to Court. Suffer any amount of reasonable inconvenience, but do not rush into courts of law. You can never be sure of what may happen. Courts of law are a luxury for the well-to-do, and the nothing-to-do, so to call them. Audacious lying and deliberate perjury often get the better of truth. Where there are men ready to swear away your reputation, your best course is to avoid coming in contact with them. Pay any small sum if you chance to stumble upon such persons, but go not to courts of law, especially with a *summary* suit, where perjury has the greatest chance of success.

SCENES IN A MOFUSSIL MAGISTRATE'S COURT.

No mortal thinks himself so happy as the Native Magistrate in the Mofussil. But there are times when even he, whose smile gives life to the evil-doer and whose frown annihilates him, feels insecure and uneasy. He does not fear the Collector, the Judge, the Revenue Commissioner, or the Governor himself. He meets the requisition of each with cheerful *nonchalance*. But whenever he hears that an English barrister is engaged to plead for a prisoner before him, or that a European soldier or sailor is defendant in a suit, the Native Magistrate loses appetite and his sleep. He studies his Penal Code as he never studied the most sacred of his *shástras*. He also reads his Compendium of English Grammar and Composition, and on the day the case is to appear, goes to Court after many prayers and supplications to the gods to "preserve his *abru*."* Poor native suitors know the Magistrate's weakness, and take all precautions they can to counteract its effects.

A few months ago one of these Magistrates had to decide a case in which the town barber was plaintiff and a discharged Irish soldier defendant. The soldier seems to have thrashed the barber for some reason best known to himself. Now the barber, who was a man of sense, knew that he could not establish his case against the white man. So, with grim Oriental humour, he made his mother-in-law plaintiff in the case, and with the aid of two or three trumpery witnesses, undertook to prove that the soldier had assaulted the "poor defenceless woman" in a field of bájri † hard by, and that the whole town knew of it. The barber had only recently married a fourth wife, with a neat little dowry; so he said, "As *Prabhu* ‡ has given me the means, I am determined to set an example." With this purpose in view, the barber went to the best pleader in his town, a very learned man,

* Reputation. † Millet. ‡ His god.

who "had once gone to Bombay." What better counsel for a good cause?

On the day fixed for hearing the court was crowded by spectators, some of them Parsi lads on a holiday tour. The Magistrate came first, looking very mild and anxious. Then came the soldier, looking very cool and careless. Third came the plaintiff's pleader, looking very warm and important, and with the pleader's robe and high-heeled creaking boots on. Last of all came the plaintiff, the barber's mother-in-law, with a crowd at her back. She seemed to have rheumatism, paralysis, and many other dreadful ailments besides.

"From the tears she shed in the streets," explained the jocular Musulman constable, "one might think we had rain last night; at any rate, there will be no need for watering the streets this noon!"

A minute or two after, the proceedings were formally opened. I shall only transcribe here the examination of the undefended soldier by the barber's counsel.

PLEADER (*with easy familiarity, and intending to procure confession for mere asking*).—Well, my man, why did you do this thing?

SOLDIER.—What thing?

PLEADER.—You know it, *is it not?*

SOLDIER.—Hanged if I do!

PLEADER.—Don't use vulgar curses; you should not be *contemptible* towards the Court.

SOLDIER.—What do ye want, thin?

PLEADER.—Did you assault *this lady*, or not?

SOLDIER (*looking at* the lady *and breaking out into a horse laugh*).—Did ye see me assault this *lady?*

PLEADER.—No, but others did. It was a most indecent and brutal outrage, and you will have at least five years for it.

SOLDIER.—You are a d—— d——. Why the dickens should I assault that hag? Ax her yeself, ye murdhering thief, and thin *git* ready (*putting himself in attitude*).

PLEADER (*in a dreadful funk, turning to the Magistrate*).—I seek your worship's protection of my person and property.

MAGISTRATE.—Chhut, chhut, Mr. Rámrás. What do you mean by *indecent* assault in this case? That word should not be imported at this stage; it is not in the original plaint.

PLEADER.—By the fifth of——

MAGISTRATE.—Nonsense, all nonsense; that applies to cases of murder only.

PLEADER (*in sulks*).—I will then leave the case to your worship. I can go to the High Court.

SOLDIER (*to the Magistrate*).—Why don't ye lave this varmint to me, Sir, and ye ax the old woman hersel.

MAGISTRATE.—Mr. Soldier, don't use bad words. Yes, I 'll ask the woman.

SOLDIER.—Begorra, ye are a handsome gintleman, yer honour.

MAGISTRATE (*to the barber's mother-in-law*).—Here, woman, stand up. Did the sahib assault you?

WOMAN (*blubbering*).—You are my father and mother!

MAGISTRATE.—You will have to be flogged if you don't answer directly. Did the sahib beat you?

WOMAN.—I am a poor widow; my husband used to shave you, *mábáp*! *

MAGISTRATE (*losing temper*).—Here, constable—now, will you answer or not? Did this *sojer* beat you?

WOMAN.—*Mábáp*, beating my son-in-law is beating me! (*Pleader hanging down his head, barber looking daggers at his dear wife's mother, magistrate tittering, and soldier smiling.*) The whole town knows it.

MAGISTRATE.—Knows what?

WOMAN.—That I am an honest woman!

MAGISTRATE.—But, woman, that is not the question.

WOMAN.—That my Lakhi's father shaved you!

MAGISTRATE (*turning in disgust to the Pleader*).—Mr. Rámrás, you see the defendant may have assaulted another person.

PLEADER (*taking up the cue*).—Did you assault this gentleman barber? (*Asking the soldier.*)

SOLDIER.—Now, say ye so, my jewel!

PLEADER (*sententiously*).—Weigh your words.

SOLDIER.—How kin I weigh my words?

PLEADER.—Sir, have you come here to *brandy* words with me?

SOLDIER.—Do ye think so?

PLEADER (*furiously*).—Now, hold *out* your tongue, Sir.

Pat seized this golden opportunity, and throwing a world of solemnity into his attitude, *held out* his tongue—a big, red, lolling thing—to the infinite amusement of the spectators, who knew not why they laughed. The Pleader was dumbfounded ; the barber looked at him with pity and contempt. The Magistrate was convulsed with laughter ; he thrust his silk handkerchief into his mouth till he was fairly suffocated.

The case was dismissed.

NATIVE MENDICANTS:

Including the Aghori.

One of the most prominent sights, though none of the pleasantest, that the visitor encounters, is the professional beggar. No people had ever before them higher ideals of charity than the Hindus. As in the new, so in the old world, charity has been the corner-stone of the edifice of Faith. But nowhere, not even in Christian Europe, have the subtler and more potent forms of charity been so fully realised as in the land of the Aryas. It was only in the recent degenerate days that ideas of charity grew vague and puerile till, since the advent of the present century, the spirit of charity has steadily deteriorated. Charity at present signifies the giving away of superfluous wealth to the worthy or the unworthy, for certain objects, especially what they call "personal distinction." It is wise of the Government to recognise public spirit by the grant of titles; but the indiscriminate showering of these empty honours is perverting our instinct of charity. No one in these days can indulge the luxury of giving away a few thousand rupees, however earned, without being overtaken for his folly by the inevitable Khán Báhádurship or some such "mark of His Excellency's favour." The grand old doctrine of THINKING WELL, SPEAKING WELL, AND ACTING WELL—the triple badge of Oriental charity, is becoming forgotten day by day, and in its stead we have a grosser, an unreal substitute, *the giving to others that which may not be of particular use to oneself*. It is hard to convince some people that there is not the least flavour of charity in the miser leaving his millions to a charitable institution. There is no merit in it. The wretch leaves his hoardings behind simply because he cannot take them with him to where both the miser and his money are equally unwelcome.

THE MENDICANT CLASS.

One of the best means, perhaps, to obtain an

insight into the principle and working of charity in this country—thus far materialised—is by a study of its mendicant class, a numerous and potential factor of the great Indian population. A study of their habits and modes of life would be highly interesting. But what I can here do is to briefly characterise each division, and leave the reader to take the cue for further investigation and comparison.

STREET PENSIONERS.

First among native mendicants we shall take the street pensioners—a numerous body of men, women, and children, partly diseased but wholly indolent, who infest the streets by day and night, and are content with a morsel of rice for a meal. They are Hindus as well as Mahomedans, and are patronised indiscriminately, though not to an equal extent. The Hindus reserve their favours more or less for their own people; and so do the Mahomedans for their people. The former generally give their pensioners what remains of the food after the household have partaken of it. The Mahomedans often do more. They cook a huge quantity of rice and *dal** on particular

* Pulse.

holidays, and it is a sight to see the lazy fellows falling to the godsend, licking their fingers and smacking their lips at short intervals.

White Mendicants.

Hebrew mendicants are not a rare sight in our streets. They are generally females with a troop of children, their own or borrowed for the occasion. It is not an offensive sight, this group of quietly-clamorous "white" beggars. But it is not a credit to the rich and influential class to which the beggars belong. In this respect, as also in another wherein the insensibility of the elders is much more reprehensible, our Hebrew brethren might easily imitate the Parsis. A sort of arrangement was, I believe, attempted some years ago, but the people break loose from it. It also seems that they cannot do without begging and the other vice. In the former avocation, if not in the latter, they have Europeans and Parsis mostly for their patrons.

Private and Professional Mendicants.

But let us return to the mendicant proper to India—the indigenous growth. He appears in various guises—the *Táin*, the *Mowlá*, the *Fakir*, the *Sádhu*, the *Bhâtu*, the *Chárana*, the *Gosáin*, the *Jogi*, the *Gora*—and their females. Some of these are public beggars, the rest being professional. They are gentle or violent in their clamours as circumstances warrant. They go from house to house and shop to shop, and adopt various expedients to obtain their "due." They sing, dance, philosophise, they cry, curse, and raise a storm, in order to move the hard-hearted Banian. They are more powerful than the police, and certainly more numerous. The respectable ones are also professional. For instance, there is the poetic mendicant, with his harp, his *veno*,* or other ricketty instrument. There is the historical mendicant, with his rag of a Sanskrit or Persian reference book; there are the astronomical, the medical, the moral mendicants, all with their peculiar hobbies and peculiar twangs, always amiable and often instructive. Then there is the friendly mendicant, generally a Mahomedan, who will button-hole you in the streets, discuss with you a variety of subjects, from polite literature to the rates of salt fish, and then, just before parting, startle you with

* A sort of guitar.

the whispered query, "By the bye, do you, Sir, happen to have a loose pie * in your pocket?"

DOMESTIC MENDICANTS.

But the most influential of all is the religious order of mendicants. It begins with the domestic priest, the Guru, and ends with that destroyer of all virtues, the Vallabhacháryan Máháráj. The Guru is as meek as he is sleek, and generally a worthy, jovial fellow, who is much, too much, trusted by the "ladies of the house." Then there is the temple priest who keeps the idol, and is, in return, kept in the best style by the worshippers. The *moorlis* † of Máháráshtra and their sisters of Bengálá are also subjects of great interest. They are fair devotees who profess to have consecrated their virginity to the favourite god. But they are very obliging creatures, very frolicsome; and as their highest merit consists in earning most for the temple, they are all anxiety to earn. Several daring youths, who once crossed the threshold of the Káli temple near Calcutta, have come out of it with recol-

* The smallest copper coin.

† Unmarried women supposed to have dedicated themselves to a favourite god or goddess.

lections of their one night's adventures which are likely to last them their whole life.

The Aghori.

We now come to the Aghori mendicant. The Aghori, as his name implies, is an atrocity. It is a human being who, by a series of exercises, has achieved the highest pitch of his ambition—the feelings, habits, the very nature of a beast. The Aghori is insensible to all bodily discomforts; in fact, he courts them. He is a very rare animal, but by no means altogether extinct. One has only to see him to realise the loathsome object. Dark, muddy, hirsute, with eyes on fire, the nostrils wide distended, the nails grown to the length of an inch, diseased in various parts of the body, which is actually being worm-eaten, with vermin in the hair of his head, vermin on his body, and generally stark-naked. Such is the Aghori. His look is that of a mad idiot. There are the insane leer, the protruding tongue, the filthy teeth. The Aghori never washes, never dresses. He takes only carrion or putrid food, and drinks foul water. In one hand he carries a human skull, in another some hideous instrument of torture and death. These are his insignia. To complete the picture of this horrible process of brutalisation, it is only to be added that the Aghori besmears himself with human ordure. He does not hold human life in the least account. Nothing is too sacred for him. He can enter any house and ask for anything. The least hesitation makes him cut himself or others frightfully. He delights in the infliction of wanton pain. He is particularly fond of human flesh and blood, and the larger the number of his victims, the higher his merit in this life and the other. With the advent of the British the Aghori has almost completely disappeared. But he still haunts remote villages, and the havoc he works by his mere appearance is incredible. His sight throws women and children into convulsions, and there are instances of premature and painful births induced by the sight of this atrocious monster.

THE MISSIONARY IN THE MOFUSSIL.

What he is Like, and How he comes into the World.

If the visitor is not altogether unlucky, he may, in course of his tour through these parts, meet with the Missionary. The Missionary is a great soul split up by many pettinesses. A man of infinite trust, but slow to trust the heathen; of sanguine hope, but always despairing of the world's future; of boundless charity, and yet very strict in judging of all outside the pale of his little communion. Learned as a book and simple as a child, too sensitive too grovel in poverty, and yet to proud to renounce it—the Christian Missionary presents a strange paradox in the economy of social life in India. There are many theories in circulation amongst the "vulgar" as to the object of England sending out so many Missionaries to India. The most original and plausible of these is that when an English pair have no children, they pray to their God, just as we pray to our gods here, to grant them at least a son, who, the parents vow, shall devote his life to "preaching Christ" to the perishing millions of heathendom; and God being, in popular estimation, a sensible sort of a person, never tires of granting such requests.

Infancy and boyhood are a period of severe discipline to the missionary *in embryo*, and of acute anxiety to the parents who, whatever their means, will not rest till the hopeful is at least an M.A. or B.D. by the time he is twenty-one. Then he comes to India, generally in connection with a school. Immediately on landing he is taken in hand by the Munshi,* the Pandit,† and the Khabardár or informant. He falls to the work of studying the vernaculars with avidity; and the stories of the Khabardár, too, he swallows with equal zest. In less than two years the *padre* is monarch of all he surveys. He bears a

* Persian and Hindustaní teacher. † Sanskrit teacher.

charmed life in the village. He is supposed to be in the Collector's confidence, a favourite with the Collector's worthy dame, or of the Engineer's elder sister, who sometimes keeps house for him. The Munshi and the Pandit have taught the *padre* just enough to give him the worst possible idea of Mahomedanism and Hinduism. "Duty" being a matter of choice with him, the Missionary never hesitates to *hold forth* whenever he can.

His Daily Duties.

Let us accompany our friend in his round of daily duties. He begins the day with a short prayer in the little church where all his "people" attend. After the prayer and a few kindly inquiries, the *padre* re-enters his little shell, from which he emerges after breakfast. A few visits to the poor, and then two or three hours of literary work. This done, he goes to school, from which he returns for afternoon tea. This is his leisure time, when many an honest inquirer reads the Book with him, and retails to him his latest spiritual experiences. About 5 o'clock, the *padre* leaves his neat little cottage on his preaching tour. He walks sometimes for miles together, and returns home exhausted. But he never complains—there is the same bright smile on his face as in the morning, and the early supper and cup of tea are gone through with much pleasant chit-chat.

Such is the Missionary in the mofussil. He is not so *stiff* as he used to be, and many of his foibles, too, he is getting under. But the good that is in him would compensate for weaknesses a hundredfold. He has a pronounced predilection for sermons; but then that is his craft, his calling, the very mission of the Missionary. It may be that he sometimes emphasizes "hell," "damnation," and such other words with a sort of frenzy, but he always means what he says.

The Missionary an Institution.

It is ridiculous to expect the Missionary to "retire" for good. He has taken deep root in the soil. He has a firmer hold on our hearts than any earlier growth. The Collector may go, the Engineer may be turned out, the Governor may be recalled, aye, the very Government of the country may change, but the Missionary will remain. He will endure to the end of time, a monument to the silent influence of his faith. As a friend of all people, adviser of the State, teacher and guide of youth, preacher of a grand idea, as general leavener of society, the Christian Missionary will always occupy a high and beneficent prominence in India.

One standing complaint against the Missionary is that he reaches the soul through the body. But is that *his* fault? The Aryan "Gentoo," of the lower order especially, has so much of body, and so little of soul, that it is impossible to reach the latter before oiling every nook and corner of the "tabernacle of flesh." The Gentoo is of the flesh, fleshy; and as *curry chowal** has a very soothing effect on the flesh and, through it, on what little of soul he may have in him, the *padre* is justified in his tactics.

The Missionary's Wife.

To write of the Missionary and omit his good wife would be a sin. She is his right hand, his real helpmete. A simple, unselfish, devoted woman, of even gentler sympathies than his, she often tames him, when under sudden provocation he forgets the obligations of his sacred office. To the sick and the starving she is an angel of

* Rice and curry.

14 *

mercy. She ministers both to the body and the soul, and in bestowing her little gifts she seems as if actually receiving them. Truly womanlike, she is the best friend of girlhood, and parents cheerfully acknowledge this. In all the lighter duties she is indispensable—at marriage, birth, baptism; whilst it would take too long to tell what good she does in school work and teaching.

SHETT JAMÁL GOTÁ, PHILANTHROPIST.

In the course of my itinerary through Gujarát I was never so much amused and shocked as when learning the particulars of a truly extraordinary life. The history of Khán Báhádur Jamál Gotá, J.P., may show, amongst other things, how certain native families have risen. Shett Jamál Gotá, I must explain, is an extreme case of social oddity.

How he Rose.

Khán Báhádur Jamál Gotá is the only son and heir of his father by his "own mother," as he proclaims to the world. Jamál Gotá *pater* was an honest liquor-shop keeper at Charub. One Christmas Day he took a bottle of country-made *mowrá* to Colonel Buttercup, Cantonment Magistrate. The Colonel and his wife, Mrs. Millicent Buttercup, were at dinner with Collector Jalap, when Jamál Gotá approached "the presence," *saláming* * repeatedly, with something like a bottle wrapped in a clean white napkin. Making his best bow to the company, Jamál unwrapped the bottle and placed it on the table; then folding his arms, as the Parsi does before his *Keblá*, orated to this effect:—"Námdár Sirkar Sáhib, it is our custom to lay before such feet as yours (Buttercup had left his feet on the field of Assaye) the first-fruits of the season. Hence the trouble, Lord Sáhib, for which your pardon, General Sáhib!" Buttercup, who neither relished the allusion to his absent feet nor the bottle in the presence of the strict Jalap, affected to be thunderstruck. After a gasp or two, he found coherent articulation enough to ask, "Are you mad, Parsi? Who are you?" Jamál Gotá, who had come prepared, hereupon fell to the ground, sobbing as if his heart would break, and whining "Oh, Sáhib, you are my *mábáp*. Is it not the duty of a son to keep his mábáp *Khush*?

* Bowing obsequiously.

Do what you like with it, but don't give me back the bottle. I am a disgraced man, and poison is my only remedy now." Buttercup could not resist the force of such reasoning, and that on a Christmas Day. So he nodded to the suppliant, remarking by way of reward, "You old humbug! How can I be your *mábáp*? We shall suppose, for the fun of it, that I am your *báp*, but how can you make me out your *má*?—unless he means you, my dear," whispered the wicked Buttercup, turning to his spouse. At this sally there was a great laugh. Jamál gathered strength, and offered to serve his *dároo* * with his own hands. The request was granted. Jamál knew he had made his fortune. In less than a week he installed himself head butler. He stuck to his shop, too, but at dinner time he would be at the bungalow, with one novelty or other to provoke appetite. It need not be said that Jamál rose rapidly in importance. He was on confidential terms with Mrs. Colonel Buttercup, they knew. She consulted him upon every concern. When there was cholera, Jamál would advise madam to fly to a distant village with her

* Wine.

dear Colonel. And off they would go, leaving everything to Jamál. When they returned, Jamál would explain how he had burnt or buried the metal, wood, or other utensils at home, for fear these should retain the germ of the horrid disease. "What is money before your health, Sáhib?" The Buttercups were delighted with Jamál's deep devotion. They made a contractor of Jamál, who in less than four years rose to be the leading Shett of the town.

But as he grew in public importance he deteriorated in domestic virtues. (This is generally the case.) Jamál found that his marriage with the present Mrs. Jamál Gotá was a mistake, that his only son and heir was also a mistake. They tried to humour him every way at home, but Shett Jamál was not to be reconciled. At last, "with the advice of friends and patrons," he took to him a second wife. Bigamy was no offence then; but the first Mrs. Jamál, whom, strange to say, her husband treated better after his second marriage, repaid the kindness by dying within three months. Young Jamál accused his father of having killed the old woman by Jadoo.* This was too much for

* The dark arts.

Shett Jamálji, who swore that he had disinherited the young "thief," and in a fit of passionate upbraiding, was carried off before he could make another will.

Jamál Gotá Fils at Home and in Public.

Come we now to the history of Jamál Gotá *Fils*, Justice of the Peace, Khán Báhádur, &c. &c. Young Jamál's first care was to look into the finances of the house. He ascertained that he was master of about five lakhs of rupees. He then counted how much he should spend every month, so as to leave a few thousands for his "brats," as he paternally called his sons. Having settled this point, he opened his campaign of luxury, dissipation, and waste. He pulled down house after house and built bungalows instead. He organised dinner parties and nautch* parties, and other immoral entertainments. He invited the *élite* of the town three times a week on one pretence or another. He took a Mehtá † in confidence, only bargaining that *he* should be supplied with what he wanted daily, the family to be reared with strict economy. He spent Rs. 1,000 one night on a party, and threatened

* Dancing. † Accountant.

the Mehtá (clerk) with dismissal next morning for allowing to the family of eleven members besides servants Rs. 2 for bazaar expense. He denied that his family had any claim upon him. "Did they bring this money?" he asked of remonstrating friends. He kicked his wife and children, and abused them frightfully in the presence of his dancing girls. He married his children with great pomp, spending large sums on dinners and other parties, and then put down double those sums against their names, explaining that each had already received his or her share of the inheritance, and that none should expect anything more. He, however, promised them their two meals a day provided they behaved themselves. The boys, seeing no future, asked to be sent to school, though already fathers themselves. Shett Jamál hereupon levelled a pistol at them, saying they wanted to dishonour him. Why should they go to school like poor people? Had they not every blessing of life—a generous parent, fine handsome wives, and a number of children? Was he not feeding them all? It was no use arguing with the man. The sons then went to the Collector who had made Jamál Gotá a Khán Báhádur, and said, "Sir, we are starving; give us to eat." The Collector gave them respectable berths under him, asking them to learn soon to qualify themselves for the posts. When Shett Jamál heard of this he ran up to the Collector, took his turban off his head, put it at the Sáhib's feet, unclasped his Khán Báhádur medal, and said, with tears in his eyes, "Sir, you made me Khán Báhádur; this great honour has given me a chair *beside Queen Victoria*; the sun smiles on me, the moon courts my smile: all this I owe to you. Now take away this honour and kill me. My *ábru** is all gone, and you, my own patron, have done this by making clerks of my sons. Oh! oh! Why did I live to see this day? What will the Queen say to this? Oh! oh! ungrateful sons! wicked wife! I would kill them all."

"You old brute," replied the infuriated Collector, "you old, vicious, stinking brute! Had I known you were a drivelling idiot like this! Talking of Queen and sun and moon, when you have no more sense than my stable-boy! Here, remove this man; take him to the Magistrate; let him be bound over to keep peace towards his

* Reputation.

unhappy family. Oh, you putrescent carcase," broke out the Collector, half laughing.

The butler was immediately sent with instructions to take the "beast" home, lest he should die of fright before the Magistrate whom he had so often fêted.

His Decline and Fall.

Khán Báhádur Jamál was *done for*. He took to his bed. He would see nobody (except his nautch girls). He would eat nothing (except sweetmeats). No, no; he had done with life. But he had still about a lakh of rupees left, safely invested by the Mehtá. He withdrew this sum, and left it with a Bombay firm which promised 12 per cent. interest. In about six months the firm broke, and it was with immense difficulty Jamál could get back about 40,000. This, with a couple of bungalows, is all that is now left to Khán Báhádur Jamál Gotá. He now leads a retired life, away from his family, whom he has altogether discarded. But, indulgent father as he is, he has still "kept his son's saláms," he explains to friends—that is, once a year his sons go to salám him from a distance, in the faint hope of getting a hundred or two from the unnatural wretch.* Vain, vain is the hope. The father is a thief and a traitor, developing a degree of selfishness which is absolutely fiendish. And still he is an ornament of mofussil society! He is ever on the alert to catch the eye of the public. He presents a stable-house to the Anjuman,* and his charity is loudly praised. "Leaders of society" crowd at his dinners, call him a public benefactor, while at the same time they know that the imbecile, whose substance they are eating up like pariahs, has a family literally starving—the sons going about from office to office for work which they have not been taught to perform, the daughters eking out a precarious existence by sewing and stitching, and the wife, the "lady of the house," daughter of a true gentleman, is ending her days in sorrow and in suffering, aggravated by the cries of adults and infants of an ever-increasing family. And honest editors immortalise the virtues of Jamál Gotá, Esquire, Justice of the Peace, Khán Báhádur, "our great philanthropist," whom they know to have been an undutiful son, a wicked husband, an unnatural parent, a false friend, so worse

* Community.

than brutal in selfishness, that the veriest brute would have blushed for him had Jamál Gotá been assigned the place in creation which he so richly deserves.

HOME LIFE IN GUJARÁT.

A few details of domestic life in Gujarát may not be uninteresting. Let us begin with the beginning—birth. The birth of a child is, of course, an *event* in the family. Want of issue is felt as a curse and a reproach by the wife as well as the husband. No Hindu can enter *Swarga*, his heaven, who does not leave a son and heir in the world to perform the *post mortem* ceremony named *Shrádha*. The Parsi is not quite free from this superstition. When conjugal life is unblessed with issue, a thousand means are tried by the poor wife. She is not an honoured wife before she becomes a mother. She appeals to gods and goddesses without number to grant her prayer. Charlatans and impostors are not wanting to take advantage of her ignorance. It would fill a volume to record the adventures of a Hindu wife in search of offspring. Suffice to say that the uneducated Hindu wife will stop at no means to get at the desired end. She is at peace when once the prize is secured, no matter how, where, or when.

BOYHOOD.

Every care and comfort is lavished on the mother expectant. She who was a few months ago the most despised of the family, even less important than the servants, now finds herself real mistress of the house. As the time of trial and triumph approaches, a dinner party is given in her honour, at which, besides some insane rites, the poor creature has to put up with many a rabid joke and ribald song. Three days after the child is born the astrologer prepares its horoscope. The young mother's heart sometimes "bursts with happiness" as she listens to the astrologer's glib forecast of the child's career. If it is a boy, the baby is taken in hand by the grandparents, who transfer all their affection for their son to the little infant. At an early age the boy has the *Janoi* * ceremony performed

* The sacred thread.

upon him, which makes a real and responsible Hindu of him. The Parsi boy likewise has the *Kusti* * ceremony performed on him, and the Mahomedan undergoes *Sunnat*.†

GIRLHOOD.

The girl is a heavy responsibility, and parents are always uneasy about her future. They anxiously look out for a suitable match, and as soon as they can they get rid of the dangerous possession. "A girl is best at her father-in-law's," says the native proverb, "as is the elephant at the Rájá's." Indeed, every parent looks upon a daughter as a "white elephant." Amongst the Hindus it is extremely difficult to find suitable husbands in one caste and suitable wives in another.

MARRIAGE AMONG HINDUS.

Not only is intermarriage between two castes nearest in customs and rites prohibited, but marriage between cousins of the remotest degree sternly is looked down upon. Such connection is incest according to Hindu law. The rarity of a

* The triple cord. † Circumcision.

really happy marriage can be conceived. And still, curious to say, a Hindu marriage seldom turns out *unhappy*. The credit of this is mainly due to the Hindu woman.

PARSI MARRIAGE.

Parsis, too, cannot marry out of caste; but there is an incipient revolt at work against this ruling, and several daring youths have taken unto them fair European brides. But this happens in rare instances, and it is not at all desirable, I believe.

But the Parsi can marry his cousin—even first cousins marry. In fact, such alliance is always preferred. To such an extent is this practice of "breeding in and in" carried by certain families, that the results have told disastrously on the progeny. Eminent medical men have strongly condemned this practice. Of one European doctor, high up in the profession, it is said that he was once called to the side of a young Parsi lady in trouble. The new comer was so slow in coming, that the mother's life was at one time despaired of. But at last she came. Her grandfather, a very wealthy merchant, looking at the tiny little girl, small enough to make a morsel for man or beast, asked the doctor very plaintively how it was that his grandchildren were so very diminutive and often deformed. The doctor replied, "My dear sir, if you keep up the practice of marrying cousins, I will not be surprised if, ten years hence, you get babies no better than half-formed ourang-outangs!" And no mistake. Too much of cousin-marriage has given us not a few ourang-outangs in physique as well as in intellect.

The Parsi is a monogamist; not so the Hindu and the Mahomedan. Polygamy obtains amongst the very highest circles or the very lowest.

A friend of mine has a *Dhobi* (a washerman), a low class Hindu, who has six wives. Being asked one day what a poor man like him could do with so many costly luxuries, the man explained, with a wicked leer, that he had originally married only one wife, of his own caste, that she was his queen-wife, and she attended to his personal wants. The second wife, he explained, he had married for mere convenience, and so also the other four. The first looked after his kitchen, the second and third earned money for the whole family, the fourth was intended for perpetuation of his race; she having failed, the fifth was taken in, and the sixth was her sister! All save the first were of lower caste than himself, and besides paying him in money for his condescension in marrying them, besides working for him like slaves, they felt honoured and happy! He did literally nothing, he continued with another horrid leer, except going to customers on pay-day. Not a bad idea!

Marital Travesties.

Marriages, both among Parsis and Hindus, especially the latter, are often very strange perpetrations. I read some time ago a graphic account of a marriage recently perpetrated at Poona. The "happy bridegroom" had just entered on his fifth year when he took to him the "blooming bride" of two-and-a-half. The parties concerned seemed to have taken the matter very lightly; so much so, that to the outsider the ceremony seemed to have been performed between the two parents who stood sponsors, and to whom the usual query, "Dost thou take him" or "her as thy lawful," &c., was addressed by the priest. The bridal preparations were complete to a degree—the groom was turned out in all the bravery of the *toga virilis* and a huge sugar-loaf turban, whilst of the bride nothing could be recognised save the blinking eyes and the cry for "the bottle" from under her heap of *trousseau*. It was a Parsi marriage, and indicates "the march of progress" characteristic of a highly advanced people. But such "marriages" are not frequent among Parsis.

Marriages among Kudwá Kunbis.

Perhaps the strangest form of this kind of "marriage" obtains amongst the Kudwá Kunbis of Gujarát, a wealthy and otherwise intelligent class in that province. The "season" for marriage among the Kudwás occurs only once in twelve years, when all marriages are settled after consulting *Mátá*, the tutelary goddess. Among these are adult marriages, child marriages, infant marriages, and marriages in the womb. The last-mentioned are highly amusing arrangements, in which the mothers expectant undergo the preliminaries. Many curious results attend these marital travesties; but the national instinct is equal to all extraordinary occasions. For instance, if the "married mothers" both give birth to girls or boys, these are looked upon as sisters or brothers, and the previous marriage annulled.

The marriage is held good only in case of one of the births being a boy, the other a girl. And in this case neither disease nor deformity, nor any physical inadaptability stands in the way of the validity of the marriage contract. Who will say, after this, that the Hindu mind is not saturated with a sense of rich and grotesque humour? Of this marriage *in embryo* and its results, I have culled an account from several curious manuscripts, in prose and verse, that came in my way during my travels. Many of the quaint incidents recorded in my idyl were witnessed by myself personally or by Hindu friends who have gone through the harrowing experiences.

An Aryan Idyl.

Motichand Zaver and Kastur Pitámber were merchant princes. They were castemen, neighbours, and friends; each was called the very "nose" of Ahmedábád society. Mrs. Moti and Mrs. Kastur were also sisters.* Many a friendly chat had the two Sheths † together, chewing *pán supári* and congratulating each other on the success of the week's "operations." Many also

* In affection.

† Leading wealthy citizens.

were the meetings between the two Shetháńis,‡ who went to the holy Máháráj together, and often examined each other's heads to detect parasites (an unfailing sign of bosom friendship). One afternoon, as Bái Devkore was looking into Bái Shámkore's locks, she pinched the latter's cheek and chid her for not having acquainted her "own sister" with an interesting secret she had only then discovered by accident.

"Sister," said Devkore, "thy heart is not clear like mine. Did I not tell thee, without asking, that I was six months gone? How far art thou?"

Then replied the modest Shámkore, "Oh, sister Devkore, I was so ashamed you would go on joking and teasing. You have done it so often—you have four already. I am five months gone, and it will be a boy, I know."

"I'll have a girl," replied the impetuous Shámkore. "What say you to a match, sister mine?"

"Oh, sister," replied the younger, "it will be an honour to our family; I'll ask my This (husband)."

* Wealthy matrons.

That night Shámkore's "This" saw Devkore's "This," and in less than a week the mothers-expectant were "married" in right Shráwak fashion.

"It is a splendid stroke, my dear," said the uxurious Kastur to his young wife that night. "That hog [his friend Moti] is worth a plum."

But unluckily for them, both gave birth to girls. This was a sore disappointment, but it was overcome by the arrangement that the next male birth should wed the promised bride. It was four years before Mrs. Kastur did present her lord with a thing which the midwife declared *would be* a boy by-and-bye. Unfeigned were the rejoicings thereupon, not so much at Kastur's house as at Shett Motichand's. Mrs. Moti was wild with joy. "Oh, sister mine, I feel as if *I* had done it, I so badly want the little rogue, my poor Mánkore (the promised bride) is growing so."

Time flies. Mánkore is now sixteen, her boy-husband is nearing twelve. Mánkore looks older than her age by at least five years. Devchand, her husband, looks nine at most. He is short, dull, consumptive. She is the reverse. But is she not his promised bride? The families now live away from each other; but the wife is informed of her husband's rapid progress, physical and mental. Mánkore is "bursting" with youth and hope; she is already a *moogdhá*;* her season of leafage is over; her wise mother has already disclosed to her enraptured gaze the mysteries of wifehood. "Oh, dear, how I long to meet my lord. I am more eager for his company than is the pea-hen for raindrops. Indeed, indeed, I must be married, mother." And married she was.

Mánkore's heart died within her when, after all these years, she beheld her lord. Her fancy had pictured another form altogether. But she would not repine. She would consecrate her life to rendering his happy.

"He is little, he is ignorant, he is ugly; but is he not my wedded lord? I'll give him my own health, my own knowledge, my own beauty. Bhugwán † will help a virtuous wife. O Brahmá! O Shiva! O Vishnu! ye thirty-three crores of *devás* and *devis*, make *me* ugly and ignorant, and give the gifts ye have given to me to my dear lord. I'll cherish him in my heart,

* Mature. † God.

I 'll soothe him in my arms, I 'll kiss him into glorious manhood, I 'll be a *motherly* wife unto him."

So reasoned Mánkore and so she vowed. The wedding ceremonies are over; the bridal party disperse; the bridegroom is carried into his room. An hour later the bride follows. All is hushed. With a light step Mánkore enters the magnificent apartment, mirrored all round, with the scented bedstead, its silk and satin trappings, its gold and silver posts, its lovely curtains. But she heeds not all these tinsel effects. The "life" of all this beauty is her lord, and he is—SNORING! There is no ecstasy of impatience on his part. He sleepeth the sleep of the innocent. Mánkore sees this and sighs. But her love for the miserable little fellow is supremely unselfish. She feasts her eyes on the object which, under other circumstances, she could not have too strongly loathed. She lays herself down gently on the floor. Oh, the horrors of this bridal night! "The water of despair extinguishes the fire of my love, but I 'll venture." Gently she nears the bed, and looking around, all fearful, she touches his feet. They are so clammy! Then, overpowered by an undefinable feeling, pity, loneliness, despair, she attempts to ravish a chaste wifely kiss from the slumbering bridegroom. But, unused to such osculatory exercise, the idiot awakes, sets up a terrible shriek: "Oh, *má*!* oh, *bápá*!† come, come! this strange woman is biting my lips!‡ oh, *má*! she is gagging my mouth! oh, she is breaking my legs! oh, oh, oh!" There is a rush into the room. The poor fainting bride is removed gently to another room by the mother-in-law. There is wondrous sympathy between these two women. The little Sheth Devchand is soothed to slumber by promise of a long holiday from school, and the Bhaiají§ sleeping with him.

And thus ends my Aryan Idyl: what followed is only known to the chief actors. The Máhárájtried to improve his opportunity. But Mánkore is not like her mother or her mother-in-law. She can only cry in corners, read Karsandás Mulji's *Moral Essays*, pray to her "true" God. She is very gently treated; her parents are gone, her husband is *going*. He cannot last over a few

* Mother.

† Father.

‡ Devchand has forgotten all about the marriage.

§ Gate-keeper.

years more. She waits upon her lord. "I am his handmaid, and I pray that he may live; I am quite happy," she reasons falsely. "Let him only live—he must survive me. Is he not my lord? What he can't give me *here* he 'll give me *there*, surely—I have learned that much." Poor child, poor child! What a wealth of faith and hope is thine! Widow of a living imbecile, amidst trials and temptations, surrounded by sin and sorrow, thou art pure of heart—a virgin immaculate! But thou canst not hide it from thyself that custom and the folly of parents have blighted thy life. May none of thy sisters realise *thy* fate!

Experiences of a Newly-Married Parsi.

An odd marriage is not a rarity among Parsis, too, as I have said—it may be odd in various ways. Here are the experiences—of a "mixed" character—of my friend Ookerji, confided to me as a friend. Any honest Parsi can vouch for the facts, though I very much doubt if any will like to be identified as the "happy" bridegroom or his dear wife's mother!

Last week I was dined by my mother-in-law. Mother-in-law is a well-endowed widow who keeps her own accounts and her own counsels. I hail from Panch Kaliani, a small possession of Nawáb Khudá Bux of Mowlághar. I was an orphan before I was born; so one might well doubt my existence. But fact is a stern thing, and so is mother-in-law, to whom at once I must return. Well, the dinner was in honour of my marrying mother-in-law's only daughter. It was an "affair of the heart," for had not mother-in-law set her heart on it? And when she sets her heart, or head, or hand, or foot on anything, there is small hope of resistance, you may be sure. Our union was arranged for just after the fury of the 1864–5 share mania had subsided into bankruptcy and suicide. One day father-in-law "was not." So mother-in-law came to Panch Kaliani a woe-begone widow to all appearance, but with small effects of large value hidden in many odd corners of her capacious motherly person. I distinctly remember this visit. My old aunt received her, and a little girl trotting behind her, at the threshold. I was busy eating raw Indian corn, but instinctively made out that the little girl was her daughter and my destiny. They lived with us for about a year, during which time our troths were plighted. Shortly after my poor old aunt died, leaving me and her neat little fortune to mother-in-law's care. We then came up to Bombay, where mother-in-law at once set up for a rich widow with no desire to become a woman again. She put us both to cheap schools—me and my wife—where we were happier than at home. Mother-in-law had a horror of over-feeding us, and whenever we cried from hunger she would remind us of the day when we would be wedded and free. And, in very sooth, she was making grand preparations for the day, and the repeated threat was, "The wedding once over, I'll lay down my aching bones in peace." This was an empty boast, for, as far as could be gathered from a respectful distance, the doctor was of opinion that her constitution was not predisposed to generating ossific substance. But I see the reader is looking out for a picture of mother-in-law. Well, she was no meet subject for a poetic pen. Horizontally and perpendicularly she measured the same. She had a fine head of hair, which grew in rank luxuriance, shooting out their delicate downy germs on the fallow surface of her facial region, notably on her upper lip and chin. In voice and manners she was more mannish than is usual.

So much for mother-in-law. As to her daughter, I am not the man to betray what is in my keeping.

How the Marriage was managed.

Well, mother-in-law worked for a successful wedding business, as I said. She set apart Rs. 5,000 for one day's expenses. She got thick placards printed in red and blue, commencing with a brief history of her house, mentioning the names of parties to be married, and concluding with an invitation to the recipient and "all with you"—meaning your whole race, including the ayás,* hymáls,† and even the next-door neighbour. Those invitation cards mother-in-law got liberally distributed by Parsi priests, who have, somehow or another, taken leave of their priestly calling, but who make excellent dry-nurses, match-makers, waiters, and errand-boys. Well, well, the day came, and with the crowing of the cock we started for the wedding-hall. A thousand cushioned chairs were scattered over the spacious grounds, while the hall inside was being swept and scoured. That day must

* Women attendants. † Men house-servants.

have cost mother-in-law ten years of her life. She lived in an acute agony of hope and fear. Would the day go off well? One local magnate would send word that he could not join, because his wife was ill; and away would go poor mother-in-law to the stubborn dame, coax, cajole, and bribe her into gracing the occasion. In some instances, she says, she positively bought brilliant silk dresses for ladies who did not care to disgrace their families by appearing in the garments their husbands could afford! By 4 o'clock visitors commenced pouring in. We were now asked to go and purify ourselves—me and the bride. This is done by repeating sundry prayers said by the priest, drinking a glass of *niranga*, and taking an oath. A rupee to the priest had changed the *niranga* into most palatable *eau de vie*. On dressing we were seated side by side, and the high priests approached with a high-and-mighty gait. One of these "holy men" managed to tread upon some rotten plantain bark. I dare not describe the result, but that evening another priest had to officiate for Dastur Banámeijad. We were soon married, and then mother-in-law came to wash my feet, according to custom. The five minutes occupied by this ceremony were to me an age. I was in constant fear of having the foot disjointed. But mother-in-law was all smiles that evening. She formulated the motherly blessing, "May I be thrown from over thy head," and then the thing was over.

I was now led to a seat outside between two venerable guests, and took a leisurely survey of the assembly. Most of the guests were Parsis, but there were some Mussulmans, Hindus, and Portuguese. How these latter gentlemen came to know our family is still a mystery to me; but mother-in-law is certain they were representatives of the Government. As far as I could guess, one of them was Dr. de Lucha, the Sonápore apothecary, and the other Mr. Annunciation, the undertaker. But each had a cocoa-nut and a nosegay in his hand, and that means they were welcome guests. I have no time to speak of the dresses of ladies and gentlemen, and of the exquisite music the former discoursed alternately with the Portuguese band.

But here's how we dined on the occasion. The guests sat at table instead of squatting on the floor, each having before him a fresh plantain leaf. On this leaf the waiter served the dinner —about two dozen little dainties from sugar, *ghee*,

16

and plantain, up to cake, custard, and cream. It was beautiful to see the liquid *ghee* meandering through the viands and making friendly overtures to the coat and trousers of the diner, while the oil-lamp was flickering from nervous exhaustion. It was beautiful to see how the dinner was eaten —the rice *dál* and plantain first, and then the solids and substantials by way of dessert. The toasting, too, was beautiful to witness. How the health of deceased ancestors was first drunk, then the health of remote descendants, and, oftener than was necessary, of the living worthies of the community. The health was, of course, drunk in what goes by the name of "wine." The toasts were proposed by professional toasters, sometimes by friends of the host and sometimes by the waiters. Have you seen the dirtiest chimney-sweep of London? Well, then, the average Parsi waiter *beats* him. There is not one white speck to relieve the dread darkness of his appearance. A cold shiver runs through your body as you see the waiter stalking out of the kitchen and serving the pudding or custard with his five dirty fingers. His appearance strikes terror into children, and I was told of a mother that was to be on whom the sight of him had a most disastrous effect. The Parsi waiter is only next in harrowing associations to the Parsi corpse-bearer. There is a subtle sympathy between the two wretches which the student of nature can easily account for.

DEATH—ITS EFFECTS ON THE LIVING.

In dealing, though very cursorily, with such a solemn subject as life, it would not be well to omit death, the twin-brother of life. Death is not a stranger to us; but he is never a welcome guest. And by none is a visit from him so much dreaded as by the Hindu wife. The death of her husband is a crushing blow to her; she cannot recover from its effects. The Hindu widow is doomed to wearing life-long weeds. The widow is not treated like a human being. Her look is "inauspicious," her touch pollutes everything. Despised, neglected, and often betrayed by the wolves of society, her woman's life often becomes a burden to her. She has nothing for it but either to abandon her pure womanhood to impure customs, or to drag on her miserable solitary sojourn to the bitter end, often reached long before it is time! I am here speaking of the YOUNG HINDU WIDOW—she who has all her life before her. The widow who has the consolation of children left to her is not so completely at the mercy of caste and custom. Indeed, the widow with grown-up boys does not think she is to be so much pitied as her neighbour who has been left "alone." Of such widows my bold but unhappy heroine, Moghi Thakrani, is a notable instance. Let me speak of her class "by her mouth."

The Confessions of Moghi Thakrani.

A Chapter of Lapses, Relapses, and Collapses.

"My father married late in life—after his forty-eighth year. My mother was then about twelve. She looked old for her age, my aunt Kevli tells me. My father was really old, having led a laborious and irregular life; but he had hoarded money, with which he bought my mother. She made a devoted wife. He, too, was kind to her in his own way. Three years after the marriage my mother gave me life and lost hers in the attempt. My father mourned her truly, but his grief was selfish and arbitrary. What grieved him was not so much her death, as her not having left him a son and heir. My father loved and was very proud of me. He would not part with me under Rs. 50,000, he used to say. I remember my youth from six years upwards. At this age I was first taken to the Máháráj's Mandir. My aunt and several of my cousins came with me. Up to nine I worshipped the Máháráj at a distance; but after my marriage with an old man I was initiated into the sacred rites of Máháráj worship. My father as well as my husband did not know, or rather pretended not to know of my dedication to the 'Source of True Bliss.' On the day of our visit my aunt decked me out in the best of clothes and richest of ornaments, murmuring softly all the while, 'Thou little lucky rogue, thy life will be blessed to-day.' And thus fell upon my life the cruellest blight that could befal womanhood. I would not have the heart to wish such a curse to fall upon my deadliest enemies. But we are all alike. After my dedication I went to live with my husband. He was an old man, with many of the infirmities of age—he was deaf and colour blind, for two things, and made dreadful mistakes through jealousy. I had scarcely been with him for three months when an undesirable acquaintance sprang up between me and an opposite neighbour. I made very light of the sin, and so we lived on for about six months. The knowledge no way interfered with my happiness. But soon came its punishment. The Brahmin cook, learning of it, besieged me, and threatened exposure when I disregarded his importunities. It is impossible to deny favours which are asked as a price for secrecy. Next year I presented my husband with an heir, who died in a few weeks. The old man himself died soon after.

"I now entered on a career of unbridled license. When inconveniently situated, I would organise pilgrimages to holy shrines, whither I would go in company of half a dozen wives and maidens, accompanied by two or three servants. Having fallen myself, I felt a kind of satisfaction in seeing others fall. I think I have this way ruined a hundred women."

Let me now give a few instances of the sad results of caste. A man being strictly forbidden to marry out of caste, and eligible girls being very few, he has to pass the best years of his life in low intrigues for the acquirement of money and the gratification of brute passions. He is nearly a wreck at the time of his marriage, and makes an indifferent guardian for what is his exclusively. After a few years of the marital foolery, the husband either dies or is quietly removed. And then the young widow, used to sin, breaks out into open profligacy, undermining the morals of all who come in contact with her.

On the other hand, when the wife dies first, leaving a son of say ten years, the father gets for him a bride of thirteen or fifteen. There is a double object in view. He cannot marry again if he is a poor man. He will have sooner or later to bring a wife for the son; so he resorts to this stratagem. Such arrangements are rare, but people know what they are made for. The re-marriage of widows and permission to marry one degree out of caste, would do away with practices the infamy of which attaches to almost all sections of uneducated Hindus.

The Thraldom of Caste—Its Approaching End.

Oh Caste! what havoc hast thou wrought in Gujarát in the name of religion, and under the sanction of antiquity! We have been thy slaves for centuries—and no slaves so abject as we Gujarátis, no tyrant so absolute as thou, cruel, cruel Caste! But thy days are numbered. Yes, the reign of King Caste is drawing to a close. Nature, the sovereign controller of all mundane affairs, is already asserting her supremacy; and though it may be years, perhaps whole decades yet, before the rightful sovereign comes into her own, I doubt not that Caste, in his more hateful aspects, is retreating. Twenty years ago, the re-marriage of a Hindu widow was an event not to be dreamt of. In the course of last year I have recorded at least fifteen such unions. The bold spirits who defy Caste in order to save their honour and secure the happiness to which instinct tells them they are entitled, have to put up with bitter persecution, even personal violence from bigots in power; but the eye of an All-wise Providence watches over the victims. The time is coming when, sanctified by Him and blessed by all sensible Gujarátis, widow re-marriage will grow up an institution of the land. Meantime, the following account of a Caste meeting may afford some cue to the observant reader as to the knowledge and power for good of the representatives of Caste, and the attitudes of the advocates of reform. The proceedings are conducted in a very primitive manner. But I need not apologise for *that*, inasmuch as it is my business to place before the reader the real pictures of life and manners, rough, crude, sometimes half-naked, but always *natural*.

A Hindu Caste Meeting.

Thákar Khokhrá, the Shett (*smoking opium from his hubble-bubble*).—Brothers, it has come to my ears that some of us here assembled are children of the devil.

Manhordás (*ardent reformer*).—Yes, *father*.

Thákar Khokhrá.—Why should it be so, *my son?*

Manhordás.—Father, if thou wilt forgive thy chhoru (child), I 'll speak.

Rangilkáka (*a gay widower*).—Yes, Manhorbhái, tell the truth and *shame the devil*.

Manhordás.—Well, then, we are going to the devil, as Khokhrá *bápá* says, because we would rather follow the devil than such a Máháráj as Chandoolálji.

Ládubhat (*orthodox priest*).—Shut up your mouth, shut up your mouth; you are to-day a sudhár awálá (reformer), but did you never worship the Máhápurasha?

Manhordás.—Never.

Ládubhat.—I have myself seen you kissing

the sacred toe. (Cries of "Shame! shame!" "The hypocrite!")

MANHORDÁS.—It is false. I can prove it false.

KHOKHRÁ SHETT.—Prove it, young man.

MANHORDÁS.—Because on the 5th *vad* of Vaishák 19—the Máháráj's toe was bitten off by rats whilst he lay exhausted after a drunken frolic. Dr. Bhan Daji * could prove it. (Hisses and groans and uproar.)

THÁKAR KHOKHRÁ (*upsetting the hubble-bubble*).—You shameless infidel! I have put you out of caste.

VESHDHÁRI (*a man who loves widows in private and hates them in public*).—I declare that Manhordás is a Kristan † fellow. He is a *vutlel* (convert). What are these Sudháráwálá? One cheats widows out of their portions; another keeps a number of widows in his house under pretence of protection; a third gambles and becomes a bankrupt: they become Sudháráwálá to please the *Sahib loques*, and that way assume importance. They are the thieves and pirates of society. Shame upon their birth!

* Our most accomplished Hindu physician and scholar of Bombay—died in 1872.

† Christian.

MANHORDÁS.—Don't make me speak out, Veshadhári. I know you and the widows of your family!

VESHADHÁRI.—They are your *mothers*, you rascal!

MANHORDÁS.—Ah! they never *keep* their children!

VESHADHÁRI (*losing temper*).—Oh, you slanderous murderer! Is not your widowed sister a witch?

MANHORDÁS (*relapsing into street Arabism*).—Your daughter, your sister, your mother!

VESHADHÁRI.—Your aunt, your grandmother—were they not Mahomedans?

MANHORDÁS.—And can you swear who is your father?

VESHADHÁRI.—Yes, and I can also swear who your real father is. Now, will you fight it out, you malicious liar?

THÁKAR KHOKHRÁ (*waking from his nap and falling back upon the hubble-bubble*).—Is the business before the meeting over?

MANHORDÁS.—No; you must listen to me.

KHOKHRÁ SHETT (*striking his belly*).—I will listen to this first. I have put you out of caste, also all your family and friends, unless you do the proper penance in time, and give three caste dinners of *ghee*, mango juice, and assafœtida. So long as I live I will trample upon *Sudhárá*. I am not such a fool as to pretend to be wiser than my fathers. Return home in peace and hope, my children, and may the blessing of the Máhá-ráj be with the faithful!

HOLIDAYS.

A HASTY glance at some of the national holidays of Gujarát may not be an unfitting conclusion of our itinerary. Chief among Hindu holidays is, of course, the far-famed

DIWÁLI.

No description of Diwáli would be complete that did not extend from nine days before Dasará to fifteen days after Diwáli proper. The holiday preceding Dasará is called *nava rátri*, "nine nights," which in vulgar parlance has come to be called *nortá*.

These nine nights are sacred to *garbás*, generally amorous ditties sung in the streets of Gujarát. A few oil-lamps are placed on a lamp-holder in the centre of an area, close to which are placed a virgin pair—"a bonny youth and maiden fair." About these a bevy of from twenty to sixty women of all ages circle round and round, taking up a refrain, and often repeating in chorus a verse sung by one and, at times, two women, keeping time to clap of hands. These *garbás* are evanescent scintillations of the genius of Dayárám, the Byron of Gujarát. The hero of the songs is Krishna, the lord of 16,000 *gopikás*,* who are maddened by love of him, who are drawn to the "nourisher of our souls" by the enchanting tones of his *murli* † in the by-lanes of Brindában, and who fly to him at early morn—one "slipping from her husband's side," another "leaving the morning duties undone," and a third without "suckling her babe," all with tumultuous delight, panting, perspiring, and half naked! There, in the wilderness of unbought love, they meet him, the "soul-subduer," and in converse with him their souls "drink delight." This legend is asserted to be no more than a poetical portraiture of the passionate yearning the soul feels towards her Maker—a feeling that surpasses in intenseness the love we feel for

* Cowherdesses.

† Flute.

children or parents, even that selfish and vehement longing we have for "the flesh of our flesh, the bone of our bone." This harmless legend is worked by Dayárám into various orgies of songs whose luscious sweetness and witchery of style have done more than any other social vagaries to perpetuate the horrors of those dens of iniquities, the Vaishnava Máhárájs' Mandirs. In this respect Dayárám's poetry works in Gujarát as "procuress of the lords of Hell." But the days of street *garbás* in Gujarát are numbered. Surat was head-quarters of these midnight songs, and attracted, during the *nava rátri*, visitors from outlying places, even from so far as Bombay.

To be allowed to join a *garbá* was an honour, and none but your Langtrys * and Wests could claim the privilege. The ambitious songstress must have a figure like the cypress, her eyes a pair of young lotuses, her mouth a full moon, her teeth a row of pearls or pomegranate seeds, her breath like citron, her lips corals, her forehead virgin marble, her nose the parrot's beak, her hair like the graceful nágavel,† her cheeks

* The bronzed counterparts of two far-famed English beauties.

† Betel plant.

dimpled love-gardens, her chin a sloping meadow, her neck like the swan's, her breast like the dove's, her waist like a liquid jet, her feet like moonbeams playing at hide-and-seek, and her dance must be like the peacock's! Her laugh must be a shower of *mogras*,* her voice sweet but varied, now simmering like the soft undulating bubbles in a bowl of Cyprian wine, then roaring and splashing like the giant Niagárá, now warbling like the silver flute of a Circassian *houri*, then thundering like the war-drum of a fierce Amazon! For months and months was the pure virgin soul saturated with sweet silly domestic legends, and thus prepared to take part in the *garbás*.

But those scenes are now, happily, "visions of the past." In place of the lovely, sylph-like, Hinduáni †—the maiden who blushes as she smiles at her heart's happiness in having been allowed to join the street song, and whose guileless glance enthrals a crowd of fluttering butterflies—you have now the substantial matron, with her brown little progeny pulling at her skirts, whose voice is formed all for gutturals, and whom the gayest dandy refuses to ogle.

* Jasmine flowers.

† Hindu lady.

Garbás sung by Males.

In other places, especially in temples, you have males keeping up the *garbás*—Banias and Bháthias swaying backwards and forwards their fat inelastic carcases, ogling one another, and "making night hideous" with their vociferous howls and hand-clapping. I know several influential Hindu merchants, Government officials, and even ministers of native states joining in the incongruous buffoonery. At Bombay you have nothing like street *garbás*, except those sung by the gipsies for hire. These are wanton wanderers of the lowest order, going about from street to street and asking the housewives, "Will you have the *garbo* sung, ladies?" The songs are rude, disjointed snatches stolen from here and there—a sort of patchwork poetry, sacred to *Amba Bhowáni.**

THE DASARÁ.

At the end of *Navarátri* you have the Dasará. This is a grand national holiday, commemorating the event of the stupendous myths, the Pandavas,† having girded their loins against their cousins,

* The Mahratta type of the dread goddess Káli.
† The heroes of the Máhábhárata.

the Kaurawas.* But the Dasará, and, in fact, the whole range of days from *Navarátri* to *Kártiki Purnimá*, is more a social than a religious holiday. It is the national harvest holiday. Pity such an interesting holiday has not yet been immortalised by any local bard. Dasará is a most auspicious day for sending children to school, for the Mahrattas marching against the enemy, &c. The housewife gets up that morning before the cock crows, cleans and sweeps and scours the house, chanting a simple hymn the same time in subdued tones, lest that sluggard of her husband be disturbed in his slumbers. She is assisted by her daughter, if the domestic circle is blessed with any such "phantom of delight." There is nothing more beautiful in the home life of the Hindu than the love between mother and daughter. Through thick and thin, through good report and evil report, the two beings cling to each other at every and any sacrifice. As soon as the master of the house gets up, there is uproarious bustle in the house. All metal gods and ornaments are furbished up, the domestic pets are fondled and decorated with flowers, the horse is

* The heroes of the Máhábhárata.

presented with a new harness, &c. Later on in the day the father and children go to a tree called *sonpatra*, worship it, pick or purchase a leaf of it, go to their friends, embrace them and get embraced (a regular bear-hug), return home, make a *havana*, feeding the fire with grain and *ghee*, partake of holiday dainties, making a sly compliment now and then to the poor drudge of a wife who waits upon her "lord" while at dinner, and then go to bed.

DHANA TERASA AND KÁLI CHANDAS.

Twenty days after Dasará is Diwáli. It commences on the 12th of the dark part of the month. That day is Vágha Bárasa or *Guru Dwádashi*. The day after Bárasa is *Dhan Teras* or *Dhan Trayodashi*, when the merchant brings together his hoards into one room, and after gloating over the heap, offers prayers to it, sprinkles it with red ochre, and kneeling, requests the presiding deity not to take unto her wings. The deity presiding over wealth is Lakshmi. Then come *Káli Chondasa* or *Narka chaturdashi*, observed in honour of Vishnu's victory over Narakásura. The most effective illumination is generally on this day. The housewife gets up early this morning, sets a lamp burning in each nook and corner of the house, rubs herself and children, and even her "lord," with ointment, and performs hot-water ablutions. The hotter the water, the greater the efficacy of the prayer following. No little urchin in the house can escape a good smothering bath, and happy he whose skin does not peel off under the operation. The mistress of the house then performs the *árti* with a lamp in a brass plate in her hand, and receives various presents.

Diwáli Proper.

Next day is Diwáli proper. The day is sacred to Saraswati, goddess of learning, when all the shop papers are solemnly worshipped. The worship is called Vahipujá. The family priest, a "little round fat oily man of God," requests Saraswati Mátá on this day not to desert his client. The merchant opens new accounts, new branches of his firm, and new business on this auspicious day. These are public ceremonies; there are private doings, too, on these occasions, drinking, gambling, and revelling. In these games the Hindu is joined heartily by the Parsi and the Mahomedan. Diwáli illuminations are enjoyed by all classes, young and old, rich and poor. The vast multitude of a hundred nationalities surging up the thoroughfares like the waves of the ocean, in all colours of the rainbow, each heart bent upon enjoying the present, and each face beaming with the enjoyment, must be a magnificent sight indeed. No one feature of the night is perhaps more attractive than the different head-gears. The Parsi "sugar-loaf," the European "chimney-pot," and the Mahratta "cart-wheel." The glory of Diwáli holidays is now almost gone. But even in these degenerate days the Hindu merchant is able to show you a decidedly larger margin on Diwáli than the Parsi or Mahomedan. And this, not because the Hindu has greater sagacity or enterprise, but because the Parsi or Mahomedan knows not what a "large revenue parsimony is" to the merchant.

Next to her marriage day and the day on which she becomes a mother, Diwáli is the most welcome occasion to the Hindu female. The poor weary heart has then some glimpses of light and sunshine; it is full of song and sweetness, and of the thousand little charities peculiar to her sex. Two days after the Diwáli is the

Bhaubij day, a holiday reminding you of patriarchal times and customs. On this day all members of the family are drawn towards the warmth of the family hearth; brothers gone to other towns on business, sisters gone to their husbands, uncles, nephews, aunts, nieces, all meet at home. The wife is nowhere this day. She must make room for her husband's sister, who cooks his food and serves him with it. In return she gets presents from him before returning to her husband's.

The Kártiki Purnimá—a Tremendous God-fight.

The last of the holidays is *Kártiki Purnimá*. It celebrates the victory of Shiva over the demon Tripurásura. The monster once upon a time grew so unmanageable that Brahmá and the other gods, whom he had driven out of Swarga, were obliged to seek redress of Shiva the Destroyer. Shiva received this deputation of deities with courtesy, and promised to make short work of their common foe. One fine morning the mighty Destroyer sallied forth. No one can say that our warrior went ill-equipped. The Earth was his chariot, with the Sun and the Moon as its wheels. No less a god than Brahmá was made his Jehu, the. Himálaya mountain served him as his bow, the Serpent King as his bowstring, and Vishnu himself as his quiver! Tripurásura fought Shiva manfully, but even *he* could not long cope with the Destroyer thus equipped. The worshippers of Shiva promote a splendid fair on the anniversary of this renowned pre-historic battle. At Bombay the fair is held at Wálkeshwar. At Surat you have it on the open maidán * about the Castle.

THE KHIÁLS OF SURAT.

The Surat fair was enlivened by the singing of Khiáls, rhymed romances and philosophical or polemic songs. There are two schools of Khiáls, the Turráwálás and the Kalagiwálás. The first worship the male essence as the prime cause, the second the female power. This is the bone of contention. The founders of the two schools are said to have been Tukangir and Allábux. Both claim divine origin and divine inspiration. Both had miraculous powers, such as bringing down rain, causing eclipses, and even reviving the dead. This used to be centuries ago, and we

* Esplanade.

had better not be too inquisitive about such miraculous doings. About fifty years ago the two schools were represented by Báhádursing and Allibhái. The former was a Pardesi,* the latter a Borá. Both were illiterate. The first served as gate-keeper for Rs. 7 a month, the second eked out a precarious existence by patching up old gunny-bags. What would Carlyle have said to this? Men who could answer, in *impromptu* verse, the most intricate questions of philosophy and metaphysics, who could thus hold forth at public meetings for a week and a fortnight: illiterate, ill-favoured men "building the lofty rhyme" with the rapidity with which fairies build enchanted castles! Few know of the struggles of these heroic souls, the "mute inglorious Miltons" of India—men like Kabir † and Nának,‡ Sahajánand,§ Tukárám,|| and Bahadursing and Allibhái.

The Kalagiwálás were remarkable for their "linked sweetness," a lively fancy, and all those

* North India man, or stranger.

† Great Sikh reformer.

‡ Founder of the Sikh faith.

§ The great Gujarát reformer.

|| The great Mahratta poet and reformer.

lovable little arts which suit and adorn the sex. The Turráwálás, on the contrary, were known for the vigour and solidity of their productions. From their lips flowed "wisdom married to immortal verse." Both schools have now sunk into obscurity, and thus one great charm of the Diwáli holidays has fled Gujarát.

THE INIMITABLE "RAMAYAN." RAMA, SITA, LAXAMAN.

ANOTHER attractive feature of the Diwáli holiday is the recitation of the epic of Rámáyan. I had the most enjoyable time of it at Baroda when listening, for a few hours every evening, to recitations from the Rámáyan.

I have read the Rámáyan, the Iliad, the Sháhnámeh, and other master-pieces of human thought, but none in the original. I never advanced much in the learned languages, though I attempted all by turn. I remember having taken up my friend Professor Bhandárkar's *First Book of Sanskrit* to keep off the agitating sensation one feels when conscious, for the first time, of having a baby at home. But baby was obstinate that night in mistaking me for the mother. I loved Sanskrit, and I loved baby, too, in a sort of way. What was I to do? Oh! happy thought. I put baby on the table, and tried to soothe it to slumber with excellent Sanskrit conjugations. But it was no use—baby conjugated with me in chorus. Now came the time to decide, and I foolishly decided to give up Sanskrit. You do enough for one man if you can manage a new baby. It is a terrible task, especially for absent-minded students. You take the little being up with a shiver of anxiety lest it should melt in your hands, or lest it should slip through your fingers; or lest, in deep "brown study," mistaking it for a plaything, you should throw it out of the window. Then, again, you have the presence of the mother to disturb your peace of mind—the mother who sleeps with one eye eternally open. Oh, it is a saddening thing; but one must do one's duty. Babies take very kindly to me, except when I am hungry, at which time they avoid me with that instinct of self-preservation which is the first law of our nature. Well, then, if I gave up Sanskrit, you see it was not on a flimsy pretext.

Popular Recitations of the National Epic.

But to return to the recitation of the Rámáyan at Baroda. These popular recitals from the

Rámáyan are done in Gujaráti in easy, flowing narrative verse. I have often listened to them, and always with increasing interest. I believe the Gujaráti rendering is by Premánand, the sweetest of our bards, and an inhabitant of Baroda. It is read out by an intelligent Brahmin to a mixed audience of all classes and both sexes. It has a powerful and perceptible influence on the Hindu character. I believe the remarkable freedom from infidelity which is to be seen in most Hindu families, in spite of their strange gregarious habits, can be traced to that influence. And little wonder.

Every true lover of poetry knows what the Rámáyan is. It is a work for all times, for all men. I have read poetry of various ages and of various climes, and it is my deliberate opinion that in the field of ancient literature, so rich in imperishable prose and verse, the Rámáyan stands pre-eminent. It is the greatest of intellectual efforts inasmuch as it has moulded the character of the mightiest nation of antiquity. I can hardly believe it to be the work of a mortal. I have great faith in the efficacy of life-long prayer and contemplation—contemplation of the eternal God, the Source of all knowledge. And thus I can see nothing unnatural in Válmiki * having been inspired by Heaven, after such a life of contemplation, to write the Rámáyan, a work which has been the most precious and the most cherished heritage of the Aryans. William Ewart Gladstone, the greatest Englishman of our times, has done much to enlighten the student on the life and times of his favourite author, the immortal Homer. Had he studied the Rámáyan, he, and Europe with him, would have known infinitely more of India in every way than at present. Yet Horace Wilson, Sir William Jones, and others too many to name and too distinguished to need being named, have rendered conspicuous service to this branch of Hindu literature; and the Hindus will cherish their memory to the latest hour of their national life. The records of ancient literature give evidence of the wondrous energy of thought and expression the old masters commanded; but none equals Válmiki in depicting those soft little domestic charities which are equally powerful to heal the wounds and bruises of severe misfortune, and to soothe the wrinkles of every-day care. Works there are to which the

* Supposed author of the epic.

human intellect owes much of its refined culture; but none so imbues, so possesses the mind with deep, calm, abiding affection, as the Rámáyan.

HERO AND HEROINE.

Look at the principal characters. There is Laxaman, lesser of the brother heroes of the solar dynasty. His generous heart recoils at the thought of living in ease and comfort when his elder brother is threatened with exile. He is indignant with the step-mother for her arts and machinations; but, obedient to his brother, he suppresses his wrath, and vows henceforth to renounce the world, and follow the brother and his bride in their forced banishment, humble as a slave, dutiful as a son unto both. Laxaman's behaviour towards her he honours with the name of "mother" is extremely tender and touching. Look at Ráma. The loving, dutiful son, the faithful brother, the tender protecting husband, the devoted friend, the magnanimous foe, in every relation of life he realises our ideal of man, while his character as sovereign, "a ruler of men," transcends all his private virtues. The picture drawn by the immortal poet is faultless, absolutely faultless in detail as in the aggregate.

And Sitá? Mistress of a thousand womanly graces—the fond faithful wife, the tender being twice transplanted by relentless fate from the bosom where she had learnt but yesterday to nestle so close—the suspected, repudiated wife, scorned of the foul-mouthed rabble, left alone by the husband in the trackless desert to the mercy of the fierce beasts and the fierce elements, leading an aimless, hopeless life; now exhausted by reason of her loneliness, now cheered by the thought of her precious burden, the pledge of her short-lived union—whose unselfish soul rises superior to all personal discomforts, and who, in the midst of insupportable misery, even in the agonies of travail, has no thought but of her Ráma, "the beloved of my heart, my true, my tender, my eternal lover, who has deserted me because he thought fit!"

Happy the nation who can claim Ráma and Sitá for their ideal. Blessed the hearth at which are offered tributes of national homage to this peerless pair, when the simple children of toil—the rough old artisan, his matter-of-fact dame, and the sweet, simple, romantic girl—mingle honest tears as the family priest recites some favourite passage out of the sacred volume!

And blessed, thrice blessed, the man (if only *man* he was) whose genius could soar up to the very fount of divine inspiration ; and who could create two beings of such exquisite grace, before whose realistic and ever-enduring nature the works of such literary giants as Homer and Firdousi look mean and distorted. With all its varied brilliancy it must be admitted that European genius pales and retreats before the fire of Oriental genius, even as the wan and sickly queen of night pales and retreats before the glorious lord of day.

The Sanskrit Language.

Sanskrit is a wonderful language ; almost each word of it has a double meaning, the esoteric and exoteric. In this respect, as in others, it is the most capable of the world's languages. And when such a poet as Válmiki writes in such a language as Sanskrit, the outcome of his labours must, of course, be inimitable. Each verse of the Rámáyan has a world of hidden meaning. Each simple line, which looks common-place at first sight, discovers, when carefully studied, an unbroken scene of beauty, under the surface, a glorious panorama of "sweetness and light," where the reader, drinking his fill of the freshest and healthiest sentiment, forgets himself in the contemplation of the genius that conjured up a creation so perfect in symmetry and proportion. At such times his first thought is to forswear his own namby-pamby puerilistics and be content in life with a loving study of the great master.

THE BALEVA.

Another popular Hindu holiday is the Baleva, or *Náliari Punema*, what the Europeans are pleased to call the Cocoa-nut Day. On this full-moon day (in August) the violence of the monsoon is supposed to have come to an end, and Father Neptune is supposed to be ready, on the customary propitiations, to allow ships to have a safe voyage. In writing of the Cocoa-nut holiday, it would not perhaps be amiss to describe the scope and significance of this peculiarly Aryan fruit in shell. What of all other nuts it most resembles in form is the human *caput*. It is indispensable on every religious occasion. Its water is considered holy nectar. The hairy surface of its coating goes to make miniature coir purses, bags, &c. The coating, or husk, itself makes excellent *hukás*, or hubble-bubbles. For this purpose the kernel is removed through the "eye" of the nut, which is otherwise kept intact. When broken into two, the shell makes good handy curry or liquor cups, and oil vessels. When burnt to cinders and mixed with vinegar or lime, the coating is very good for ringworm and other cutaneous eruptions. If burnt by a peculiar process, the coating yields an oil, which is said to be peculiarly efficacious for the above purpose. Thus far the shell. Its kernel is good for children. Taken with date or molasses, it is excellent food for travellers. It enters into the composition of a thousand dishes, and is much relished alike by Hindus and Mahomedans. Its "milk." makes a very good hair-restorer, and one may often see Mahomedan and other lads buy a piece of the kernel, chew it, take the fluid in the hollow of the hand, apply it to the hair, and eat the remainder! Cocoa-nut oil is used in cooking. The oil is also a mild, pleasant burner. But at religious performances it is indispensable. It makes the ambrosia of the gods if mixed with *ghee* and sugar. When given to strangers, it means welcome; on the other hand, the phrase "to give the cocoa-nut" also means a peremptory and ignominious dismissal, exactly corresponding to your "give him the sack." But I presume this must mean the *empty shell.*

The Cocoa-nut holiday is a great day in Bombay. Your Gujarati servants generally become ill a fortnight before the day. You have to grant them leave, or they will stay away without any thought of the future. But this is not because of the cocoa-nut day; the whole month of Shráwan is a prolonged feast-day: there is a little fair every day of it at Walkeshwar. The Mondays are sacred to the goddess of revelry and song. The Vaishnava Máhárájs have the jolliest time of it all through the month.

At Bombay the Esplanade and Back Bay, and of late years Mody Bay, are worth a visit on *Baleva* day. The fair commences after three, and is kept up till very late. Merchants and traders first go to the sea, propitiate the deity with a cocoa-nut and some flowers duly consecrated. The merchant then receives the Brahman's blessing, with a thread on his wrist, and wends his way homewards through the slow-moving mob, picking up cheap things here and there from the stalls and booths erected on the Esplanade. Some people take a short cruise on the sea by way of first trial; others do the housewarming, and others still have the *nautch* performed. But on the whole, compared with other national festivals, Baleva is a tame affair as could be guessed. The show is mostly held on the seashore, and therefore affords a picturesque spectacle for griffins* and up-country Anglo-Indians.

The most comprehensive of Hindu holidays, so to speak, is the—

SHRÁWAN MÁS.

In this holy *Shráwan Más* Hindus of all castes, and of all parts of the country, keep their high carnival. The whole month is a prolonged holiday, with the four Mondays as special red-letter days. To the stranger the Shráwan festival is the most innocent and least grotesque of the numerous so-called national festivals. It resembles the Christmas more than any other Hindu holiday. Members of a family that may have left the family-hearth on various purposes, meet again; old quarrels are made up, the sacred thread is changed, the new dress is put on (in too many cases the only new dress of the year!), the flower and fruit offerings are placed before the gods. Taking your morning constitutional

* Fresh-arrived Europeans.

by the Queen's Road (Bombay) you are sure to encounter, during these days, bevies of Hindu maids and matrons, tripping by, singing softly to themselves, and discussing the kindness of their respective husbands and mothers-in-law. For, be it remembered, that in this holy season the heart even of the mother-in-law is too joyous to seek quarrels. Here you see a group of fair Maráthins, with lissome figures, passing demurely by, with downcast eyes and a gentle cautious tread. She is very lightly, but still always becomingly dressed, this fair daughter of Maháráshtra. Her national *sári* and *choli* sit æsthetically on her graceful person—grace beyond the reach of art. Her raven-black hair is gathered up into a knot (chignon) at the back of the head, which knot is adorned by a pretty little gold ornament, or a prettier flower of the season.

A few paces behind her is the robustious Márwáran, shuffling past in her cumbrous ugly petticoat. She is a big strapping body, and the tread of her bejewelled foot is extremely assertive. She, or perhaps her lord, has peculiar notions of personal adornment. She throws her *sári* around, or, rather, shrouds herself in her *sári*, till every vestige of her face is invisible. She wears ivory bangles or rings on her arms—both arms are literally covered by these ponderous articles. The palms of her hands, and the nails, the Márwáran dyes red, and the lips and teeth black! Her swathing petticoat she wears so far down as her ancle, and below she has ornaments, silver and brass, or both. The Márwáran is more parsimonious than her lord, and though she is constrained to take some cheap offering to the gods once or twice in the year, she does not scruple to bring part of it back, thus cheating deity itself! The Márwáran is a rare phenomenon in Native society. She is purchased by the husband at a fearful cost. The Márwári does not marry till late in life. He comes to Hindustan, or the Deccan, only with his *dhoti** and his *loti*†. After ten years or so, he goes home to see his mother. As long as a relative is alive, the Márwári does not care for a wife. But when he has accumulated "a sum," and when he sees he is waxing old, he invests a good fat slice of his fortune in a wife. But she is a luxury in the buying only. As soon as that is over, the husband never repents him of the bargain. For, whatever

* Waist garment. † A small brass ewer.

mathematicians might think of it, it is a well-known fact that the Márwári and the Márwáran between them spend exactly a half of what the Máwári used to spend singly. This may be a lesson to Miss Susie Trots, the railway-guard's wife. The Márwáran is not visible to the vulgar gaze, except during the *Holi* holidays. She is then in her element. She squirts paint and water on the gallants that serenade her, and gives them back joke for joke with the keenest relish. But all this while her face is veiled. In fact, few young Márwárans are seen unveiled. And those who *know* are of opinion that it is a mercy the Márwáran does not show herself to the public in all the reality of her swarthy countenance.

But by no fair Hinduáni are the joys of the *Shráwan Más* drunk with such avidity as by your Vaishnava lasses—the Bháttia and Baniá females. To them it is a month of love and liberty. And, thanks to the pious Máhárájs, the month passes as swiftly as a dream. Wife, widow, and maiden, each has the jolliest time of it in *Shráwan*. There are the dances to be danced before the Máhá-ráj, plays to be played, songs to be sung; his Holiness to be washed and dressed and fed. Oh, the joys of *Shráwan*!—to the Vaishnavas. The beauteous *Shráwan Más*, when "the days are devoted to singing, and when the fair Rádhá is flattered by a whirlwind of love. All fair sisters go to the Jamna for holy ablutions, their foreheads adorned by *Kaisari*,* and their graceful feet coloured. The fair ones worship *Gowri* with wreaths and flowers in one hand, in the other hand the box of *Kunkun* colour, and the name of *Shri Gopál* on their lips. Four *pohoras* † the lovely ones devote to singing songs, forsaking sleep; the night is short, and the sports are long. "Oh, I tremble lest the envious morn soon breaks in upon our joys!" So sings the fair Gujarátan.

The PARSI has many holidays, but none of such deep religious import, as the Hindus, unless it was the Muktád.

THE MUKTÁD HOLIDAYS.

Muktád reads like a Zend term, closely allied to Sanskrit, and means the "saved," or "released." It alludes to what the Occidentals call "Emancipated spirits." *Doslá* is a *prákrit* Hindu term, and means, if anything, "the old puts," "the old fellows," what some English news-

* Saffron. † A *pahora* equals three hours.

papers call "the venerable departed worthies." This is the origin: Muktád is of Pagan growth, not belonging to Zoroastrianism "pure and simple." Zoroastrians in Iran, over twelve hundred years ago, had between five and ten days set apart every year "for prayers and fasting," as expiation for their own sins, and more as offerings for "repose of the souls" of their relatives. But all this is changed in India. The praying is changed into gambling, and the fasting into feasting. The simple ceremonial sank into a gross and debasing pagan rite.

Twenty years ago (the Parsis have since improved) this was the explanation of the *Doslá* holidays. Those of our departed relatives who had been "good boys" on earth, and therefore admitted to Heaven, were allowed every year a long holiday for eighteen days to return to earth and live with their earthly friends. There are proofs positive of these "spirits" having visited our grandmothers and mothers-in-law (in their dreams, of course), and telling them what good things of earth they would like to have for their creature comforts during their holiday sojourn "here below." Their wants were often unconfined. But generally they consisted of the following: Brand-new clothes, various dishes of fowl, fish, and fruit; good country wine and toddy, and, in short, all those things they had a relish for during their earthly existence. They also required things for amusement, such as paper kites, tops, packs of cards, &c. This is how the dear ones were received: The best room in the house was reserved for them; it was washed, scoured, and furnished with pictures. In the centre was placed a many-branched iron frame; on the top of the frame was placed a tray of choicest flowers (the only redeeming feature in this whole heathen ceremonial), along with the flowers there were fruits. On all sides of the frame were placed metal pots filled with crystal water, and by virgins, female and male. Surrounding the frame, on the floor, were arranged steaming dishes of edibles and rows of favourite playthings. The priest (Dastur) consecrated the food and other things, and took a mouthful from every dish (a full distended priestly mouth seldom measures under 5 inches by 7), he then declared the feast open to the enjoyment of the spirits visitant. These entered the room unperceived, except by the priest and the grandmother or mother-in-law; they washed themselves with the water, and fell to. This degrading farce was carried on for eighteen days, three times a day. Many Parsi families have got rid of this tom-foolery, but still it lingers on. The whole thing is intended for the good of two, the priest (Dastur) and the cook. These eighteen days are a carnival to these fellows. To the paterfamilias, and his son who is an unemployed graduate of the University, they are the worst days in the year. The old gentleman has to spend his cash without stint, and the young gentleman has to submit every now and then to the bitter reproaches of his progenitor, who turns fiercely upon him and says: "See, you idle unskilful vagabond! Look at the barber* of a cook; we have to pay him Rs. 30 for eighteen days, and he knows not how to make an omelet. And you, sirrah, you are what they call B.A., and M.A., and your education alone has cost me Rs. 5,000. And what do you earn? Nothing. Oh, why did not your mother re-marry before you were born!" The old man is justified in complaining, though the logic of his concluding remark is eminently Hibernian. And who can help pitying the poor "B.A. and M.A."?

* Any utterly useless fellow.

But look at the rotund, fatuous Dastur. How busy he is! What a roaring trade he drives! Though he visits a dozen houses in swift succession, there is only one room for him at every house, and that is the well-stocked prayer-room, "the Mecca of his appetite." He lives in "a paradise of pies and puddings." He prays, eats, and sleeps; sleeps, eats, and prays. While muttering the meaningless prayer, his eyes are on the solids—"the substantials, Sir Giles, the substantials." The jargon he mutters is *dry*, "so he moistens his words in his cups." And when, with his inner man thus fortified, he proceeds to prayers, "his words are of marrow, unctuous dropping fatness." He is a droll fellow, this Parsi Levite, and laughs over the folly of those on whose substance he fattens. He has materials in him of a good divine and a scholar, but he is born in an atmosphere of hollow imposture and sham, and lives and dies a cheat and a charlatan. To this man is due the invention and perpetuation of the thick haze of superstition which envelops the pure and simple form of worship bequeathed to us by the Prophet-Priest of Iran.

The MAHOMEDAN holiday of the year, if holiday it may be called, is the Mo'haram.

THE MO'HARAM.

"Hai Hassan, Hai Hussein," are the wails of genuine grief that pierce the dense air of Imámbárá on Mo'haram night. "Hai Hassan, Hai Hussein," form the interlude to the touching national elegy, recited to the echo of frantic breast-beating by sturdy hard-favoured Moguls and Seedies (African Mussulmans), who abandon themselves for the nonce to uncontrollable woe. It is the last night of the Passion week throughout Islam, when the Shehá Moslem enacts his Passion Play, and the Sooni Mahomedan keeps up his High Carnival. In the month of Mo'haram, "holiest of the holy," eight days are sacred to the memory of Hassan and Hussein, grandsons of the Prophet by his beloved daughter Fátimá, and his no less beloved disciple Ali. The youthful heroes are said to have fallen victims to partisan fury. The Shehás, by all accounts the true believers, who acknowledge Ali as heir and successor to the Founder of Islam, spend the early part of the week in erecting the *taboot*, the paper mausoleum which is supposed to hold the murdered hopes of the Prophet's house, in reading the *fáthiá*, the initial verses of the

Korán, before it, and in other religious rites. On a raised seat squats the venerable Mohla, surrounded by the Hadjees and other dignitaries and elders of the Moslem Church; and at a distance squat vast multitudes of the faithful. To the breathless audience the voice of the Mohla is "more than the miraculous harp." In tones of intense anguish does he recite the tale of woe—how one of the heroes was poisoned by the foul assassin at Yezd, how the other was slaughtered by the dastard soldiery of Damasens, on the field of Kerbalá. In the course of the recital, the High Priest lays solemn emphasis on an incident here and there, swaying his portly person backward and forward. At such times his deep-drawn sigh generally makes itself heard at a distance—a sigh that seems "to shatter his bulk." This prolonged inspiration is taken up by the audience, converted into a loud sob, a united but discordant groan, decidedly more striking to the ear than harmonious. Here the agonised spirit finds vent in moans of "Hai Hassan, Hai Hussein." Here ply the brawny hands on the livid breast—a cruel torture unfelt, owing to the self-abandonment of the hour, though to the onlooker the breast is a piece of raw flesh besprinkled with the vital fluid.

Then supervenes a simultaneous hush as the Mohla's lips are observed quivering in a painful effort to speak. The sigh is subdued, the pain endured in silence. The grief surging up the breast empties itself at the eyes. It is not the hired lip-homage of the Hindu mourner, this Marsiá song of the Moslem. The cold philosophy of the fatalist is nowhere this evening. His emotion has usurped the seat of reason. Here are no external "trappings and suits of woe"—the grief is genuine, of and in the heart.

Given the time, the place, the frantic enthusiasm of the Moslem nature, and the awfulness of the tale of murder and assassination, and the veriest day-drudge will develop into a hero and a patriot, the most arrant coward will raise himself into a sympathising martyr. Wonderful is the influence of Islam on the believer's mind; and a faith that has such a hold on men's minds will endure with the sun. It was years ago I first witnessed the *Marsiá*, and in other place than the Imámbárá of Bombay. It was in Gujarat, in the season of early youth, but the impression still remains, in spite of the assertion of the half-true poet, that "youth holds no fellowship with woe."

The Soonis, that is, the Indian converts to

Islam, get up a frightful caricature of the proceeding. They look upon Hussan and Hussein (*Anglicè*, Hobson, Dobson) as pretenders. If you speak to the Sooni of the premature death of the brother-heroes, he will reply in mock sympathy "Pity they died not earlier." This is mortal offence to the parties concerned, but as "the dead feel no resentment," their friends the Moguls and other Shehás take up the cudgels for them. Hence bleeding noses, broken pates, and other paraphernalia of carnage. The hatred the two sects bear each other is imperishable. The Sooni's idea of the holiday is to make merry at his rival's expense. He keeps up mad revels all these days exactly in proportion to the intensity of the Shehá's mourning. He will become a monkey, a bear, a tiger, an old hag, a mock Mohlá, a pious dust-begrimed Darvish, a street dancer, a *bairágí*, and anything and everything, in fact, except a respectable human being. If he is well-to-do, and middle-aged, he enters on a career of indiscriminate hospitality, where the invitation to the guest is in the golden language of the ancients, "Drink or depart." I need not say many prefer the former alternative. When he comes out into the street with his very much mixed following, he looks "a thing of shreds and patches." Altogether, the Sooni makes a most discreditable figure during the sacred season which he converts into a perfect saturnalia. But he is little to blame, poor fellow. Government don't seem so anxious to dispel his mental fog, his own people won't wash and clean him. There is no Jamsetjee Jejibhoy institution for him. He has contrived to earn a bad name; and he can no easier get rid of it than can the dog in the proverb. He won't respect law, because he looks upon law as a *hocus-pocus*. Who interprets the law to him? It is rather unjust, therefore, to think Kásam is always rife for treason. Why, he cannot commit treason even if he wished, because he has no soul. I am quoting political philosophy. And as for judgment, why, sir, Kásam has not the judgment of a "malt horse." Sir, he has not so much as "a thought in his belly," so utterly barren he is. He will chat and strut bravely. I allow he will "pluck the moon out of her sphere *if she let him*."

Perhaps the most popular, though certainly not at all reputable, of Gujarát holidays is the

UNHOLY HOLI.

Holi is not a holy institution wholly, but it is

a jolly holiday nevertheless. It is the season of free love and free language, not only among the Vaishnavas, but the lower castes of Gujarát, the saturnalia of indecent song, the high carnival of mad carousal. It is the season of *rang* and *rág*, which two innocent-looking monosyllables the High Court Translator may translate as "red paint and music," but which, in reality, mean the luxuries of love's embrace, the sporting of *Káma** and *Rati*.† The origin of Holi has been a subject of ardent speculation by philosophers and theosophists. It ought to be credited with divine beginning, if Hindu antiquaries are to be believed. But as Hindu antiquaries are far too mystic and imaginative for this age, it would be better to be content with a more rational genesis. It is this: Once upon a time, when civilisation was not, there lived in a certain nagri‡ a great Barna sowcár—a merchant prince more opulent than Crœsus. This great sowcár, we are told, had an immense lot of goods and chattels, an immense lot of servants and slaves, an immense lot of wives and handmaids. But he had no heir to perpetuate his name. By dint of prayers and penances he, however, prevailed upon the gods to give him

* Cupid. † His wife. ‡ Great town.

issue. This was promised to be a son; but the sowcár happening to offend one of the deities, he got at last only a daughter. But he was content. Why, he thought, the gods could have given me anything or nothing! *Their* will be done.

That brings me to the sowcár with an only daughter. She was a lovely thing, became lovelier as she grew, and at the age of thirteen she was absolutely bewitching. She sat at the window every cool evening, dressed handsomer than Cleopatra, chewing *pán sopári* and slyly squirting the red nectar amongst the enthralled crowd below. The marble forehead, the silken tresses, the swan-like neck, those rainbow brows, and those coral lips sent the gallants raving mad. But who could openly aspire to her hand? Every prodigal son of an impoverished race (and of such are your gallants) was the sowcár's debtor. With what face could he ask for the hand of the sowcár's only daughter, when he had not been able to return a paltry sum of money! So Huliká (that was her name) grew in the loveliness and loneliness, till one moonlit night she espied a lovable Rajput youth, deep in her father's debt. They looked at each other, their eyes met, their hearts went out to each other, &c. &c. Huliká directly sent her *dási**, her "dearer than mother," after the youth. A meeting was arranged, and their "united fate" discussed. Their troths were plighted on the spot. But it was hopeless to win the father over, in whose iron safe was locked up the lover's destiny, in the shape of promissory notes and such other documents of *high interest.* Elopement was the only way, and that the lover proposed. At first Huliká shrank from the proposal; but, like a wise young woman she was, in less than five minutes she succumbed to the arts of the sweet enchanter. But Huliká was a virtuous Helen, look you; and she therefore took the *dási* (old nurse) with them. She left a note for dear papa, stating she was carried away against her wishes, but that she could not survive this vile treatment for a week; however, she had the old maid-servant with her, and that she hoped she would shortly become *suttee* if her honour were not saved. They took a good many valuable nick-nacks with them, and with rare temerity took lodgings in the same street. The town was in an uproar in the morning, and the old sowcár instituted a rigorous search in the neighbouring cities. Huliká ascer-

* Female attendant.

tained that day that in spite of the innocent little note she had left behind, the women of the town took her to be a party to a scandalous amour. Her virtuous instincts were outraged, and from the depths of her woman's resources she at once evolved a plan by which her reputation should be saved. She got up at the dead of night, locked the old woman, who was asleep, in the room, locked all doors save one from inside, and coolly set fire to the house in various parts. When she saw no human efforts could save the house, she dressed herself as a *jogini*,* getting her astonished lover to do likewise. And locking the remaining door from outside, this daughter of Gujarát left the town. A few hours later the house was found to be on fire. Efforts were made to save it; but before daylight it was all a wreck. In the morning they found the sowcár's old *dási* burnt to death, but easy of recognition. Then it was that the wise women of the town proclaimed that Huliká the virtuous had committed *suttee*, and that the immortal gods had taken her up from the grasp of the cruel but baffled seducer. Huliká henceforward came to be recognised as one of the saints; and there was no one, not even the old

* A female ascetic.

dási, thanks to Huliká's precaution, to contradict the general belief. This is one version of *Holi*, given by the blind bard of Gujarát, but which I, for my part, cannot quite accept.

The Holi of the day is supposed to be the annual celebration of this *suttee* affair. It is a national holiday, and has a wonderful power for demoralisation over the infatuated Vaishnava, the sturdy Márathá (the lower order only, I believe), and the stingy Márwári. You can in Bombay see *Holi* in full swing in two places, the Máháráj's Mandir and the Márwári Bazar. In the former could be witnessed, for days together, a promiscuous assemblage of devoted worshippers, without distinction of age, sex, or social position, revelling in hideous orgies such as the Western imagination could hardly picture. Modest young women are submitted to showers of coloured water and clouds of red paint. They are handled to a degree of indecent familiarity incredible to the outside public. At one exhibition like this hundreds of young women are liable to go astray from the inborn modesty of their nature. It is a wonder how, with such social customs as these, the Vaishnavas lead such happy, contented, and respectable lives. But these malign associations of *Holi* are happily dying out. In the streets you may still encounter respectable Vaishnava merchants pelting each other with coloured curd, cow-dung, mud, and such other delectable missiles. But to have a vivid idea of the wild delirium excited by this holiday, one has (in Bombay) to stand for an hour in the Márwári Bazar at Mumbádevi. He can there see what extraordinary social antics the usually sober, money-grubbing Márwári is capable of. How a crowd of these *bháng**-intoxicated bacchanals will besiege a neighbour's Zenana, by way of a serenade, I suppose, and shout their rude amorous ditties in unmistakable language and with significant gestures and attitudes. The filthy epithets, the wanton glances, the obscene gestures, defy description; but these are rewarded, on the part of the dusky Márwáran, by equally shameless ogling and the squirting of red paint. This is the only holiday the stingy sojourner in Gujarát enjoys, according to his lights. Never is the morose Márwári more free, more frolicsome, more abandoned, than on this occasion.

* Hemp-juice.

April, 1883.

BOOKS, &c.,

ISSUED BY

MESSRS. W. H. ALLEN & Co.,

Publishers & Literary Agents to the India Office,

COMPRISING

MISCELLANEOUS PUBLICATIONS IN GENERAL LITERATURE.

MILITARY WORKS, INCLUDING THOSE ISSUED BY THE GOVERNMENT.

INDIAN AND MILITARY LAW.

MAPS OF INDIA, &c.

13, WATERLOO PLACE, LONDON, S.W.

Works issued from the India Office, and Sold by W. H. ALLEN & Co.

Illustrations of Ancient Buildings in Kashmir.

Prepared at the Indian Museum under the authority of the Secretary of State for India in Council. From Photographs, Plans, and Drawings taken by Order of the Government of India. By Henry Hardy Cole, Lieut. R.E., Superintendent Archæological Survey of India, North-West Provinces. In One vol.; half-bound, Quarto. Fifty-eight plates. £3 10s.

The Illustrations in this work have been produced in Carbon from the original negatives, and are therefore permanent.

Pharmacopœia of India.

Prepared under the Authority of the Secretary of State for India. By Edward John Waring, M.D. Assisted by a Committee appointed for the Purpose. 8vo. 6s.

The Stupa of Bharhut. A Buddhist Monument.

Ornamented with numerous Sculptures illustrative of Buddhist Legend and History in the Third Century B.C. By Alexander Cunningham, C.S.I., C.I.E., Major-General, Royal Engineers (Bengal Retired); Director-General Archæological Survey of India. 4to. Fifty-seven Plates. Cloth gilt. £3 3s.

Archæological Survey of Western India.

Report of the First Season's Operations in the Belgâm and Kaladgi Districts. January to May, 1874. Prepared at the India Museum and Published under the Authority of the Secretary of State for India in Council. By James Burgess, Author of the "Rock Temples of Elephanta," &c., &c., and Editor of "The Indian Antiquary." Half-bound. Quarto. 58 Plates and Woodcuts. £2 2s.

Archæological Survey of Western India. Vol. II.

Report on the Antiquities of Kâthiâwâd and Kachh, being the result of the Second Season's Operations of the Archæological Survey of Western India. 1874–75. By James Burgess, F.R.G.S., M.R.A.S., &c., Archæological Surveyor and Reporter to Government, Western India. 1876. Half-bound. Quarto. Seventy-four Plates and Woodcuts. £3 3s.

Archæological Survey of Western India. Vol. III.

Report on the Antiquities in the Bidar and Aurungabad Districts in the Territory of H.H. the Nizam of Haidarabad, being the result of the Third Season's Operations of the Archæological Survey of Western India. 1875–1876. By James Burgess, F.R.G.S., M.R.A.S., Membre de la Societé Asiatique, &c., Archæological Surveyor and Reporter to Government, Western India. Half-bound. Quarto. Sixty-six Plates and Woodcuts. £2 2s.

Illustrations of Buildings near Muttra and Agra,

Showing the Mixed Hindu-Mahomedan Style of Upper India Prepared at the India Museum under the authority of the Secretary of State for India in Council, from Photographs, Plans, and Drawings taken by Order of the Government of India. By Henry Hardy Cole, Lieut. R.E., late Superintendent Archæological Survey of India, North-West Provinces. 4to. With Photographs and Plates. £3 10s.

The Cave Temples of India.

By James Fergusson, D.C.L., F.R.A.S., V.P.R.A.S., and James Burgess, F.R.G.S., M.R.A.S., &c. Printed and Published by Order of Her Majesty's Secretary of State, &c. Royal 8vo. With Photographs and Woodcuts. £2 2s.

Aberigh-Mackay (G.) Twenty-one Days in India.
Being the Tour of Sir ALI BABA, K.C.B. By GEORGE ABERIGH-MACKAY. Post 8vo. 4s.
An Illustrated Edition. 8vo. 10s. 6d.

Æsop, the Fables of, and other Eminent Mythologists.
With Morals and Reflections. By Sir ROGER L'ESTRANGE, kt. A facsimile reprint of the Edition of 1669. Folio, antique, sheep. 21s.

Akbar. An Eastern Romance.
By Dr. P. A. S. VAN LIMBURG-BROUWER. Translated from the Dutch by M. M. With Notes and Introductory Life of the Emperor Akbar, by CLEMENTS R. MARKHAM, C.B., F.R.S. Crown 8vo. 10s. 6d.

Alberg (A.) Snowdrops: Idylls for Children.
From the Swedish of Zach Topelius. By ALBERT ALBERG, Author of "Whisperings in the Wood." 3s. 6d.

—— **Whisperings in the Wood**: Finland Idylls for Children. From the Swedish of Zach Topelius. By ALBERT ALBERG, Author of "Fabled Stories from the Zoo," and Editor of "Chit-Chat by Puck," "Rose Leaves," and "Woodland Notes." 3s. 6d.

Allen's Series.

1.—Ansted's World We Live In. 2s.

2.—Ansted's Earth's History. 2s.

3.—Ansted's 2000 Examination Questions in Physical Geography. 2s.

4.—Geography of India. (See page 13.) 2s.

5.—Ansted's Elements of Physiography. 1s. 4d.

6.—Hall's Trigonometry. (See page 14.) 2s.

7.—Wollaston's Elementary Indian Reader. 1s. (See p. 43.)

Ameer Ali. The Personal Law of the Mahommedans (according to all the Schools). Together with a Comparative Sketch of the Law of Inheritance among the Sunnis and Shiahs. By SYED AMEER ALI, Moulvi, M.A., LL.B., Barrister-at-Law, and Presidency Magistrate at Calcutta. 8vo. 15s.

Anderson (Ed. L.) How to Ride and School a Horse.
With a System of Horse Gymnastics. By Edward L. Anderson. Cr. 8vo. 2s. 6d.

—— A System of School Training for Horses.
By Edward L. Anderson, Author of "How to Ride and School a Horse." Crown 8vo. 2s. 6d.

Anderson (P.) The English in Western India. 8vo. 14s.

Anderson (T.) History of Shorthand.
With an analysis and review of its present condition and prospects in Europe and America. By Thomas Anderson, Parliamentary Reporter, &c. With Portraits. Crown 8vo. 12s. 6d.

—— Catechism of Shorthand; being a Critical Examination of the various Styles, with special reference to the question, Which is the best English System of Shorthand? By Thomas Anderson, Author of "Synopsis of a New System of Shorthand Writing," "History of Shorthand," &c. Fcap. 1s.

Andrew (W. P.) India and Her Neighbours.
By W. P. Andrew, Author of "Our Scientific Frontier," "The Indus and Its Provinces," "Memoir of the Euphrates Route." With Two Maps. 8vo. 15s.

—— Our Scientific Frontier.
With Sketch-Map and Appendix. 8vo. 6s.

Ansted (D. T.) Physical Geography.
By Professor D. T. Ansted, M.A., F.R.S., &c. Fifth Edition. Post 8vo., with Illustrative Maps. 7s.

Contents:—Part I.—Introduction.—The Earth as a Planet.—Physical Forces.—The Succession of Rocks. Part II.—Earth—Land.—Mountains.—Hills and Valleys.—Plateaux and Low Plains. Part III.—Water.—The Ocean.—Rivers.—Lakes and Waterfalls.—The Phenomena of Ice.—Springs Part IV.—Air.—The Atmosphere. Winds and Storms.—Dew, Clouds, and Rain.—Climate and Weather. Part V.—Fire.—Volcanoes and Volcanic Phenomena.—Earthquakes. Part VI.—Life—The Distribution of Plants in the different Countries of the Earth.—The Distribution of Animals on the

Earth.—The Distribution of Plants and Animals in Time.—Effects of Human Agency on Inanimate Nature.

"The Book is both valuable and comprehensive, and deserves a wide circulation."—*Observer.*

Ansted (D. T.) Elements of Physiography.

For the use of Science Schools. Fcap. 8vo. 1s. 4d.

—— The World We Live In.

Or First Lessons in Physical Geography. For the use of Schools and Students. By D. T. ANSTED, M.A., F.R.S., &c. Fcap. 2s. 25th Thousand, with Illustrations.

—— The Earth's History.

Or, First Lessons in Geology. For the use of Schools and Students. By D. T. ANSTED. Third Thousand. Fcap. 2s.

—— Two Thousand Examination Questions in Physical Geography. pp. 180. Price 2s.

—— Water, and Water Supply.

Chiefly with reference to the British Islands. Part I.—Surface Waters. 8vo. With Maps. 18s.

—— and Latham (R. G.) Channel Islands. Jersey, Guernsey, Alderney, Sark, &c.

THE CHANNEL ISLANDS. Containing: PART I.—Physical Geography. PART II.—Natural History. PART III.—Civil History. PART IV.—Economics and Trade. By DAVID THOMAS ANSTED, M.A., F.R.S., and ROBERT GORDON LATHAM, M.A.. M.D., F.R.S. New and Cheaper Edition in one handsome 8vo. Volume, with 72 Illustrations on Wood by Vizetelly, Loudon, Nicholls, and Hart; with Map. 8vo. 16s.

"This is a really valuable work. A book which will long remain the standard authority on the subject. No one who has been to the Channel Islands, or who purposes going there will be insensible of its value."—*Saturday Review.*

"It is the produce of many hands and every hand a good one."

Archer (Capt. J. H. Lawrence) Commentaries on the Punjaub Campaign—1848-49, including some additions to the History of the Second Sikh War, from original sources. By Capt. J. H LAWRENCE-ARCHER, Bengal H. P. Crown 8vo. 8s.

Armstrong (Annie E.) Ethel's Journey to Strange Lands in Search of Her Doll. By ANNIE E. ARMSTRONG. Cr. 8vo. With Illustrations by CHAS. WHYMPER. 2s. 6d.

Army and Navy Calendar for the Financial Year 1883-84. Being a Compendium of General Information relating to the Army, Navy, Militia, and Volunteers, and containing Maps, Plans, Tabulated Statements, Abstracts, &c. Compiled from authentic sources 2s. 6d.

Army and Navy Magazine.
Vols. I. to IV. are issued, each containing Six Cabinet Photographs of Celebrated Officers. Volumes 7s. 6d. each.

Aynsley (Mrs.) Our Visit to Hindustan, Kashmir, and Ladakh.
By Mrs. J. C. MURRAY AYNSLEY. 8vo. 14s.

Baildon (S.) The Tea Industry in India.
A Review of Finance and Labour, and a Guide for Capitalists and Assistants. By SAMUEL BAILDON, Author of "Tea in Assam." 8vo. 10s. 6d.

Belgium of the East (The).
By the Author of "Egypt under Ismail Pasha," "Egypt for the Egyptians," &c. Crown 8vo. 6s.

Bellew (Capt.) Memoirs of a Griffin; or, A Cadet's First Year in India. By Captain BELLEW. Illustrated from Designs by the Author. A New Edition. Cr. 8vo. 10s. 6d.

Black (C. I.) The Proselytes of Ishmael.
Being a short Historical Survey of the Turanian Tribes in their Western Migrations. With Notes and Appendices. By CHARLES INGRAM BLACK, M.A., Vicar of Burley-in-Wharfedale, near Leeds. Second Edition. Crown 8vo. 6s.

Blanchard (S.) Yesterday and To-day in India.
By SIDNEY LAMAN BLANCHARD. Post 8vo. 6s.

CONTENTS.—Outward Bound.—The Old Times and the New.—Domestic Life.—Houses and Bungalows.—Indian Servants.—The Great Shoe Question.—The Garrison Hack.—The Long Bow in India.—Mrs. Dulcimer's Shipwreck.—A Traveller's Tale, told in a Dark Bungalow.—Punch in India.—Anglo-Indian Literature.—Christmas in India.—The Seasons in Calcutta.—Farmers in Muslin.—Homeward Bound.—India as it Is.

Blenkinsopp (Rev. E. L.) Doctrine of Development in the Bible and in the Church. By Rev. E. L. Blenkinsopp, M.A., Rector of Springthorp. 2nd edition. 12mo. 6s.

Boileau (Major-General J. T.)
A New and Complete Set of Traverse Tables, showing the Differences of Latitude and the Departures to every Minute of the Quadrant and to Five Places of Decimals. Together with a Table of the lengths of each Degree of Latitude and corresponding Degree of Longitude from the Equator to the Poles; with other Tables useful to the Surveyor and Engineer. Fourth Edition, thoroughly revised and corrected by the Author. Royal 8vo. 12s. London, 1876.

Boulger (D. C.) History of China. By Demetrius Charles Boulger, Author of "England and Russia in Central Asia," &c. 8vo. vol. I. With Portrait. 18s. Vol. II. 18s.

—— **England and Russia in Central Asia.** With Appendices and Two Maps, one being the latest Russian Official Map of Central Asia. 2 vols. 8vo. 36s.

—— **Central Asian Portraits**; or the Celebrities of the Khanates and the Neighbouring States. By Demetrius Charles Boulger, M.R.A.S. Crown 8vo. 7s. 6d.

—— **The Life of Yakoob Beg**, Athalik Ghazi and Badaulet, Ameer of Kashgar. By Demetrius Charles Boulger, M.R.A.S. 8vo. With Map and Appendix. 16s.

Bowles (Thomas Gibson) Flotsam and Jetsam. A Yachtman's Experiences at Sea and Ashore. By Thomas Gibson Bowles, Master Mariner. Cr. 8vo. 7s. 6d.

Boyd (R. Nelson) Chili and the Chilians, during the War 1879–80. By R. Nelson Boyd, F.R.G.S., F.G.S., Author of Coal Mines Inspection. Cloth, Illustrated. Cr. 8vo. 10s. 6d.

—— **Coal Mines Inspection:** Its History and Results. 8vo. 14s.

Bradshaw (John) The Poetical Works of John Milton, with Notes, explanatory and philological. By John Bradshaw, LL.D., Inspector of Schools, Madras. 2 vols., post 8vo. 12s. 6d.

Brandis' Forest Flora of North-Western and Central India. By Dr. Brandis, Inspector General of Forests to the Government of India. Text and Plates. £2 18s.

Brereton (W. H.) The Truth about Opium.
Being the Substance of Three Lectures delivered at St. James's Hall. By WILLIAM H. BRERETON, late of Hong Kong, Solicitor. 8vo. 7s. 6d. Cheap edition, sewed, 1s.

Briggs (Gen. J.) India and Europe Compared. Post 8vo. 7s.

Bright (W.) Red Book for Sergeants.
Fifth and Revised Edition, 1880. By W. BRIGHT, late Colour-Sergeant, 19th Middlesex R.V. Fcap. interleaved. 1s.

Buckland (C. T.) Whist for Beginners. Second Edition. 1s.

Buckle (the late Capt. E.) Bengal Artillery.
A Memoir of the Services of the Bengal Artillery from the formation of the Corps. By the late CAPT. E. BUCKLE, Assist.-Adjut. Gen. Ben. Art. Edit. by SIR J. W. KAYE. 8vo. Lond, 1852. 10s.

Buckley (R. B.) The Irrigation Works of India, and their Financial Results. Being a brief History and Description of the Irrigation Works of India, and of the Profits and Losses they have caused to the State. By ROBERT B. BUCKLEY, A.M.I.C.E., Executive Engineer of the Public Works Department of India. 8vo. With Map and Appendix. 9s.

Burke (P.) Celebrated Naval and Military Trials.
By PETER BURKE, Serjeant-at-Law. Author of "Celebrated Trials connected with the Aristocracy." Post 8vo. 10s. 6d.

By the Tiber.
By the Author of "Signor Monaldini's Niece." 2 vols. 21s.

Carlyle (Thomas), Memoirs of the Life and Writings of,
With Personal Reminiscences and Selections from his Private Letters to numerous Correspondents. Edited by RICHARD HERNE SHEPHERD, Assisted by CHARLES N. WILLIAMSON. 2 Vols. With Portrait and Illustrations. Crown 8vo. 21s.

Challenge of Barletta (The).
By MASSIMO D'AZEGLIO. Rendered into English by Lady LOUISA MAGENIS. 2 vols. Crown 8vo. 21s.

Collette (C. H.) The Roman Breviary.
A Critical and Historical Review, with Copious Classified Extracts. By CHARLES HASTINGS COLLETTE. 2nd Edition. Revised and enlarged. 8vo. 5s.

Collette (C. H.) Henry VIII.
An Historical Sketch as affecting the Reformation in England. By CHARLES HASTINGS COLLETTE. Post 8vo. 6s.

Colquhoun (Major J. A. S.) With the Kurrum Force in the Caubul Campaign of 1878–79. By Major J. A. S. COLQUHOUN, R.A. With Illustrations from the Author's Drawings, and two Maps. 8vo. 16s.

Cooper's Hill College. Calendar of the Royal Indian Engineering College, Cooper's Hill. Published by authority in January each year. 5s.

CONTENTS.—Staff of the College; Prospectus for the Year; Table of Marks; Syllabus of Course of Study; Leave and Pension Rules of Indian Service; Class and Prize Lists; Past Students serving in India; Entrance Examination Papers, &c.

Corbet (M. E.) A Pleasure Trip to India, during the Visit of H.R.H. the Prince of Wales, and afterwards to Ceylon. By Mrs. CORBET. Illustrated with Photos. Crown 8vo. 7s. 6d.

Cowdery (Miss E.) Franz Liszt, Artist and Man.
By L. RAMANN. Translated from the German by Miss E. COWDERY. 2 vols. Crown 8vo. 21s.

Crosland (Mrs. N.) Stories of the City of London; Retold for Youthful Readers. By Mrs. NEWTON CROSLAND. With ten Illustrations. Cr. 8vo. 6s.

These Stories range from the early days of Old London Bridge and the Settlement of the Knights Templars in England to the time of the Gordon Riots with incidents in the Life of Brunel in relation to the Thames Tunnel; narrated from Personal recollections.

Cruise of H.M.S. "Galatea,"
Captain H.R.H. the Duke of Edinburgh, K.G., in 1867–1868. By the REV. JOHN MILNER, B.A., Chaplain; and OSWALD W. BRIERLY. Illustrated by a Photograph of H.R.H. the Duke of Edinburgh; and by Chromo-Lithographs and Graphotypes from Sketches taken on the spot by O. W. BRIERLY. 8vo. 16s.

Cunningham (H. S.) British India, and its Rulers.
By H. S. CUNNINGHAM, M.A., one of the Judges of the High Court of Calcutta, and late Member of the Famine Commission. 10s. 6d.

Daumas (E.) Horses of the Sahara, and the Manners of the Desert. By E. DAUMAS, General of the Division Commanding at Bordeaux, Senator, &c., &c. With Commentaries by the Emir Abd-el-Kadir (Authorized Edition). 8vo. 6s.

"We have rarely read a work giving a more picturesque and, at the same time, practical account of the manners and customs of a people, than this book on the Arabs and their horses."—*Edinburgh Courant.*

Deighton (K.) Shakespeare's King Henry the Fifth. With Notes and an Introduction. By K. DEIGHTON, Principal of Agra College. Crown 8vo. 5s.

Destruction of Life by Snakes, Hydrophobia, &c., in **Western** India. By an EX-COMMISSIONER. Fcap. 2s. 6d.

Dickins, (F. V.) Chiushingura: or the Loyal League. A Japanese Romance. Translated by FREDERICK V. DICKINS, Sc.B., of the Middle Temple, Barrister-at-Law. With Notes and an Appendix containing a Metrical Version of the Ballad of Takasako, and a specimen of the Original Text in Japanese character. Illustrated by numerous Engravings on Wood, drawn and executed by Japanese artists and printed on Japanese paper. 8vo. 10s. 6d.

Diplomatic Study on the Crimean War, 1852 to 1856. (Russian Official Publication.) 2 vols. 8vo. 28s.

Doran (Dr. J.) "Their Majesties Servants": Annals of the English Stage. Actors, Authors, and Audiences, From Thomas Betterton to Edmund Kean. By Dr. DORAN, F.S.A., Author of "Table Traits," "Lives of the Queens of England of the House of Hanover." &c. Post 8vo. 6s.

"Every page of the work is barbed with wit, and will make its way point foremost. . . . . provides entertainment for the most diverse tastes."—*Daily News.*

Douglas (M.) Countess Violet; or, What Grandmamma saw in the Fire. A Book for Girls. By MINNIE DOUGLAS. Author of "Two Rose Trees." Illustrated. 5s.

Drury (Col. H.) The Useful Plants of India, With Notices of their chief value in Commerce, Medicine, and the Arts. By COLONEL HEBER DRURY. Second Edition, with Additions and Corrections. Royal 8vo. 16s.

Dutton (Major Hon. C.) Life in India. By Major the Hon. CHARLES DUTTON. Crown 8vo. 2s. 6d.

Dwight (H. O.) Turkish Life in War Time.
By Henry O. Dwight. Crown 8vo. 12s.

Edwards (G. Sutherland) A Female Nihilist.
By Ernest Lavigne. Translated from the French by G. Sutherland Edwards. Crown 8vo. 9s.

Edwards (H. S.) The Lyrical Drama: Essays on Subjects, Composers, and Executants of Modern Opera. By H. Sutherland Edwards, Author of "The Russians at Home and Abroad," &c. Two vols. Crown 8vo. 21s.

—— **The Russians At Home and the Russians Abroad.**
Sketches, Unpolitical and Political, of Russian Life under Alexander II. By H. Sutherland Edwards. 2 vols. Crown 8vo. 21s.

Ensor (F. Sydney) The Queen's Speeches in Parliament, from Her Accession to the present time. A Compendium of the History of Her Majesty's Reign told from the Throne. Edited and Compiled by F. Sydney Ensor, Author of "Through Nubia to Darfoor." Crown 8vo. 7s. 6d.

—— **Incidents of a Journey through Nubia to Darfoor.**
By F. Sydn y Ensor, C.E. 10s. 6d.

Eyre (Major-General Sir V.), K.C.S.I., C.B. The Kabul Insurrection of 1841–42. Revised and corrected from Lieut. Eyre's Original Manuscript. Edited by Colonel G. B. Malleson, C.S.I. Crown 8vo., with Map and Illustrations. 9s.

Fearon (A.) Kenneth Trelawny.
By Alec Fearon. Author of "Touch not the Nettle." 2 vols. Crown 8vo. 21s.

Forbes (Capt. C. J. F. S.) **Comparative Grammar of the** Languages of Further India. A Fragment; and other Essays, the Literary Remains of Captain C. J. F. S. Forbes, of the British Burma Commission. Author of "British Burma and its People: Sketches of Native Manners, Customs, and Religion." 6s.

Foreign Office, Diplomatic and Consular Sketches. Reprinted from "Vanity Fair." Cr. 8vo. 6s.

Fraser (Lieut.-Col. G. T.) Records of Sport and Military Life in Western India. By the late Lieut.-Colonel G. T. Fraser, formerly of the 1st Bombay Fusiliers, and more recently attached to the Staff of H.M.'s Indian Army. With an Introduction by Colonel G. B. MALLESON, C.S.I. 7s. 6d.

Garrick (H. B. W.) Mansukhi and Sundar Singh.
A Hindu Tale in Hindustani. With 24 Illustrations. By H. B. W. GARRICK. 4to. 1s. 6d.

Gazetteers of India.
Thornton, 4 vols., 8vo. £2 16s.
„ 8vo. 21s.
„ (N.W.P., &c.) 2 vols., 8vo. 25s.

Gazetteer of Southern India.
With the Tenasserim Provinces and Singapore. Compiled from original and authentic sources. Accompanied by an Atlas, including plans of all the principal towns and cantonments. Royal 8vo. with 4to. Atlas. £3 3s.

Geography of India.
Comprising an account of British India, and the various states enclosed and adjoining. Fcap. pp. 250. 2s.

Geological Papers on Western India.
Including Cutch, Scinde, and the south-east coast of Arabia. To which is added a Summary of the Geology of India generally. Edited for the Government by HENRY J. CARTER, Assistant Surgeon, Bombay Army. Royal 8vo. with folio Atlas of maps and plates; half-bound. £2 2s.

Gibney (Major R. D.) Earnest Madement; a Tale of Wiltshire. By MAJOR R. D. GIBNEY, late Adjutant 1st Wilts Rifle Volunteers. Cr. 8vo. 6s. (Dedicated by permission to Lieut.-Gen. Sir Garnet Wolseley, G.C.B.)

Gillmore (Parker) Encounters with Wild Beasts.
By PARKER GILLMORE, Author of "The Great Thirst Land," "A Ride Through Hostile Africa," &c. With Ten full-page Illustrations. Cr. 8vo. 7s. 6d.

—— **Prairie and Forest.** A description of the Game of North America, with Personal Adventures in its Pursuit. By PARKER GILLMORE (Ubique). With Thirty-Seven Illustrations. Crown 8vo. 7s. 6d.

Goldstucker (Prof. Theodore), The late. The Literary Remains of. With a Memoir. 2 vols. 8vo. 21s.

Graham (Alex.) Genealogical and Chronological Tables, illustrative of Indian History. 4to. 5s.

Grant (Jas.) Derval Hampton: A Story of the Sea. By JAMES GRANT, Author of the "Romance of War," &c. 2 vols. Crown 8vo. 21s.

Greene (F. V.) The Russian Army and its Campaigns in Turkey in 1877–1878. By F. V. GREENE, First Lieutenant in the Corps of Engineers, U.S. Army, and lately Military Attaché to the United States Legation at St. Petersburg. 8vo. With Atlas. 32s. Second Edition.

—— **Sketches of Army Life in Russia.** Crown 8vo. 9s.

Griesinger (Theodor) The Jesuits; a Complete History of their Open and Secret Proceedings from the Foundation of the Order to the Present Time. Told to the German People. By THEODOR GRIESINGER. Translated by A. J. SCOTT, M.D. 2 vols. 8vo. Illustrated. 24s.

Griffith (Ralph T. H.) Birth of the War God. A Poem. By KALIDASA. Translated from the Sanscrit into English Verse. By RALPH T. H. GRIFFITH. 8vo. 5s.

Hall (E. H.) Lands of Plenty, for Health, Sport, and Profit British North America. A Book for all Travellers and Settlers. By E. HEPPLE HALL, F.S.S. Crown 8vo., with Maps. 6s.

Hall's Trigonometry.
The Elements of Plane and Spherical Trigonometry. With an Appendix, containing the solution of the Problems in Nautical Astronomy. For the use of Schools. By the REV. T. G. HALL, M.A., Professor of Mathematics in King's College, London. 12mo. 2s.

Hancock (E. C.) The Amateur Pottery and Glass Painter. With Directions for Gilding, Chasing, Burnishing, Bronzing, and Groundlaying. By E. CAMPBELL HANCOCK. Illustrated with Chromo-Lithographs and numerous Woodcuts. Fourth Edition. 8vo. 6s.

—— **Copies for China Painters.**
By E. CAMPBELL HANCOCK. With Fourteen Chromo-Lithographs and other Illustrations. 8vo. 10s.

Handbook of Reference to the Maps of India.
Giving the Lat. and Long. of places of note. 18mo. 3s. 6d.

**** This will be found a valuable Companion to Messrs. Allen & Cos.' Maps of India.*

Harcourt (Maj. A. F. P.) Down by the Drawle.
By MAJOR A. F. P. HARCOURT, Bengal Staff Corps, author of "Kooloo, Lahoul, and Spiti," "The Shakespeare Argosy," &c. 2 Vols. in one, crown 8vo. 6s.

Heine (Heinrich) The Book of Songs. By HEINRICH HEINE. Translated from the German by STRATHIER. Cr. 8vo. 7s. 6d.

Helms (L. V.) Pioneering in the Far East, and Journeys to California in 1849, and to the White Sea in 1878. By LUDWIG VERNER HELMS. With Illustrations from original Sketches and Photographs, and Maps. 8vo. 18s.

Hensman (Howard) The Afghan War, 1879–80.
Being a complete Narrative of the Capture of Cabul, the Siege of Sherpur, the Battle of Ahmed Khel, the brilliant March to Candahar, and the Defeat of Ayub Khan, with the Operations on the Helmund, and the Settlement with Abdur Rahman Khan. By HOWARD HENSMAN, Special Correspondent of the "Pioneer" (Allahabad) and the "Daily News" (London). 8vo. With Maps. 21s.

General Sir Frederick Roberts writes in regard to the letters now re-published :—

"Allow me to congratulate you most cordially on the admirable manner in which you have placed before the public the account of our march from Cabul, and the operations of 31st August and 1st September around Candahar. *Nothing could be more accurate or graphic.* I thought your description of the fight at Chara-ai was one that any soldier might have been proud of writing; but your recent letters are, if possible, even better."

Holden (E. S.) Sir William Herschel. His Life and Works. By Edward S. Holden, United States Naval Observatory Washington. Cr. 8vo. 6s.

Holland.
By Edmondo de Amicis. Translated from the Italian by Caroline Tilton. Crown 8vo. 10s. 6d.

Hough (Lieut.-Col. W.) Precedents in Military Law.
8vo. cloth. 25s.

Hughes (Rev. T. P.) Notes on Muhammadanism.
Second Edition, Revised and Enlarged. Fcap. 8vo. 6s.

Hunt and Kenny. On Duty under a Tropical Sun.
Being some Practical Suggestions for the Maintenance of Health and Bodily Comfort, and the Treatment of Simple Diseases; with Remarks on Clothing and Equipment for the Guidance of Travellers in Tropical Countries. By Major S. Leigh Hunt, Madras Army, and Alexander S. Kenny, M.R.C.S.E., A.K.C., Senior Demonstrator of Anatomy at King's College, London, Author of "The Tissues and their Structure." Crown 8vo. 4s.

Hutton (J.) Thugs and Dacoits of India.
A Popular Account of the Thugs and Dacoits, the Hereditary Garotters and Gang Robbers of India. By James Hutton. Post 8vo. 5s.

India Directory (The).
For the Guidance of Commanders of Steamers and Sailing Vessels. Founded upon the Work of the late Captain James Horsburgh, F.R.S.

Part I.—The East Indies, and Interjacent Ports of Africa and South America. Revised, Extended, and Illustrated with Charts of Winds, Currents, Passages, Variation, and Tides. By Commander Alfred Dundas Taylor, F.R.G.S., Superintendent of Marine Surveys to the Government of India. £1 18s.

Part II.—The China Sea, with the Ports of Java, Australia and Japan and the Indian Archipelago Harbours, as well as those of New Zealand. Illustrated with Charts of the Winds, Currents, Passages, &c. By the same. (*In preparation.*)

Indian and Military Law.

Mahommedan Law of Inheritance, &c. A Manual of the Mahommedan Law of Inheritance and Contract; comprising the

Doctrine of the Soonee and Sheea Schools, and based upon the text of Sir H. W. MACNAGHTEN's Principles and Precedents, together with the Decisions of the Privy Council and High Courts of the Presidencies in India. For the use of Schools and Students. By STANDISH GROVE GRADY, Barrister-at-Law, Reader of Hindoo, Mahommedan, and Indian Law to the Inns of Court. 8vo. 14s.

Hedaya, or Guide, a Commentary on the Mussulman Laws, translated by order of the Governor-General and Council of Bengal. By CHARLES HAMILTON. Second Edition, with Preface and Index by STANDISH GROVE GRADY. 8vo. £1 15s.

Institutes of Menu in English. The Institutes of Hindu Law or the Ordinances of Menu, according to Gloss of Collucca. Comprising the Indian System of Duties, Religious and Civil, verbally translated from the Original, with a Preface by SIR WILLIAM JONES, and collated with the Sanscrit Text by GRAVES CHAMNEY HAUGHTON, M.A., F.R.S., Professor of Hindu Literature in the East India College. New edition, with Preface and Index by STANDISH G. GRADY, Barrister-at-Law, and Reader of Hindu, Mahommedan, and Indian Law to the Inns of Court. 8vo., cloth. 12s.

Indian Code of Criminal Procedure. Being Act X. of 1872, Passed by the Governor-General of India in Council on the 25th of April, 1872. 8vo. 12s.

Indian Code of Civil Procedure. Being Act X. of 1877. 8vo. 6s.

Indian Code of Civil Procedure. In the form of Questions and Answers, with Explanatory and Illustrative Notes. By ANGELO J. LEWIS. Barrister-at-law 12mo. 12s. 6d.

Indian Penal Code. In the Form of Questions and Answers. With Explanatory and Illustrative Notes. BY ANGELO J. LEWIS, Barrister-at-Law. Post 8vo. 7s. 6d.

Hindu Law. Defence of the Daya Bhaga. Notice of the Case on Prosoono Coomar Tajore's Will. Judgment of the Judicial Committee of the Privy Council. Examination of such Judgment. By JOHN COCHRANE, Barrister-at-Law. Royal 8vo. 20s.

Law and Customs of Hindu Castes, within the Dekhan Provinces subject to the Presidency of Bombay, chiefly affecting Civil Suits. By ARTHUR STEELE. Royal 8vo. £1 1s.

Moohummudan Law of Inheritance. (See page 35.)

Chart of Hindu Inheritance. With an Explanatory Treatise, By ALMARIC RUMSEY. 8vo. 6s. 6d.

Manual of Military Law. For all ranks of the Army, Militia and Volunteer Services. By Colonel J. K. PIPON, Assist. Adjutant General at Head Quarters, & J. F. COLLIER, Esq., of the Inner Temple, Barrister-at-Law. Third and Revised Edition. Pocket size. 5s.

Precedents in Military Law; including the Practice of Courts-Martial; the Mode of Conducting Trials; the Duties of Officers at Military Courts of Inquests, Courts of Inquiry, Courts of Requests, &c., &c. The following are a portion of the Contents:—

1. Military Law. 2. Martial Law. 3. Courts-Martial. 4. Courts of Inquiry. 5. Courts of Inquest. 6. Courts of Request. 7. Forms of Courts-Martial. 8. Precedents of Military Law. 9. Trials of Arson to Rape (Alphabetically arranged.) 10. Rebellions. 11. Riots. 12. Miscellaneous. By Lieut.-Col. W. Hough, late Deputy Judge-Advocate-General, Bengal Army, and Author of several Works on Courts-Martial. One thick 8vo. vol. 25s.

The Practice of Courts Martial. By Hough & Long. Thick 8vo. London, 1825. 26s.

Indian Criminal Law and Procedure,

Including the Procedure in the High Courts, as well as that in the Courts not established by Royal Charter; with Forms of Charges and Notes on Evidence, illustrated by a large number of English Cases, and Cases decided in the High Courts of India; and an Appendix of selected Acts passed by the Legislative Council relating to Criminal matters. By M. H. Starling, Esq., LL.B. & F. B. Constable, M.A. Third edition. 8vo. £2 2s.

Indian Infanticide.

Its Origin, Progress, and Suppression. By John Cave-Brown, M.A. 8vo. 5s.

Irwin (H. C.) The Garden of India; or, Chapters on Oudh History and Affairs. By H. C. Irwin, B.A. Oxon., Bengal Civil Service. 8vo. 12s.

Jackson (Lt.-Col. B.) Military Surveying, &c. 8vo. 14s. (See page 28).

Jackson (Lowis D'A.) Hydraulic Manual and Working Tables, Hydraulic and Indian Meteorological Statistics. Published under the patronage of the Right Honourable the Secretary of State for India. By Lowis D'A. Jackson. 8vo. 28s.

—— Canal and Culvert Tables.

Based on the Formula of Kutter, under a Modified Classification, with Explanatory Text and Examples. By Lowis D'A. Jackson, A.M.I.C.E., author of "Hydraulic Manual and Statistics," &c. Roy. 8vo. 28s.

Jackson (Lowis D'A.) Pocket Logarithms and other Tables for Ordinary Calculations of Quantity, Cost, Interest, Annuities, Assurance, and Angular Functions, obtaining Results correct in the Fourth figure. By LOWIS D'A. JACKSON. Cloth, 2s. 6d.; leather, 3s. 6d.

—— Accented Four-Figure Logarithms, and other Tables. For purposes both of Ordinary and of Trigonometrical Calculation, and for the Correction of Altitudes and Lunar Distances. Arranged and accented by LOWIS D'A. JACKSON, A.M.I.C.E., Author of "Canal and Culvert Tables," "Hydraulic Manual," &c. Crown 8vo. 9s.

—— Units of Measurement for Scientific and Professional Men. By LOWIS D'A. JACKSON. Cr. 4to. 2s.

James (A. G. F. Eliot) Indian Industries.
By A. G. F. ELIOT JAMES, Author of "A Guide to Indian Household Management," &c. Crown 8vo. 9s.

CONTENTS:—Indian Agriculture; Beer; Cacao; Carpets; Cereals; Chemicals; Cinchona; Coffee; Cotton; Drugs; Dyeing and Colouring Materials; Fibrous Substances; Forestry; Hides; Skins and Horns; Gums and Resins; Irrigation; Ivory; Mining; Oils; Opium; Paper; Pottery; Ryots; Seeds; Silk; Spices; Sugar; Tea; Tobacco; Wood; Wool. Table of Exports. Index.

Jenkinson (Rev. T. B.) Amazulu.
The Zulu People. their Manners, Customs, and History, with Letters from Zululand descriptive of the Present Crisis. By THOMAS B. JENKINSON, B.A., sometime of Springvale, Natal, and Canon of Maritzburg. Crown 8vo. 6s.

Jerrold (Blanchard) at Home in Paris.
2 Vols. Post 8vo. 16s.

Joyner (Mrs.) Cyprus: Historical and Descriptive.
Adapted from the German of Herr FRANZ VON LÖHER. With much additional matter. By Mrs. A. BATSON JOYNER. Crown 8vo. With 2 Maps. 10s. 6d.

Kaye (Sir J. W.) The Sepoy War in India.
A History of the Sepoy War in India, 1857—1858. By Sir JOHN WILLIAM KAYE, Author of "The History of the War in Afghanistan." Vol. I., 8vo. 18s. Vol. II. £1. Vol. III. £1.

CONTENTS OF VOL. I.:—BOOK I.—INTRODUCTORY.—The Conquest of the Punjab and Pegu.—The "Right of Lapse."—The Annexation of Oude.—Progress of Englishism. BOOK II.—The

SEPOY ARMY: ITS RISE, PROGRESS, AND DECLINE.—Early History of the Native Army.—Deteriorating Influences.—The Sindh Mutinies.—The Punjaub Mutinies. Discipline of the Bengal Army. BOOK III.—THE OUTBREAK OF THE MUTINY.—Lord Canning and his Council.—The Oude Administration and the Persian War.—The Rising of the Storm.—The First Mutiny.—Progress of Mutiny.—Excitement in Upper India.—Bursting of the Storm.—APPENDIX.

CONTENTS OF VOL II.:—BOOK IV.—THE RISING IN THE NORTH-WEST.—The Delhi History.—The Outbreak at Meerut.—The Seizure of Delhi.—Calcutta in May.—Last Days of General Anson.—The March upon Delhi. BOOK V.—PROGRESS OF REBELLION IN UPPER INDIA.—Benares and Allahabad.—Cawnpore.—The March to Cawnpore.—Re-occupation of Cawnpore. BOOK VI.—THE PUNJAB AND DELHI.—First Conflicts in the Punjab.—Peshawur and Rawul Pinder.—Progress of Events in the Punjab.—Delhi.—First Weeks of the Siege.—Progress of the Siege.—The Last Succours from the Punjab.

CONTENTS OF VOL III.:—BOOK VII.—BENGAL, BEHAR, AND THE NORTH-WEST PROVINCES.—At the Seat of Government.—The Insurrection in Behar.—The Siege of Arrah.—Behar and Bengal. BOOK VIII.—MUTINY AND REBELLION IN THE NORTH-WEST PROVINCES.—Agra in May.—Insurrection in the Districts.—Bearing of the Native Chiefs.—Agra in June, July, August and September. BOOK IX.—LUCKNOW AND DELHI.—Rebellion in Oude.—Revolt in the Districts.—Lucknow in June and July.—The siege and Capture of Delhi.

(For continuation, *see* "History of the Indian Mutiny," by Colonel G. B. MALLESON, p. 23.)

Kaye (Sir J. W.) History of the War in Afghanistan.
New edition. 3 Vols. Crown 8vo. £1. 6s.

Keatinge (Mrs.) English Homes in India.
By MRS. KEATINGE. Part I.—The Three Loves. Part II.—The Wrong Turning. Two vols., Post 8vo. 16s.

Keene (H. G.) Mogul Empire.
From the death of Aurungzeb to the overthrow of the Mahratta Power, by HENRY GEORGE KEENE, B.C.S. Second edition. With Map. 8vo. 10s. 6d.

This Work fills up a blank between the ending of Elphinstone's and the commencement of Thornton's Histories.

Keene (H. G.) Administration in India.
Post 8vo. 5s.

—— **Peepul Leaves.**
Poems written in India. Post 8vo 5s.

—— **The Turks in India.**
Historical Chapters on the Administration of Hindostan by the Chugtai Tartar, Babar, and his Descendants. 12s. 6d.

King (D. B.) The Irish Question. By DAVID BENNETT KING, Professor in Lafayette College, U.S.A. Cr. 8vo. 9s.

Lane-Poole (S.) Studies in a Mosque. By STANLEY LANE-POOLE, Laureat de l'Institut de France. 8

Latham (Dr. R. G.) Russian and Turk,
From a Geographical, Ethnological, and Historical Point of View. 8vo 18s.

Laurie (Col. W. F. B.) Our Burmese Wars and Relations with Burma. With a Summary of Events from 1826 to 1879, including a Sketch of King Theebau's Progress. With various Local, Statistical, and Commercial Information. By Colonel W. F. B. LAURIE, Author of "Rangoon," "Narrative of the Second Burmese War," &c. 8vo. With Plans and Map. 16s.

—— **Ashé Pyee, the Superior Country**; or the great attractions of Burma to British Enterprise and Commerce. By Col. W. F. B. LAURIE, Author of "Our Burmese Wars and Relations with Burma." Crown 8vo. 5s.

Lee (F. G.) The Church under Queen Elizabeth.
An Historical Sketch. By the Rev. F. G. LEE, D.D. Two Vols., Crown 8vo. 21s.

—— **Reginald Barentyne**; or Liberty Without Limit. A Tale of the Times. By FREDERICK GEORGE LEE. With Portrait of the Author. Crown 8vo. Second Edition. 5s.

—— **The Words from the Cross**: Seven Sermons for Lent, Passion-Tide, and Holy Week. By the Rev. F. G. LEE, D.D. Third Edition revised. Fcap. 3s. 6d.

—— **Order Out of Chaos.** Two Sermons.
By the Rev. FREDERICK GEORGE LEE, D.D. Fcap. 2s. 6d.

Lee's (Dr. W. N.) Drain of Silver to the East. Post 8vo. 8s.

Le Messurier (Maj. A.) Kandahar in 1879. Being the Diary of Major A. Le Messurier, R.E., Brigade Major R.E. with the Quetta Column. Crown 8vo. 8s.

Lethbridge (R.) High Education in India. A Plea for the State Colleges. By Roper Lethbridge, C.I.E., M.A. Crown 8vo. 5s.

Lewin (T. H.) Wild Races of the South Eastern Frontier of India. Including an Account of the Loshai Country. By Capt. T. H. Lewin, Dep. Comm. of Hill Tracts. Post 8vo. 10s. 6d.

Lewis (A. J.) Indian Penal Code In the Form of Questions and Answers. With Explanatory and Illustrative Notes. By Angelo J. Lewis. Post 8vo. 7s. 6d.

—— Indian Code of Civil Procedure. In the Form of Questions and Answers. With Explanatory and Illustrative Notes. By Angelo J. Lewis. Post 8vo. 12s. 6d.

Liancourt's and Pincott's Primitive and Universal Laws of the Formation and Development of Language; a Rational and Inductive System founded on the Natural Basis of Onomatops. 8vo. 12*s.* 6*d.*

Lloyd (J. S.) Shadows of the Past. Being the Autobiography of General Kenyon. Edited by J. S. Lloyd, Authoress of "Ruth Everingham," "The Silent Shadow," &c. Second Edition. Crown 8vo. 6s.

—— Honesty Seeds, and How they Grew; or, Tony Wigston's Firm Bank. Cr. 8vo. Illustrated. 2s. 6d.

Lockwood (Ed.) Natural History, Sport and Travel. By Edward Lockwood, Bengal Civil Service, late Magistrate of Monghyr. Crown 8vo. With numerous Illustrations. 9s.

Lovell (Vice-Adm.) Personal Narrative of Events from 1799 to 1815. With Anecdotes. By the late Vice-Adm. Wm. Stanhope Lovell, R.N., K.H. Second edition. Crown 8vo. 4s.

Lupton (J. I.) The Horse, as he Was, as he Is, and as he Ought to Be. By James Irvine Lupton, F.R.C.V.S., Author of "The External Anatomy of the Horse," &c. &c. Illustrated. 3s. 6d.

Macdonald (D. G. F.) Grouse Disease; its Causes and Remedies. By DUNCAN GEORGE FORBES MACDONALD, LL.D., C.E., J.P., F.R.G.S., Author of "What the Farmers may do with the Land," "Estate Management," "Cattle, Sheep, and Deer," &c. 8vo. Illustrated. 10s. 6d.

MacGregor (Col. C. M.) Narrative of a Journey through the Province of Khorassan and on the N. W. Frontier of Afghanistan in 1875. By Colonel C. M. MACGREGOR, C.S.I., C.I.E., Bengal Staff Corps. 2 vols. 8vo. With map and numerous illustrations. 30s.

—— **Wanderings in Balochistan.** By MAJOR-GENERAL SIR C. M. MACGREGOR, K.C.B., C.S.I., C.I.E., Bengal Staff Corps, and Quartermaster-General in India. 8vo. With Illustrations and Map. 18s.

Mackay (C.) Luck, and what came of it. A Tale of our Times. By CHARLES MACKAY, LL.D. Three vols. 31s. 6d.

Mackenzie (Capt. C. F.) The Romantic Land of Hind. By EL MUSANNIF (Capt. C. F. MACKENZIE). Crown 8vo. 6s.

Maggs (J.) Round Europe with the Crowd. Crown 8vo. 5s.

Magenis (Lady Louisa) The Challenge of Barletta. By Massimo D'Azeglio. Rendered into English by Lady LOUISA MAGENIS. 2 vols., crown 8vo. 21s.

Malabari (B. M.) Gujerat and the Gujeratis. Pictures of Men and Manners taken from Life. By BEHRAMJI M. MALABARI, Author of "The Indian Muse in English Garb," "Pleasures of Morality," &c. Crown 8vo. 6s.

Malleson (Col. G. B.) Final French Struggles in India and on the Indian Seas. Including an Account of the Capture of the Isles of France and Bourbon, and Sketches of the most eminent Foreign Adventurers in India up to the period of that Capture. With an Appendix containing an Account of the Expedition from India to Egypt in 1801. By Colonel G. B. MALLESON, C.S.I. Crown 8vo. 10s. 6d.

—— **History of the Indian Mutiny, 1857–1858,** commencing from the close of the Second Volume of Sir John Kaye's History of the Sepoy War. Vol. I. 8vo. With Map. 20s.

CONTENTS.—Calcutta in May and June.—William Tayler and Vincent Eyre.—How Bihar and Calcutta were saved.—Mr. Colvin and Agra.—Jhansi and Bandalkhand.—Colonel Durand and Holkar.—Sir George Lawrence and Rajputana.—Brigadier Polwhele's great battle and its results.—Bareli, Rohilkhand, and Farakhabad.—The relation of the annexation of Oudh to the Mutiny.—Sir Henry Lawrence and the Mutiny in Oudh.—The siege of Lakhnao.—The first relief of Lakhnao.

VOL. II.—The Storming of Delhi, the Relief of Lucknow, the Two Battles of Cawnpore, the Campaign in Rohilkhand, and the movements of the several Columns in the N.W. Provinces, the Azimgurh District, and on the Eastern and South-Eastern Frontiers. 8vo. With 4 Plans. 20s.

VOL. III.—Bombay in 1857. Lord Elphinstone. March of Woodburn's Column. Mr. Seton-Karr and the Southern Maratha Country. Mr. Forjett and Bombay. Asirgarh. Sir Henry Durand. March of Stuart's Column. Holkar and Durand. Malwa Campaign. Haidarabad. Major C. Davidson and Salar Jang. Sagar and Narbadi Territory. Sir Robert Hamilton and Sir Hugh Rose. Central India Campaign. Whitlock and Kirwi. Sir Hugh Rose and Gwaliar. Le Grand Jacob and Western India. Lord Canning's Oudh policy. Last Campaign in, and pacification of, Oudh. Sir Robert Napier, Smith, Michell, and Tantia Topi. Civil Districts during the Mutiny. Minor Actions at Out-stations. Conclusion. 8vo. With Plans. 20s.

Malleson (Col. G. B.) History of Afghanistan, from the Earliest Period to the Outbreak of the War of 1878. 8vo. Second Edition. With Map. 18s.

—— **Herat: The Garden and Granary of Central Asia.** With Map and Index. 8vo. 8s.

—— **The Decisive Battles of India,** from 1746 to 1849 inclusive, with a Portrait of the Author, a Map, and 3 Plans. By Colonel G. B. MALLESON, C.S.I. 8vo. 18s.

—— **Founders of the Indian Empire.** Clive, Warren Hastings, and Wellesley. Vol. I.—LORD CLIVE. By Colonel G. B. MALLESON, C.S.I., Author of "History of the French in India," &c. 8vo., with Portraits and 4 Plans. 20s.

Manning (Mrs.) Ancient and Mediæval India. Being the History, Religion, Laws, Caste, Manners and Customs, Language, Literature, Poetry, Philosophy, Astronomy, Algebra, Medicine, Architecture, Manufactures, Commerce, &c., of the Hindus, taken from their writings. Amongst the works consulted and gleaned from may be named the Rig Veda, Sama Veda, Yajur Veda, Sathapatha Brahmana, Bhagavat Gita, The Puranas, Code of Manu, Code of Yajnavalkya, Mitakshara, Daya Bhaga, Mahabharata, Atriya, Charaka, Susruta, Ramayana, Raghu Vansa, Bhattikavya, Sakuntala, Vikramorvasi, Malati and Madhava, Mudra Rakshasa, Ratnavali, Kumara Sambhava, Prabodha, Chandrodaya, Megha Duta, Gita Govinda, Panchatantra, Hitopadesa, Katha Sarit, Sagara, Ketala, Pancnavinsati, Dasa Kumara Charita, &c. By Mrs. MANNING, with Illustrations. 2 vols., 8vo. 30s.

Marvin (Chas.) Merv, the Queen of the World and the Scourge of the Men-stealing Turcomans. By CHARLES MARVIN, author of "The Disastrous Turcoman Campaign," and "Grodekoff's Ride to Herat." With Portraits and Maps. 8vo. 18s.

—— **Colonel Grodekoff's Ride from Samarcand to Herat,** through Balkh and the Uzbek States of Afghan Turkestan. With his own March-route from the Oxus to Herat. By CHARLES MARVIN. Crown 8vo. With Portrait. 8s.

—— **The Eye-Witnesses' Account of the Disastrous Russian** Campaign against the Akhal Tekke Turcomans: Describing the March across the Burning Desert, the Storming of Dengeel Tepe, and the Disastrous Retreat to the Caspian. By CHARLES MARVIN. With numerous Maps and Plans. 8vo. 18s.

Matson (Nellie) Hilda Desmond, or Riches and Poverty. Crown 8vo. 10s. 6d.

Mayhew (Edward) Illustrated Horse Doctor. Being an Accurate and Detailed Account, accompanied by more than 400 Pictorial Representations, characteristic of the various Diseases to which the Equine Race are subjected; together with the latest Mode of Treatment, and all the requisite Prescriptions written in Plain English By EDWARD MAYHEW, M.R.C.V.S. 8vo. 18s. 6d.

CONTENTS.—The Brain and Nervous System.—The Eyes.—The Mouth.—The Nostrils.—The Throat.—The Chest and its contents.—The Stomach, Liver, &c.—The Abdomen.—The Urinary Organs.—The Skin.—Specific Diseases.—Limbs.—The Feet.—Injuries.—Operations.

"The book contains nearly 600 pages of valuable matter, which reflects great credit on its author, and, owing to its practical details, the result of deep scientific research, deserves a place in the library of medical, veterinary, and non-professional readers."—*Field.*

"The book furnishes at once the bane and the antidote, as the drawings show the horse not only suffering from every kind of disease, but in the different stages of it, while the alphabetical summary at the end gives the cause, symptoms and treatment of each."—*Illustrated London News.*

Mayhew (Edward) Illustrated Horse Management.

Containing descriptive remarks upon Anatomy, Medicine, Shoeing, Teeth, Food, Vices, Stables; likewise a plain account of the situation, nature, and value of the various points; together with comments on grooms, dealers, breeders, breakers, and trainers; Embellished with more than 400 engravings from original designs made expressly for this work. By E. MAYHEW. A new Edition, revised and improved by J. I. LUPTON. M.R.C.V.S. 8vo. 12s.

CONTENTS.—The body of the horse anatomically considered. PHYSIC.—The mode of administering it, and minor operations. SHOEING.—Its origin, its uses, and its varieties. THE TEETH.—Their natural growth, and the abuses to which they are liable.

FOOD.—The fittest time for feeding, and the kind of food which the horse naturally consumes. The evils which are occasioned by modern stables. The faults inseparable from stables. The so-called "incapacitating vices," which are the results of injury or of disease. Stables as they should be. GROOMS.—Their prejudices, their injuries, and their duties. POINTS.—Their relative importance and where to look for their development. BREEDING.—Its inconsistencies and its disappointments. BREAKING AND TRAINING.—Their errors and their results.

Mayhew (Henry) German Life and Manners.

As seen in Saxony. With an account of Town Life—Village Life—Fashionable Life—Married Life—School and University Life, &c. Illustrated with Songs and Pictures of the Student Customs at the University of Jena. By HENRY MAYHEW, 2 vols., 8vo., with numerous illustrations. 18s.

A Popular Edition of the above. With illustrations. Cr. 8vo. 7s.

"Full of original thought and observation, and may be studied with profit by both German and English—especially by the German." ***Athenæum.***

McCarthy (T. A.) An Easy System of Calisthenics and Drilling. Including Light Dumb-Bell and Indian Club Exercises. By T. A. McCARTHY, Chief Instructor at Mr. Moss's Gymnasium, Brighton. Fcap. 1s. 6d.

McCosh (J.) Advice to Officers in India.
By JOHN McCOSH, M.D. Post 8vo. 8s.

Meadow (T.) Notes on China.
Desultory Notes on the Government and People of China and on the Chinese Language. By T. T. MEADOWS. 8vo. 9s.

Menzies (S.) Turkey Old and New: Historical, Geographical, and Statistical. By SUTHERLAND MENZIES. With Map and numerous Illustrations. 2 vols., 8vo. 32s.

Military Works—chiefly issued by the Government.

Field Exercises and Evolutions of Infantry. Pocket edition, 1s.

Queen's Regulations and Orders for the Army. Corrected to 1881. 8vo. 3s. 6d. Interleaved, 5s. 6d. Pocket Edition, 1s. 6d.

Musketry Regulations, as used at Hythe. 1s.

Dress Regulations for the Army. (Reprinting.)

Infantry Sword Exercise. 1875. 6d.

Infantry Bugle Sounds. 6d.

Handbook of Battalion Drill. By Lieut. H. C. SLACK. 2s; or with Company Drill, 2s. 6d.

Handbook of Brigade Drill. By Lieut. H. C. SLACK. 3s.

Red Book for Sergeants. By WILLIAM BRIGHT, Colour-Sergeant, 19th Middlesex R.V. 1s.

Handbook of Company Drill; also of Skirmishing, Battalion, and Shelter Trench Drill. By Lieut. CHARLES SLACK. 1s.

Elementary and Battalion Drill. Condensed and Illustrated, together with duties of Company Officers, Markers, &c., in Battalion. By Captain MALTON. 2s. 6d.

Cavalry Regulations. For the Instruction, Formations, and Movements of Cavalry. Royal 8vo. 4s. 6d.

Manual of Artillery Exercises, 1873. 8vo. 5s.

Manual of Field Artillery Exercises. 1877. 3s.

Standing Orders for Royal Artillery. 8vo, 3s.

Principles and Practice of Modern Artillery. By Lt.-Col. C. H. OWEN, R.A. 8vo. Illustrated. 15s.

Artillerist's Manual and British Soldiers' Compendium. By Major F. A. GRIFFITHS. 11th Edition. 5s.

Compendium of Artillery Exercises—Smooth Bore, Field, and Garrison Artillery for Reserve Forces. By Captain J. M. McKenzie. 3s. 6d.

Principles of Gunnery. By JOHN T. HYDE, M.A., late Professor of Fortification and Artillery, Royal Indian Military College, Addiscombe. Second edition, revised and enlarged. With many Plates and Cuts, and Photograph of Armstrong Gun. Royal 8vo. 14s.

Notes on Gunnery. By Captain Goodeve. Revised Edition. 1s.

Text Book of the Construction and Manufacture of Rifled Ordnance in the British Service. By STONEY & JONES. Second Edition. Paper, 3s. 6d., Cloth, 4s. 6d.

Treatise on Fortification and Artillery. By Major HECTOR STRAITH. Revised and re-arranged by THOMAS COOK, R.N., by JOHN T. HYDE, M.A. 7th Edition. Royal 8vo. Illustrated and Four Hundred Plans, Cuts, &c. £2 2s.

Elementary Principles of Fortification. A Text-Book for Military Examinations. By J. T. HYDE, M.A. Royal 8vo. With numerous Plans and Illustrations. 10s. 6d.

Military Surveying and Field Sketching. The Various Methods of Contouring, Levelling, Sketching without Instruments, Scale of Shade, Examples in Military Drawing, &c., &c., &c. As at present taught in the Military Colleges. By Major W. H. RICHARDS, 55th Regiment, Chief Garrison Instructor in India, Late Instructor in Military Surveying, Royal Military College, Sandhurst. Second Edition, Revised and Corrected. 12s.

Treatise on Military Surveying; including Sketching in the Field, Plan-Drawing, Levelling, Military Reconnaissance, &c. By Lieut.-Col. BASIL JACKSON, late of the Royal Staff Corps. The Fifth Edition. 8vo. Illustrated by Plans, &c. 14s.

Instruction in Military Engineering. Vol. 1., Part III. 4s.

Military Train Manual. 1s.

The Sappers' Manual. Compiled for the use of Engineer Volunteer Corps. By Col. W. A. FRANKLAND, R.E. With numerous Illustrations. 2s.

Ammunition. A descriptive treatise on the different Projectiles Charges, Fuzes, Rockets, &c., at present in use for Land and Sea Service, and on other war stores manufactured in the Royal Laboratory. 6s.

Hand-book on the Manufacture and Proof of Gunpowder. as carried on at the Royal Gunpowder Factory, Waltham Abbey. 5s.

Regulations for the Training of Troops for service in the Field and for the conduct of Peace Manœuvres. 2s.

Hand-book Dictionary for the Militia and Volunteer Services, Containing a variety of useful information, Alphabetically arranged. Pocket size, 3s. 6d.; by post, 3s. 8d.

Gymnastic Exercises, System of Fencing, and Exercises for the Regulation Clubs. In one volume. Crown 8vo. 1877. 2s.

Text-Book on the Theory and Motion of Projectiles; the History, Manufacture, and Explosive Force of Gunpowder; the History of Small Arms. For Officers sent to School of Musketry. 1s. 6d.

Notes on Ammunition. 4th Edition. 1877. 2s. 6d.

Regulations and Instructions for Encampments. 6d.

Rules for the Conduct of the War Game. 2s.

Medical Regulations for the Army, Instructions for the Army, Comprising duties of Officers, Attendants, and Nurses, &c. 1s. 6d.

Purveyors' Regulations and Instructions, for Guidance of Officers of Purveyors' Department of the Army. 3s.

Priced Vocabulary of Stores used in Her Majesty's Service. 4s.

Lectures on Tactics for Officers of the Army, Militia, and Volunteers. By Major F. H. DYKE, Garrison Instructor, E.D. 3s. 6d.

Transport of Sick and Wounded Troops. By DR. LONGMORE. 5s.

Precedents in Military Law. By LT-COL. W. HOUGH. 8vo. 25s.

The Practice of Courts-Martial, by HOUGH & LONG. 8vo. 26s.

Manual of Military Law. For all ranks of the Army, Militia, and Volunteer Services. By Colonel J. K. PIPON, and J. F. COLLIER, Esq. Third and Revised Edition. Pocket size. 5s.

Regulations applicable to the European Officer in India. Containing Staff Corps Rules, Staff Salaries, Commands, Furlough and Retirement Regulations, &c. By GEORGE E. COCHRANE late Assistant Military Secretary, India Office. 1 vol., post 8vo. 7s. 6d.

Reserve Force; Guide to Examinations, for the use of Captains and Subalterns of Infantry, Militia, and Rifle Volunteers, and for Serjeants of Volunteers. By Capt. G. H. GREAVES. 2nd edit. 2s.

The Military Encyclopædia; referring exclusively to the Military Sciences, Memoirs of distinguished Soldiers, and the Narratives of Remarkable Battles. By J. H. STOCQUELER. 8vo. 12s.

The Operations of War Explained and Illustrated. By Col. HAMLEY. New Edition Revised, with Plates. Royal 8vo. 30s.

Lessons of War. As taught by the Great Masters and Others; Selected and Arranged from the various operations in War. By FRANCE JAMES SOADY, Lieut.-Col., R.A. Royal 8vo. 21s.

The Surgeon's Pocket Book, an Essay on the best Treatment of Wounded in War. By Surgeon Major J. H. PORTER. 7s. 6d.

A Precis of Modern Tactics. By COLONEL HOME. 8vo. 8s. 6d.

Armed Strength of Austria. By Capt. COOKE. 2 pts. £1 2s.

Armed Strength of Denmark. 3s.

Armed Strength of Russia. Translated from the German. 7s.

Armed Strength of Sweden and Norway. 3s. 6d.

Armed Strength of Italy. 5s. 6d.

Armed Strength of Germany. Part I. 8s. 6d.

The Franco-German War of 1870—71. By CAPT. C. H. CLARKE. Vol. I. £1 6s. Sixth Section. 5s. Seventh Section 6s. Eighth Section. 3s. Ninth Section. 4s. 6d. Tenth Section. 6s. Eleventh Section. 5s. 3d. Twelfth Section. 4s. 6d.

The Campaign of 1866 in Germany. Royal 8vo. With Atlas, 21s.

Celebrated Naval and Military Trials. By PETER BURKE. Post 8vo., cloth. 10s. 6d.

Military Sketches. By SIR LASCELLES WRAXALL. Post 8vo. 6s.

Military Life of the Duke of Wellington. By JACKSON and SCOTT. 2 Vols. 8vo. Maps, Plans, &c. 12s.

Single Stick Exercise of the Aldershot Gymnasium. 6*d.*

Treatise on Military Carriages, and other Manufactures of the Royal Carriage Department. 5s.

Steppe Campaign Lectures. 2s.

Manual of Instructions for Army Surgeons. 1s.

Regulations for Army Hospital Corps. 9d.

Manual of Instructions for Non-Commissioned Officers, Army Hospital Corps. 2s.

Handbook for Military Artificers. 3s.

Instructions for the use of Auxiliary Cavalry. 2s. 6d.

Equipment Regulations for the Army. 5s. 6d.

Statute Law relating to the Army. 1s. 3d.

Regulations for Commissariat and Ordnance Department 2s.

Regulations for the Commissariat Department. 1s. 6d.

Regulations for the Ordnance Department. 1s. 6d.

Artillerist's Handbook of Reference for the use of the Royal and Reserve Artillery, by WILL and DALTON. 5s.

An Essay on the Principles and Construction of Military Bridges, by SIR HOWARD DOUGLAS. 1853. 15s.

Mill's History of British India,
With Notes and Continuation. By H. H. Wilson. 9 vols. cr. 8vo. £2 10s.

Mitchinson (A. W.) The Expiring Continent; A Narrative of Travel in Senegambia, with Observations on Native Character; Present Condition and Future Prospects of Africa and Colonisation. By Alex. Will. Mitchinson. With Sixteen full-page Illustrations and Map. 8vo. 18s.

Mitford (Maj. R. C. W.) To Caubul with the Cavalry Brigade. A Narrative of Personal Experiences with the Force under General Sir F. S. Roberts, G.C.B. With Map and Illustrations from Sketches by the Author. By Major R. C. W. Mitford, 14th Beng. Lancers. 8vo. Second Edit. 9s.

Muller's (Max) Rig-Veda-Sanhita.
The Sacred Hymns of the Brahmins; together with the Commentary of Sayanacharya. Published under the Patronage of the Right Honourable the Secretary of State for India in Council. 6 vols., 4to. £2 10s. per volume.

Misterton, or, Through Shadow to Sunlight. By Unus. Crown 8vo. 5s.

Mysteries of the Vatican;
Or Crimes of the Papacy. From the German of Dr. Theodor Griesenger. 2 Vols. post 8vo. 21s.

Neville (Ralph) The Squire's Heir.
By Ralph Neville, Author of "Lloyd Pennant." Two Vols. 21s.

Nicholson (Capt. H. W.) From Sword to Share; or, a Fortune in Five Years at Hawaii. By Capt. H. Whalley Nicholson. Crown 8vo. With Map and Photographs. 12s. 6d.

Nirgis and Bismillah.
Nirgis; a Tale of the Indian Mutiny, from the Diary of a Slave Girl: and Bismillah; or, Happy Days in Cashmere. By Hafiz Allard. Post 8vo. 10s. 6d.

Norris-Newman (C. L.) In Zululand with the British, throughout the War of 1879. By Charles L. Norris-Newman, Special Correspondent of the London "Standard," Cape Town "Standard and Mail," and the "Times" of Natal. With Plans and Four Portraits. 8vo. 16s.

Norris-Newman (C. L.) With the Boers in the Transvaal and Orange Free State in 1880–81. By C. L. NORRIS-NEWMAN, Special War Correspondent, Author of "In Zululand with the British." 8vo. With Maps. 14s.

Notes on the North Western Provinces of India.
By a District Officer. 2nd Edition. Post 8vo., cloth. 5s.
CONTENTS.—Area and Population.—Soils.—Crops.—Irrigation.—Rent.—Rates.—Land Tenures.

O'Donoghue (Mrs. P.) Ladies on Horseback.
Learning, Park Riding, and Hunting. With Notes upon Costume, and numerous Anecdotes. By Mrs. POWER O'DONOGHUE, Authoress of "The Knave of Clubs," "Horses and Horsemen," "Grandfather's Hunter," "One in Ten Thousand," &c. &c. Cr. 8vo. With Portrait. Second Edition. 5s.

Oldfield (H. A.) Sketches from Nipal, Historical and Descriptive; with Anecdotes of the Court Life and Wild Sports of the Country in the time of Maharaja Jang Bahadur, G.C.B.; to which is added an Essay on Nipalese Buddhism, and Illustrations of Religious Monuments, Architecture, and Scenery, from the Author's own Drawings. By the late HENRY AMBROSE OLDFIELD, M.D., of H. M.'s Indian Army, many years Resident at Khatmandu. Two vols. 8vo. 36s.

Oliver (Capt. S. P.) On and Off Duty.
Being Leaves from an Officer's Note Book. Part I.—Turania; Part II.—Lemuria; Part III.—Columbia. By Captain S. P. OLIVER. Crown 4to. With 38 Illustrations. 14s.

—— On Board a Union Steamer.
A compilation. By Captain S. P. OLIVER. To which is added "A Sketch Abroad," by MISS DOVETON. 8vo. With Frontispiece. 8s.

Osborne (Mrs. W.) Pilgrimage to Mecca (A).
By the Nawab Sikandar Begum of Bhopal. Translated from the Original Urdu. By MRS. WILLOUGHBY OSBORNE. Followed by a Sketch of the History of Bhopal. By COL. WILLOUGHBY OSBORNE, C.B. With Photographs, and dedicated, by permission, to HER MAJESTY, QUEEN VICTORIA. Post 8vo. £1. 1s.

This is a highly important book, not only for its literary merit, and the information it contains, but also from the fact of its being the first work written by an Indian lady, and that lady a Queen.

Oswald (Felix S.) Zoological Sketches: a Contribution to the Out-door Study of Natural History. By FELIX S. OSWALD, Author of "Summer-land Sketches of Mexico and Central America." 8vo., with 36 Illustrations by Hermann Faber. 7s. 6d.

Owen (Sidney) India on the Eve of the British Conquest. A Historical Sketch. By SIDNEY OWEN. M.A. Reader in Indian Law and History in the University of Oxford. Formerly Professor of History in the Elphinstone College, Bombay. Post 8vo. 8s.

Oxenham (Rev. H. N.) Catholic Eschatology and Universalism. An Essay on the Doctrine of Future Retribution. Second Edition, revised and enlarged. Crown 8vo. 7s. 6d.

—— **Catholic Doctrine of the Atonement.** An Historical Inquiry into its Development in the Church, with an Introduction on the Principle of Theological Development. By H. NUTCOMBE OXENHAM, M.A. 3rd Edition and Enlarged. 8vo. 14s.

"It is one of the ablest and probably one of the most charmingly written treatises on the subject which exists in our language."—*Times.*

—— **The First Age of Christianity and the Church.** By JOHN IGNATIUS DÖLLINGER, D.D., Professor of Ecclesiastical History in the University of Munich, &c., &c. Translated from the German by HENRY NUTCOMBE OXENHAM, M.A., late Scholar of Baliol College, Oxford. Third Edition. 2 vols. Crown 8vo. 18s.

Ozanam's (A. F.) History of Civilisation in the Fifth Century. From the French. By The Hon. A. C. GLYN. 2 Vols., post 8vo. 21s.

Pebody (Charles) Authors at Work. Francis Jeffrey—Sir Walter Scott—Robert Burns—Charles Lamb—R. B. Sheridan—Sydney Smith—Macaulay—Byron Wordsworth—Tom Moore—Sir James Mackintosh. Post 8vo. 10s. 6d.

Pelly (Sir Lewis). The Miracle Play of Hasan and Husain. Collected from Oral Tradition by Colonel Sir LEWIS PELLY, K.C.B., K.C.S.I., formerly serving in Persia as Secretary of Legation, and Political Resident in the Persian Gulf.

Revised, with Explanatory Notes, by Arthur N. Wollaston, H.M. Indian (Home) Service, Translator of Anwar-i-Suhaili, &c. 2 Vols. royal 8vo. 32s.

Pen and Ink Sketches of Military Subjects. By "Ignotus." Reprinted by permission from the "Saturday Review." Crown 8vo. 5s.

Pincott (F.) Analytical Index to Sir John Kaye's History of the Sepoy War, and Col. G. B. Malleson's History of the Indian Mutiny. (Combined in one volume.) By Frederic Pincott, M.R.A.S. 8vo. 10s. 6d.

Pipon and Collier's Manual of Military Law.
By Colonel J. K. Pipon, and J. F. Collier, Esq., of the Inner Temple, Barrister-at-Law. 5s.

Pittenger (Rev. W.) Capturing a Locomotive.
A History of Secret Service in the late American War. By Rev. W. Pittenger. Crown 8vo. With 13 Illustrations. 6s.

Pollock (Field Marshal Sir George) Life & Correspondence.
By C. R. Low. 8vo. With portrait. 18s.

Pope (G. U.) Text-book of Indian History; with Geographical Notes, Genealogical Tables, Examination Questions, and Chronological, Biographical, Geographical, and General Indexes. For the use of Schools, Colleges, and Private Students. By the Rev. G. U. Pope, D.D., Principal of Bishop Cotton's Grammar School and College, Bangalore; Fellow of the Madras University. Third Edition, thoroughly revised. Fcap. 4to. 12s.

Practice of Courts Martial.
By Hough & Long. 8vo. London. 1825. 26s.

Prichard's Chronicles of Budgepore, &c.
Or Sketches of Life in Upper India. 2 Vols., Foolscap 8vo. 12s.

Prinsep (H. T.) Historical Results.
Deducible from Recent Discoveries in Affghanistan. By H. T. Prinsep. 8vo. Lond. 1844. 15s.

—— **Tibet, Tartary, and Mongolia.**
By Henry T. Prinsep, Esq. Second edition. Post 8vo. 5s.

Prinsep (H. T.) Political and Military Transactions in India. 2 Vols. 8vo. London, 1825. 18s.

Private Theatricals.
Being a Practical Guide to the Home Stage, both before and behind the Curtain. By AN OLD STAGER. Illustrated with Suggestions for Scenes after designs by Shirley Hodson. Crown 8vo. 3s. 6d.

Ramann (L.) Franz Liszt, Artist and Man, 1811–1840. By L. RAMANN. Translated from the German by Miss E. Cowdery. 2 vols. 21s.

Richards (Major W. H.) Military Surveying, &c. 12s. (See page 28.)

Rowe (R.) Picked up in the Streets; or, Struggles for Life among the London Poor. By RICHARD ROWE, "Good Words" Commissioner, Author of "Jack Afloat and Ashore," &c. Crown 8vo. Illustrated. 6s.

Rumsey (Almaric) Moohummudan Law of Inheritance, and Rights and Relations affecting it. Sunni Doctrine. Comprising, together with much collateral information, the substance, greatly expanded, of the author's "Chart of Family Inheritance." By ALMARIC RUMSEY, of Lincoln's Inn, Barrister-at-Law, Professor of Indian Jurisprudence at King's College, London. Author of "A Chart of Hindu Family Inheritance." 8vo. 12s.

—— A Chart of Hindu Family Inheritance.
Second Edition, much enlarged. 8vo. 6s. 6d.

Sachau (Dr. C. Ed.) The Chronology of Ancient Nations. An English Version of the Arabic Text of the Athar-ut Bâkiya of Albîrûnî, or "Vestiges of the Past." Collected and reduced to writing by the Author in A.H. 390–1, A.D. 1,000. Translated and Edited, with Notes and Index, by Dr. C. EDWARD SACHAU, Professor in the Royal University of Berlin. Published for the Oriental Translation Fund of Great Britain and Ireland. Royal 8vo. 42s.

Sanderson (G. P.) Thirteen Years among the Wild Beasts of India; their Haunts and Habits, from Personal Observation; with an account of the Modes of Capturing and Taming Wild Elephants. By G. P. SANDERSON, Officer in

Charge of the Government Elephant Keddahs at Mysore. With 21 full page Illustrations and three Maps. Second Edition. Fcp. 4to. £1 5s.

Scudamore (F. I.) France in the East.
A Contribution towards the consideration of the Eastern Question. By Frank Ives Scudamore, C.B. Crown 8vo. 6s.

Sewell (R.) Analytical History of India.
From the earliest times to the Abolition of the East India Company in 1858. By Robert Sewell, Madras Civil Service. Post 8vo. 8s.

*** The object of this work is to supply the want which has been felt by students for a condensed outline of Indian History which would serve at once to recall the memory and guide the eye, while at the same time it has been attempted to render it interesting to the general reader by preserving a medium between a bare analysis and a complete history.

Shadow of a Life (The) A Girl's Story.
By Beryl Hope. 3 vols., post 8vo. 31s. 6d.

Sherer (J. W.) The Conjuror's Daughter.
A Tale. By J. W. Sherer, C.S.I. With Illustrations by Alf. T. Elwes and J. Jellicoe. Cr. 8vo. 6s.

—— Who is Mary?
A Cabinet Novel, in one volume. By J. W. Sherer, Esq., C.S.I. 10s. 6d.

Signor Monaldini's Niece.
A Novel of Italian Life. Crown 8vo. 6s.

Simpson (H. T.) Archæologia Adelensis; or, a History of the Parish of Adel, in the West Riding of Yorkshire. Being an attempt to delineate its Past and Present Associations, Archæological, Topographical, and Scriptural. By Henry Traill Simpson, M.A., late Rector of Adel. With numerous etchings by W. Lloyd Ferguson. Roy. 8vo. 21s.

Small (Rev. G.) A Dictionary of Naval Terms, English and Hindustani. For the use of Nautical Men trading to India, &c. By Rev. G. Small, Interpreter to the Strangers' Home for Asiatics. Fcap. 2s. 6d.

Solymos (B.) Desert Life. Recollections of an Expedition in the Soudan. By B. Solymos (B. E. Falkonberg), Civil Engineer. 8vo. 15s.

Songs of a Lost World.
By a New Hand. Crown 8vo. 6s.

Starling (M. H.) Indian Criminal Law and Procedure.
Third edition. 8vo. £2 2s. See page 18.

Steele (A.) Law and Customs of Hindu Castes.
By Arthur Steele. Royal 8vo. £1. 1s. (See page 18.)

Stent (G. C.) Entombed Alive,
And other Songs and Ballads. (From the Chinese.) By George Carter Stent, M.R.A.S., of the Chinese Imperial Maritime Customs Service, author of "Chinese and English Vocabulary," "Chinese and English Pocket Dictionary," "The Jade Chaplet," &c. Crown 8vo. With four Illustrations. 9s.

—— **Scraps from my Sabretasche.** Being Personal Adventures while in the 14th (King's Light) Dragoons. By George Carter Stent, M.R.A.S., Author of "The Jade Chaplet," "Entombed Alive," &c. Crown 8vo. 6s.

Stothard (R. T.) The A B C of Art.
Being a system of delineating forms and objects in nature necessary for the attainments of a draughtsman. By Robert T. Stothard, F.S.A., late H.D.S.A. Fcap. 1s.

Swinnerton (Rev. C.) The Afghan War. Gough's Action at Futtehabad. By the Rev. C. Swinnerton, Chaplain in the Field with the First Division, Peshawur Valley Field Force. With Frontispiece and Two Plans. Crown 8vo. 5s.

Tayler (W.) Thirty-eight Years in India, from Juganath to the Himalaya Mountains. By William Tayler, Esq., Retired B.C.S., late Commissioner of Patna. In 2 vols. 25s. each.

Contains a memoir of the life of Mr. William Tayler, from 1829 to 1867—during the Government of eight Governors General—from Lord William Bentinck to Lord Lawrence, comprising numerous incidents and adventures, official, personal, tragic, and comic, "from grave to gay, from lively to severe" throughout that period. These volumes contain upwards of two hundred illustrations, reproduced by Mr. Tayler himself, from original sketches taken by him on the spot, in Bengal, Behar, N.W. Provinces, Darjeeling, Nipal, and Simla.

Tayler (Wm.) The Patna Crisis; or Three Months at Patna during the Insurrection of 1857. By WILLIAM TAYLER, late Commissioner of Patna. Third Edition. Fcap. 2s.

Thoms (J. A.) A Complete Concordance to the Revised Version of the New Testament, embracing the Marginal Readings of the English Revisers as well as those of the American Committee. By JOHN ALEXANDER THOMS. 6s.

Thomson's Lunar and Horary Tables.

For New and Concise Methods of Performing the Calculations necessary for ascertaining the Longitude by Lunar Observations, or Chronometers; with directions for acquiring a knowledge of the Principal Fixed Stars and finding the Latitude of them. By DAVID THOMSON. Sixty-fifth edit. Royal 8vo. 10s.

Thornton (P. M.) Foreign Secretaries of the Nineteenth Century. By PERCY M. THORNTON.

Contains—Memoirs of Lord Grenville, Lord Hawkesbury, Lord Harrowby, Lord Mulgrave, C. J. Fox, Lord Howick, George Canning, Lord Bathurst, Lord Wellesley (together with estimate of his Indian Rule by Col. G. B. Malleson, C.S.I.), Lord Castlereagh, Lord Dudley, Lord Aberdeen, and Lord Palmerston. Also, Extracts from Lord Bexley's Papers, including lithographed letters of Lords Castlereagh and Canning, which, bearing on important points of public policy, have never yet been published; together with other important information culled from private and other sources. With Ten Portraits, and a View shewing Interior of the old House of Lords. (Second Edition.) 2 vols. 8vo. 32s. 6d.

Vol. III. 8vo. With Portraits. 18s

Thornton's History of India.

The History of the British Empire in India, by Edward Thornton, Esq. Containing a Copious Glossary of Indian Terms, and a Complete Chronological Index of Events, to aid the Aspirant for Public Examinations. Third edition. 1 vol. 8vo. With Map. 12s.

*** *The Library Edition of the above in 6 volumes, 8vo., may be had, price £2 8s.*

Thornton's Gazetteer of India.

Compiled chiefly from the records at the India Office. By EDWARD THORNTON. 1 vol., 8vo., pp. 1015. With Map. 21s.

**** The chief objects in view in compiling this Gazetteer are:—*

1st. To fix the relative position of the various cities, towns, and villages with as much precision as possible, and to exhibit with the greatest practicable brevity all that is known respecting them; and

2ndly. To note the various countries, provinces, or territorial divisions, and to describe the physical characteristics of each, together with their statistical, social, and political circumstances.

To these are added minute descriptions of the principal rivers and chains of mountains; thus presenting to the reader, within a brief compass, a mass of information which cannot otherwise be obtained, except from a multiplicity of volumes and manuscript records.

The Library Edition.

4 vols., 8vo. Notes, Marginal References, and Map. £2 16s.

—— Gazetteer of the Punjaub, Affghanistan, &c.

Gazetteer of the Countries adjacent to India, on the north-west, including Scinde, Affghanistan, Beloochistan, the Punjaub, and the neighbouring States. By EDWARD THORNTON, Esq. 2 vols. 8vo. £1 5s.

Thornton (T.) East India Calculator.

By T. THORNTON. 8vo. London, 1823. 10s.

—— History of the Punjaub,

And of the Rise, Progress, and Present Condition of the Sikhs. By T. THORNTON. 2 Vols. Post 8vo. 8s.

Tilley (H. A.) Japan, the Amoor and the Pacific.

With notices of other Places, comprised in a Voyage of Circumnavigation in the Imperial Russian Corvette *Rynda*, in 1858–1860. By HENRY A. TILLEY. Eight Illustrations. 8vo. 16s.

Tod (Col. Jas.) Travels in Western India.

Embracing a visit to the Sacred Mounts of the Jains, and the most Celebrated Shrines of Hindu Faith between Rajpootana and the Indus, with an account of the Ancient City of Nehrwalla. By the late Lieut.-Col. JAMES TOD, Illustrations. Royal 4to. £3 3s.

**** This is a companion volume to Colonel Tod's Rajasthan.*

Torrens (W. T. McC.) Reform of Procedure in Parliament to Clear the Block of Public Business. By W. T. McCullagh Torrens, M.P. Second Edition. Crown 8vo. 5s.

Trimen (Capt. R.) Regiments of the British Army, Chronologically arranged. Showing their History, Services, Uniform, &c. By Captain R. Trimen, late 35th Regiment. 8vo. 10s. 6d.

Trotter (L. J.) History of India. The History of the British Empire in India, from the Appointment of Lord Hardinge to the Death of Lord Canning (1844 to 1862). By Captain Lionel James Trotter, late Bengal Fusiliers. 2 vols. 8vo. 16s. each.

—— Lord Lawrence. A Sketch of his Career. Fcap. 1s. 6d.

—— Warren Hastings, a Biography. By Captain Lionel James Trotter, Bengal H. P., author of a "History of India," "Studies in Biography," &c. Crown 8vo. 9s.

Tupper (M. F.) Three Five-Act Plays and Twelve Dramatic Scenes. Suitable for Private Theatricals or Drawing-room Recitation. By Martin F. Tupper, Author of "Proverbial Philosophy," &c. Crown 8vo. Gilt. 5s.

Under Orders: a Novel. By the Author of "Invasions of India from Central Asia." Third Edition. 3 vols. 31s. 6d.

Underwood (A. S.) Surgery for Dental Students. By Arthur S. Underwood, M.R.C.S., L.D.S.E., Assistant Surgeon to the Dental Hospital of London. 5s.

Valbezen (E. De) The English and India. New Sketches. By E. De Valbezen, late Consul-General at Calcutta, Minister Plenipotentiary. Translated from the French (with the Author's permission) by a Diplomate. 8vo. 18s.

Vambery (A.) Sketches of Central Asia. Additional Chapters on My Travels and Adventures, and of the Ethnology of Central Asia. By Armenius Vambery. 8vo. 16s.

"A valuable guide on almost untrodden ground."—*Athenæum.*

Vibart (Major H. M.) The Military History of the Madras Engineers and Pioneers. By Major H. M. Vibart, Royal (late Madras) Engineers. In 2 vols., with numerous Maps and Plans. 2 vols. 8vo. 32s. each.

Victoria Cross (The) An Official Chronicle of Deeds of Per-sonal Valour achieved in the presence of the Enemy during the Crimean and Baltic Campaigns and the Indian, Chinese, New Zealand, and African Wars. From the Institution of the Order in 1856 to 1880. Edited by Robert W. O'Byrne. Crown 8vo. With Plate. 5s.

Vyse (G. W.) Egypt: Political, Financial, and Strategical. Together with an Account of its Engineering Capabilities and Agricultural Resources. By Griffin W. Vyse, late on special duty in Egypt and Afghanistan for H.M.'s Government. Crown 8vo. With Maps. 9s.

Waring (E. J.) Pharmacopœia of India.
By Edward John Waring, M.D., &c. 8vo. 6s. (See page 2.)

Watson (M.) Money.
By Jules Tardieu. Translated from the French by Margaret Watson. Crown 8vo. 7s. 6d.

Watson (Dr. J. F.) and J. W. Kaye, Races and Tribes of Hindostan. The People of India. A series of Photographic Illustrations of the Races and Tribes of Hindustan. Prepared under the Authority of the Government of India, by J. Forbes Watson, and John William Kaye. The Work contains about 450 Photographs on mounts, in Eight Volumes, super royal 4to. £2. 5s. per volume.

Webb (Dr. A.) Pathologia Indica.
Based upon Morbid Specimens from all parts of the Indian Empire. By Allan Webb, B.M.S. Second Edit. 8vo. 14s.

Wellesley's Despatches.
The Despatches, Minutes, and Correspondence of the Marquis Wellesley, K.G., during his Administration in India. 5 vols. 8vo. With Portrait, Map, &c. £6. 10s.

This work should be perused by all who proceed to India in the Civil Services.

Wellington in India.
Military History of the Duke of Wellington in India. 1s.

White (S. D.) Indian Reminiscences.
By Colonel S. Dewe' White, late Bengal Staff Corps. 8vo. With 10 Photographs. 14s.

Wilberforce (E.) Franz Schubert.
A Musical Biography, from the German of Dr. Heinrich Kreisle von Hellborn. By Edward Wilberforce, Esq., Author of "Social Life in Munich." Post 8vo. 6s.

Wilk's South of India.
3 vols. 4to. £5. 5s.

Wilkin (Mrs.) The Shackles of an Old Love.
By Mârâ (Mrs. Wilkin). Crown 8vo. 7s. 6d.

Wilkins (W. N.) Visual Art; or Nature through the Healthy Eye. With some remarks on Originality and Free Trade, Artistic Copyright, and Durability. By Wm. Noy Wilkins, Author of "Art Impressions of Dresden," &c. 8vo. 6s.

Williams (F.) Lives of the English Cardinals.
The Lives of the English Cardinals, from Nicholas Breakspeare (Pope Adrien IV.) to Thomas Wolsey, Cardinal Legate. With Historical Notices of the Papal Court. By Folkestone Williams. 2 vols., 8vo. 14s.

—— Life, &c., of Bishop Atterbury.
The Memoir and Correspondence of Francis Atterbury, Bishop of Rochester, with his distinguished contemporaries. Compiled chiefly from the Atterbury and Stuart Papers. By Folkestone Williams, Author of "Lives of the English Cardinals," &c., 2 vols. 8vo. 14s.

Wilson (H. H.) Glossary of Judicial and Revenue Terms, and of useful Words occurring in Official Documents relating to the Administration of the Government of British India. From the Arabic, Persian, Hindustani, Sanskrit, Hindi, Bengali, Uriya, Marathi, Guzarathi, Telugu, Karnata, Tamil, Malayalam, and other Languages. Compiled and published under the authority of the Hon. the Court of Directors of the E. I. Company. 4to., cloth. £1 10s.

Wollaston (Arthur N.) Anwari Suhaili, or Lights of Canopus. Commonly known as Kalilah and Damnah, being an adaptation of the Fables of Bidpai. Translated from the Persian. Royal 8vo., 42s.; also in royal 4to., with illuminated borders, designed specially for the work, cloth, extra gilt. £3 13s. 6d.

—— Elementary Indian Reader.
Designed for the use of Students in the Anglo-Vernacular Schools in India. Fcap. 1s.

Woolrych (Serjeant W. H.)
Lives of Eminent Serjeants-at-Law of the English Bar. By Humphry W. Woolrych, Serjeant-at-Law. 2 vols. 8vo. 30s.

Wraxall (Sir L., Bart.) Caroline Matilda.
Queen of Denmark, Sister of George 3rd. From Family and State Papers. By Sir Lascelles Wraxall, Bart. 3 vols., 8vo. 18s.

Young (J. R.) Course of Mathematics.
A Course of Elementary Mathematics for the use of candidates for admission into either of the Military Colleges; of applicants for appointments in the Home or Indian Civil Services; and of mathematical students generally. By Professor J. R. Young. In one closely-printed volume. 8vo., pp. 648. 12s.

"In the work before us he has digested a complete Elementary Course, by aid of his long experience as a teacher and writer; and he has produced a very useful book. Mr. Young has not allowed his own taste to rule the distribution, but has adjusted his parts with the skill of a veteran."—*Athenæum.*

Young (M.) and Trent (R.) A Home Ruler.
A Story for Girls. By Minnie Young and Rachel Trent, Illustrated by C. P. Colnaghi. Crown 8vo. 3s. 6d.

Works in the Press.

THE HISTORY OF INDIA, AS TOLD BY ITS OWN HISTORIANS; the Local Muhammadan Dynasties. Vol. I. Guzerat. By John Dowson, M.R.A.S., late Professor of the Staff College. Forming a Sequel in two or more volumes to Sir H. M. Elliott's Original work on the Muhammadan period of the History of India; already edited, annotated, and amplified by the same Author. Published under the Patronage of H.M.'s Secretary of State for India.

QUEER PEOPLE. A Selection of Short Stories. From the Swedish of "Leah." By Albert Alberg, Author of "Whisperings in the Wood," &c. 2 vols.

THE ORDERS OF CHIVALRY. English and Foreign, existing and extinct, brought down to the present time. Compiled from original authorities by Major J. H. Lawrence-Archer. With Illustrations.

REMINISCENCES OF AN INDIAN OFFICIAL. By Sir Orfeur Cavenagh.

LIFE OF ALEXANDER II., EMPEROR OF ALL THE RUSSIAS. By the Author of "Science, Art, and Literature in Russia;" "Life and Times of Alexander I."

A HISTORY OF LONDON GOLDSMITHS AND PLATE-WORKERS, with their Marks stamped on Plate, copied in fac-simile from celebrated Examples and the Earliest Records preserved at Goldsmith's Hall, with their Names, Addresses, and Dates of Entry. Preceded by an Introductory Essay on the Goldsmiths' Art. By William Chaffers, Author of "Hall Marks on Plate," "Marks and Monograms on Pottery and Porcelain," "The Keramic Gallery," &c. 2,500 Illustrations. 12s. 6d.

THE FAMILY REGISTER. A Key to such Official Entries of Births, Marriages, and Deaths at the Registrar-General's Office as may refer to any Particular Family, and for the Preservation of Genealogical Data essential to evidence of Pedigree, with explanatory Introduction. Edited by Alfred George Taunton.